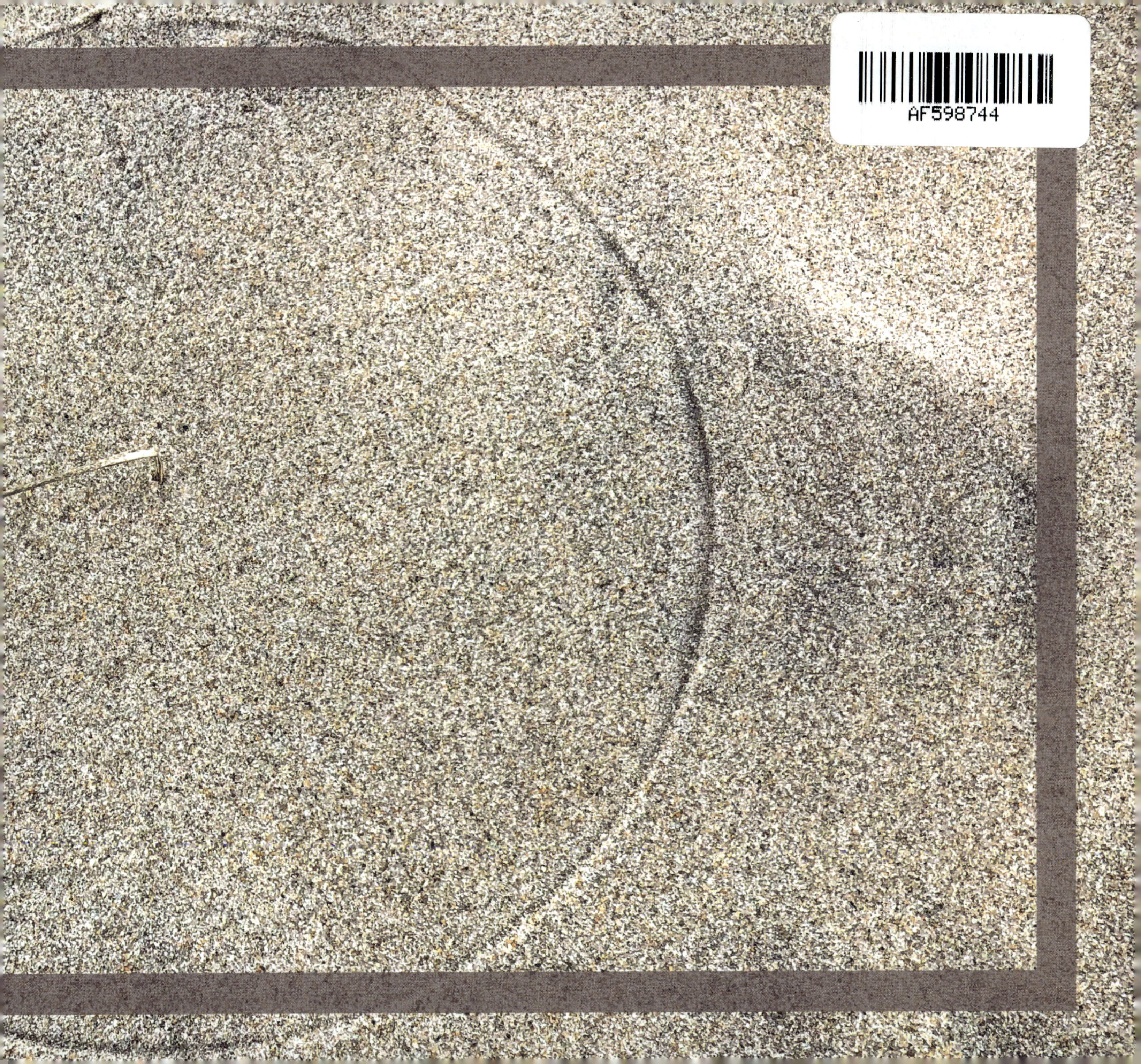

AF598744

CAPE COD

Once around the Sun

A PHOTOGRAPHIC NATURAL HISTORY OF THE SEASONS ON CAPE COD

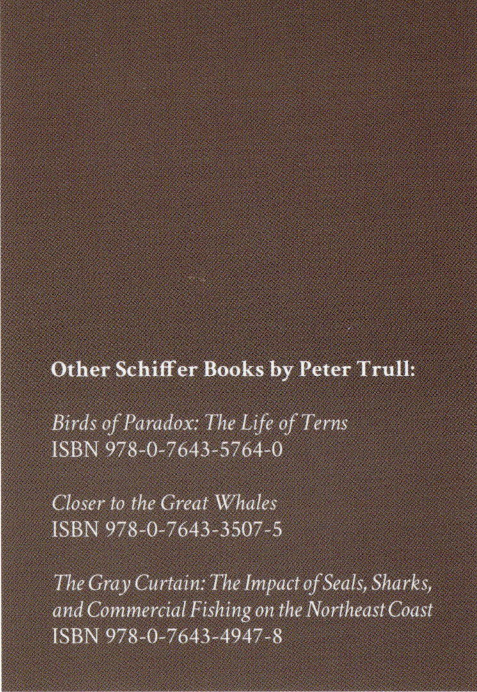

Other Schiffer Books by Peter Trull:

Birds of Paradox: The Life of Terns
ISBN 978-0-7643-5764-0

Closer to the Great Whales
ISBN 978-0-7643-3507-5

The Gray Curtain: The Impact of Seals, Sharks, and Commercial Fishing on the Northeast Coast
ISBN 978-0-7643-4947-8

Library of Congress Control Number: 2022944441

Designed by Christopher Bower
Cover design by Christopher Bower
Type set in Crimson

ISBN: 978-0-7643-6603-1
Printed in China
Published by Schiffer Publishing, Ltd.
4880 Lower Valley Road
Atglen, PA 19310
Phone: (610) 593-1777; Fax: (610) 593-2002
Email: Info@schifferbooks.com
Web: www.schifferbooks.com

For our complete selection of fine books on this and related subjects, please visit our website at www.schifferbooks.com. You may also write for a free catalog.

Schiffer Publishing's titles are available at special discounts for bulk purchases for sales promotions or premiums. Special editions, including personalized covers, corporate imprints, and excerpts, can be created in large quantities for special needs. For more information, contact the publisher.

We are always looking for people to write books on new and related subjects. If you have an idea for a book, please contact us at proposals@schifferbooks.com.

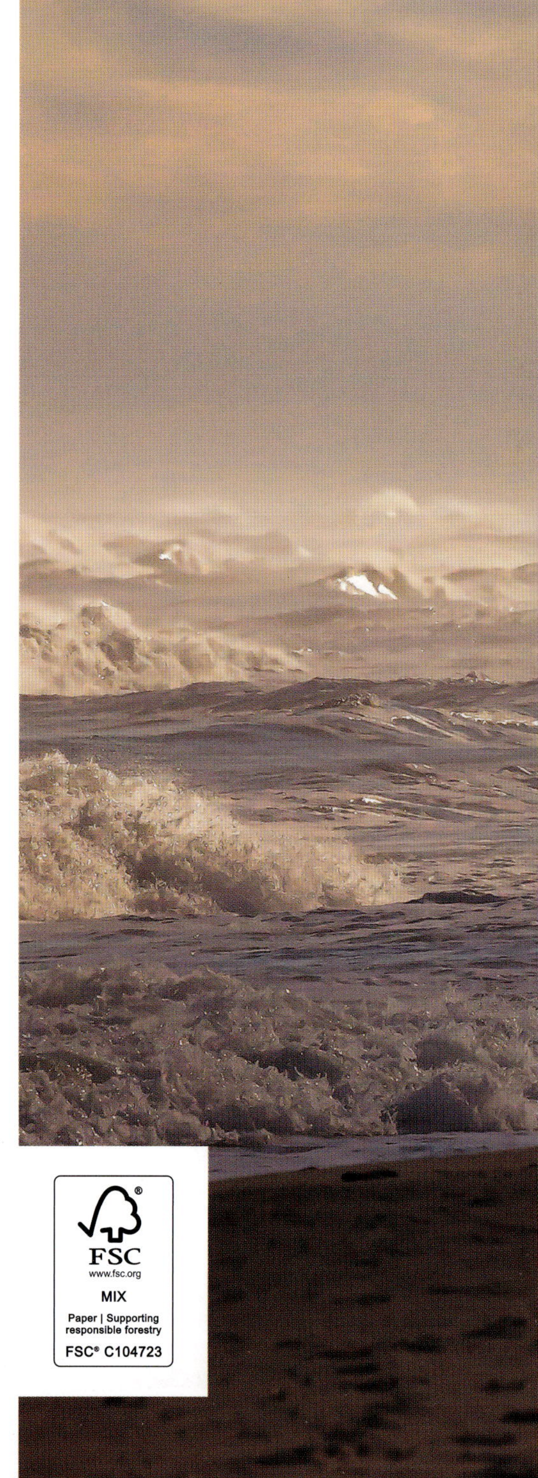

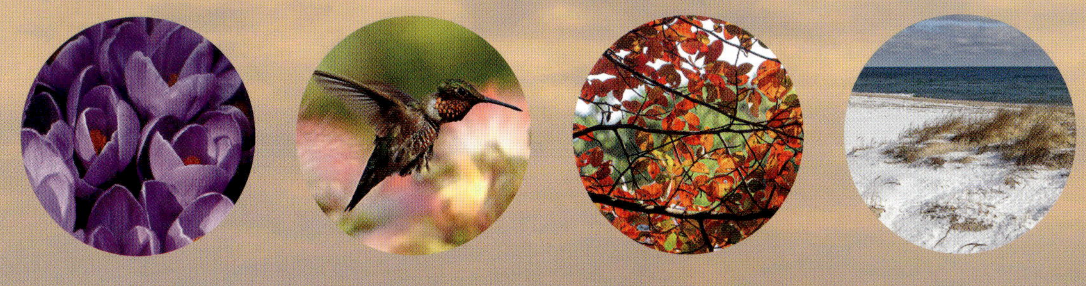

CAPE COD

Once around the Sun

TEXT AND PHOTOGRAPHY
BY
PETER TRULL

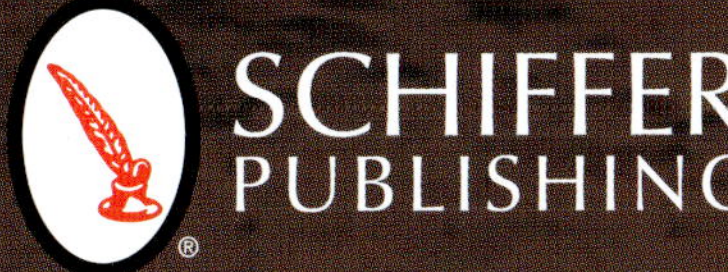

4880 Lower Valley Road • Atglen, PA 19310

Dedicated to the memory and writings of John Hay, who in 1961 wrote *Nature's Year*. His classic book, and the times we spent together watching one of our favorite subjects, terns, inspired me nearly sixty years later to put into photographs my own interpretation of his title. I call it *Cape Cod: Once around the Sun*. For John Hay.

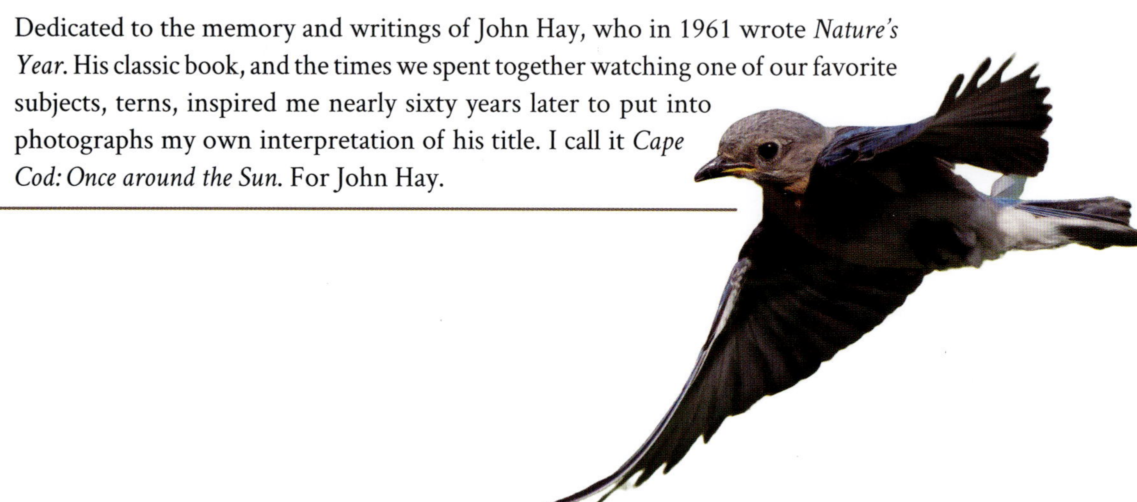

CONTENTS

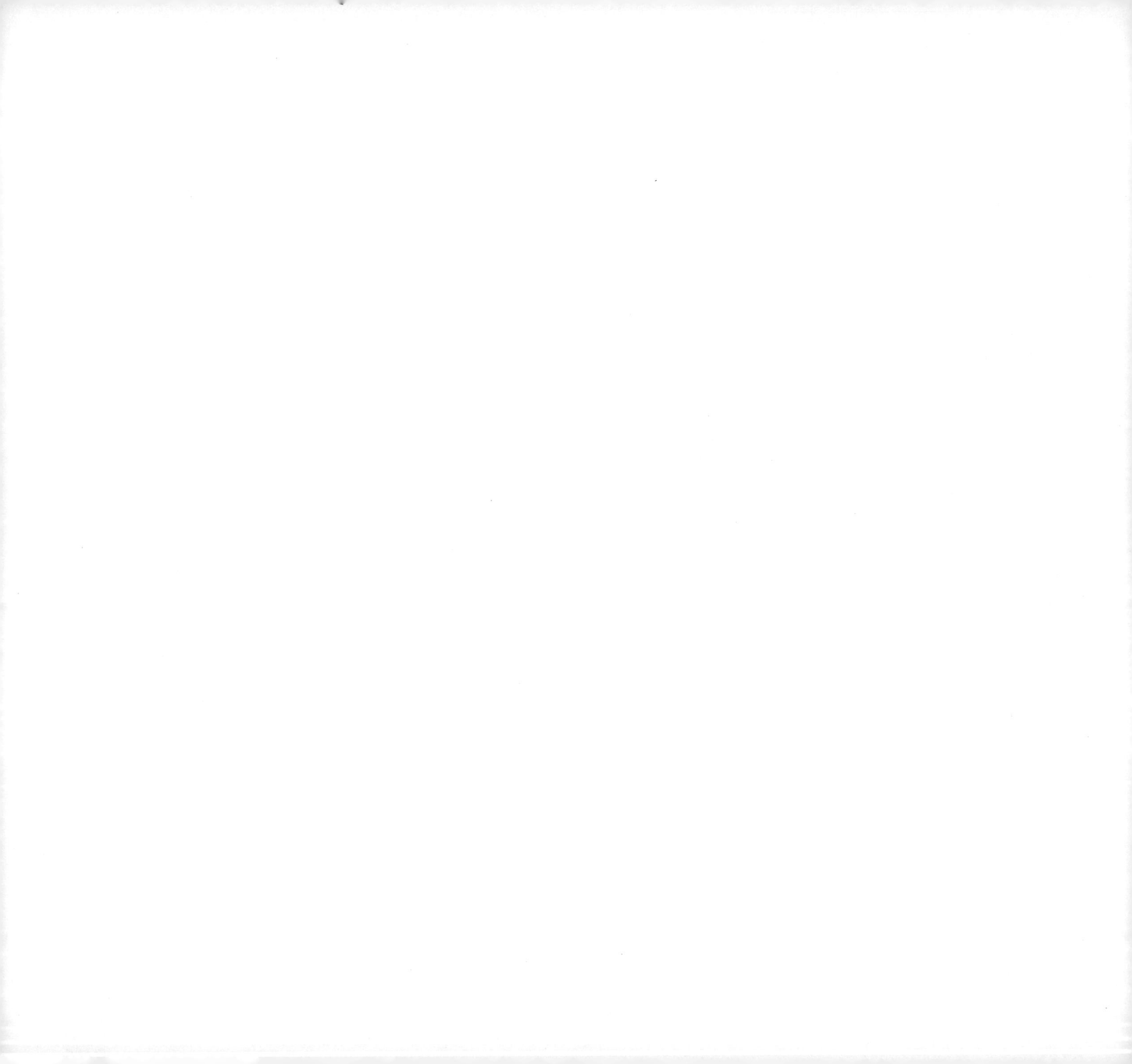

INTRODUCTION

A year of natural-history events on Cape Cod could be written over and over, and the accounts would all be different. Nature's cycles and events, though often predictable, are never the same. Some, like the first snowfall, may occur from year to year over a period spanning two to three months, while you can be sure that the first Baltimore oriole song or the spring arrival of a palm warbler may differ by only a matter of a few days from year to year. John Hays writes of these events in his 1961 book of eloquent prose, *Nature's Year.* His words become colors and scenes in our minds. We hear the gulls clamoring to grab herring at the Brewster gristmill, and we feel the chill as "a walloping, tugging, brutal wind sets in" during the month of January.

As a teacher, I tried to instill in my seventh-grade students a love and understanding of these seasonal and even daily or weekly events. After all, we make this celestial orbit around the sun over and over again, giving us a lot to look forward to each year. I wait for the first rainy night after the March full moon to go and observe the extraordinary spectacle of spotted salamanders emerging from woodland hibernation to frenzied, whirling, breeding masses of black and yellow in nearby vernal pools. As long as I live, I can be sure it will occur in March. During a John Hay seminar I taught with colleague Susannah Remillard, we visited his secluded writing cabin on Dry Hill in the Brewster woods, and our twelve- and thirteen-year-old students read and interpreted his words. We also visited some of the areas John wrote about. Susannah, a writer and Fulbright scholar, talked with me at length about this tribute to John Hay, and I thank her for the inspiration.

As a warden and researcher for the Massachusetts Audubon Society, heading up their coastal seabird (tern) program in the 1970s and 1980s, it was my honor to have John along on a few of my forays, where we talked at length about his beloved terns. His books *Spirit of Survival* (1974) and *Bird of Light* (1991) chronicled the lives of our beloved seabirds.

Here, through the lens of my camera, through knowledge gained over many journeys around the sun, I pay tribute to *Nature's Year.* I hope you enjoy these images of events that you can look forward to on your yearly journeys around the sun.

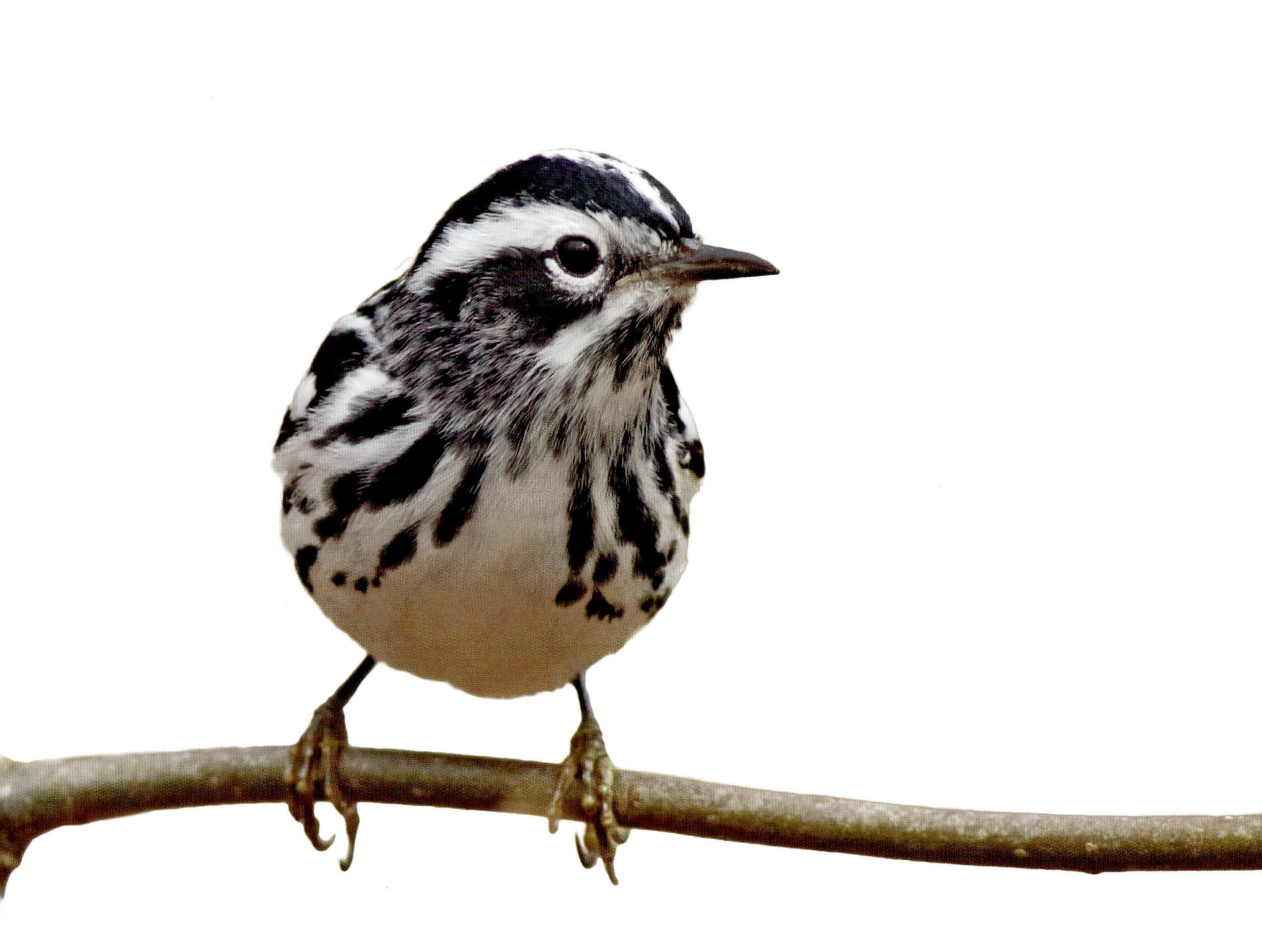

MAY AND JUNE
Nature's Energy-Burning Months

We wait for May. March and April herald the end of winter and the early spring, and although we see the daffodils blooming and the herring running, the air is still cool around us. If we don't get those southern breezes to warm us up in April, it may be spring, but on Cape Cod it will be darn cold. Nevertheless, southern migrants begin to arrive, and by early to mid-May, warbler migration is in full swing. Terns have arrived from their wintering grounds in South America to nest on the cape's sandy beaches and islands, while other local songbirds have begun to nest. Leaves begin to emerge from dormant twigs, and woodlands become rich with a variety of wild flowers. Insects begin to stir, bringing tree swallows and barn swallows from their South American wintering grounds.

Hummingbirds and catbirds have arrived in our yards, and warbler migration activity increases as the days warm. Warblers are tiny, colorful birds, woodland sprites that have wintered in Central America and South America, now returning to their nesting grounds in our northern forests, many as far north as the boreal forest of Canada. They move through during early May in waves, clamoring, whirling, swirling through the budding oaks. So much fun, and such a challenge to identify, even for the experienced birder.

Life on the ponds erupts in May and June, slowly at first as the winter waters warm. Insects metamorphose, and swallows, eastern kingbirds, and other insectivorous birds delight in the May insect swarms. Dragonflies and damselflies emerge from pond bottoms where they have spent up to two years in their larval stage; through the process of metamorphosis, they emerge as a beautiful and colorful Odonata. The many graceful dragonflies and damselflies are predators in their own right, eating small moths and other insects, but they are prey as well, feeding marsh and pond inhabitants such as frogs, birds, and even each other!

Snapping turtles climb the sandy banks of winter ponds to lay their eggs in early June, and many of our local birds are incubating eggs and feeding young throughout the month. Bluebirds, tree swallows, and black-capped chickadees are but a few of the cavity-nesting birds that will welcome the sight of a nesting box. Bird conservation through the careful placement of nest boxes is important to those species that can't find hollow trees that were once so abundant in local woodlands and yards. June is the month of raising young. It's during the busy months of May and June that Nature is immersed in the richness and fertility of summer.

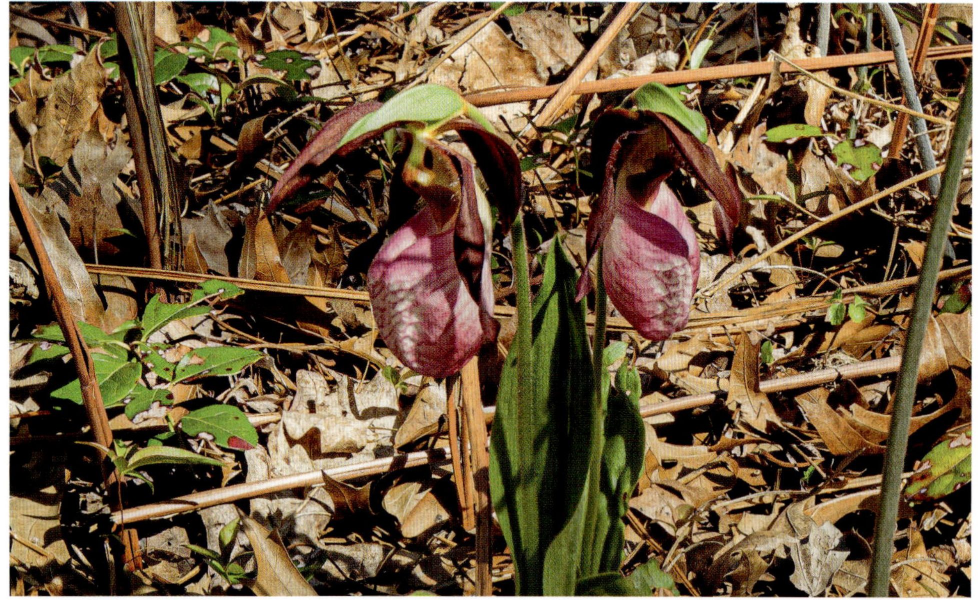

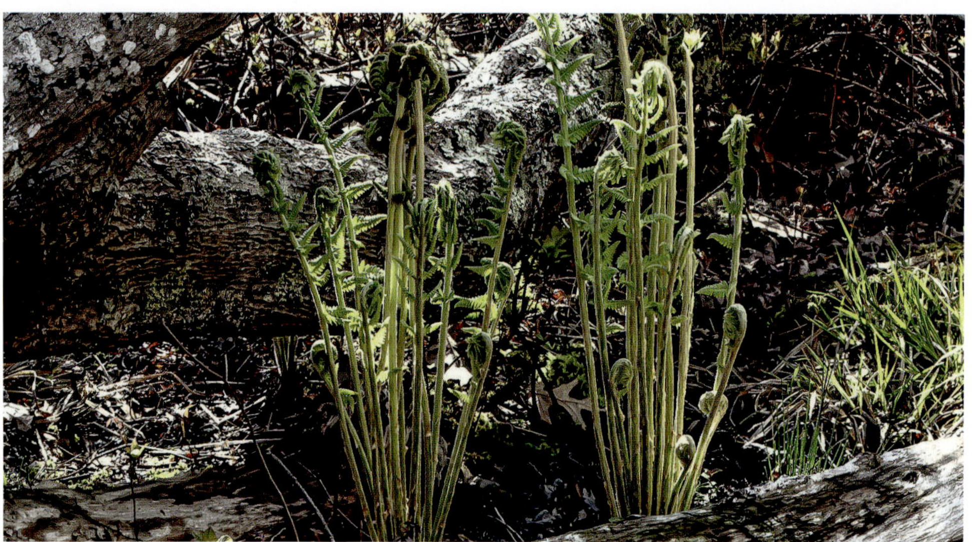

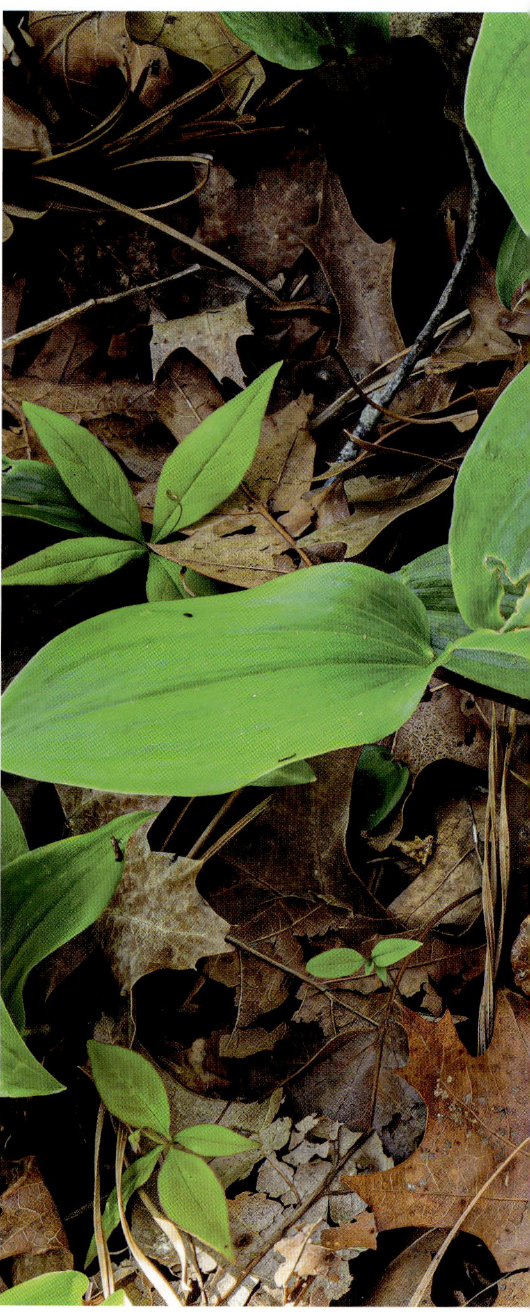

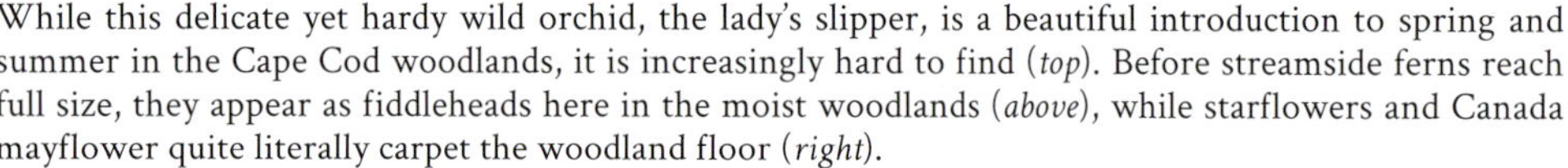

While this delicate yet hardy wild orchid, the lady's slipper, is a beautiful introduction to spring and summer in the Cape Cod woodlands, it is increasingly hard to find (*top*). Before streamside ferns reach full size, they appear as fiddleheads here in the moist woodlands (*above*), while starflowers and Canada mayflower quite literally carpet the woodland floor (*right*).

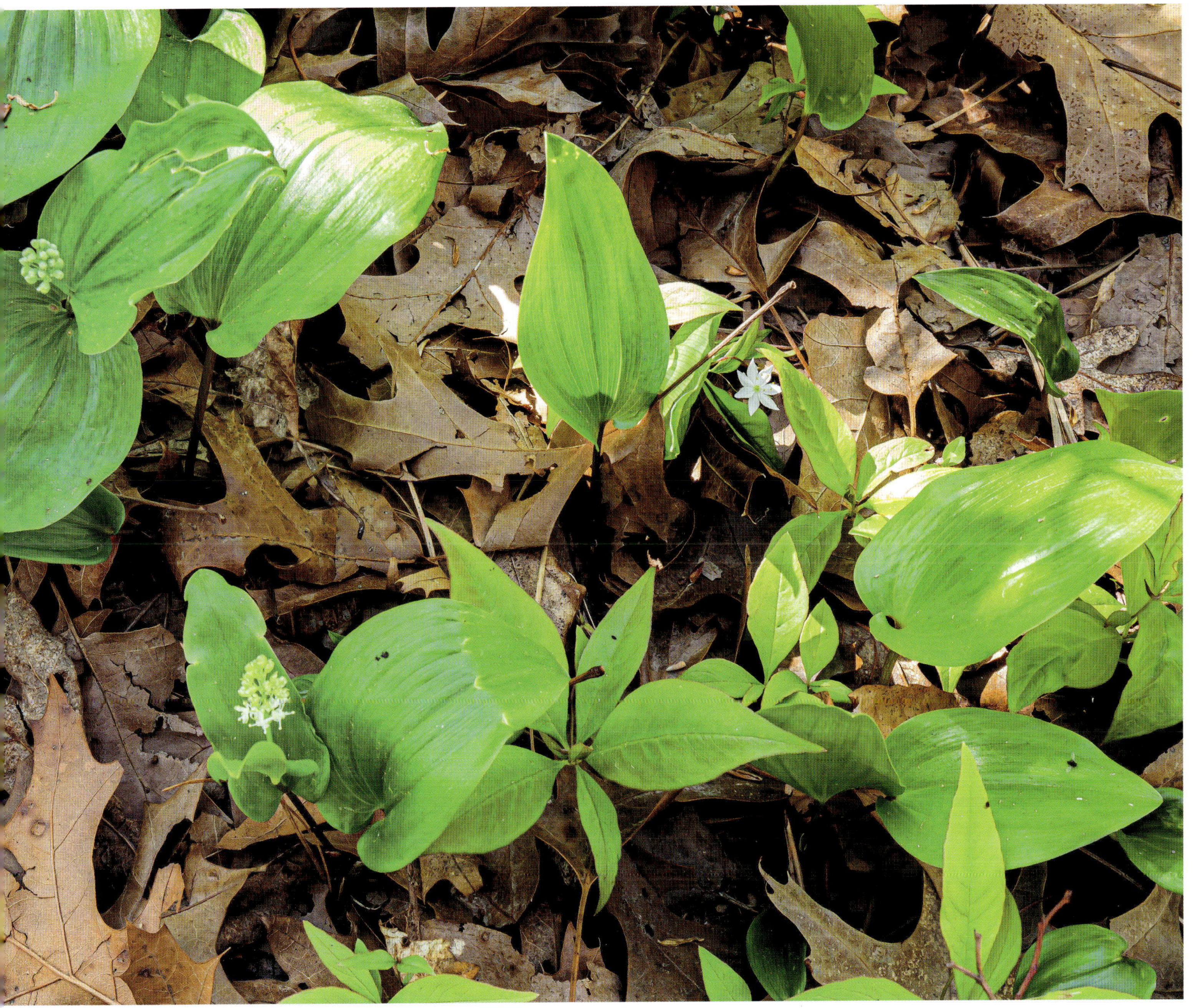

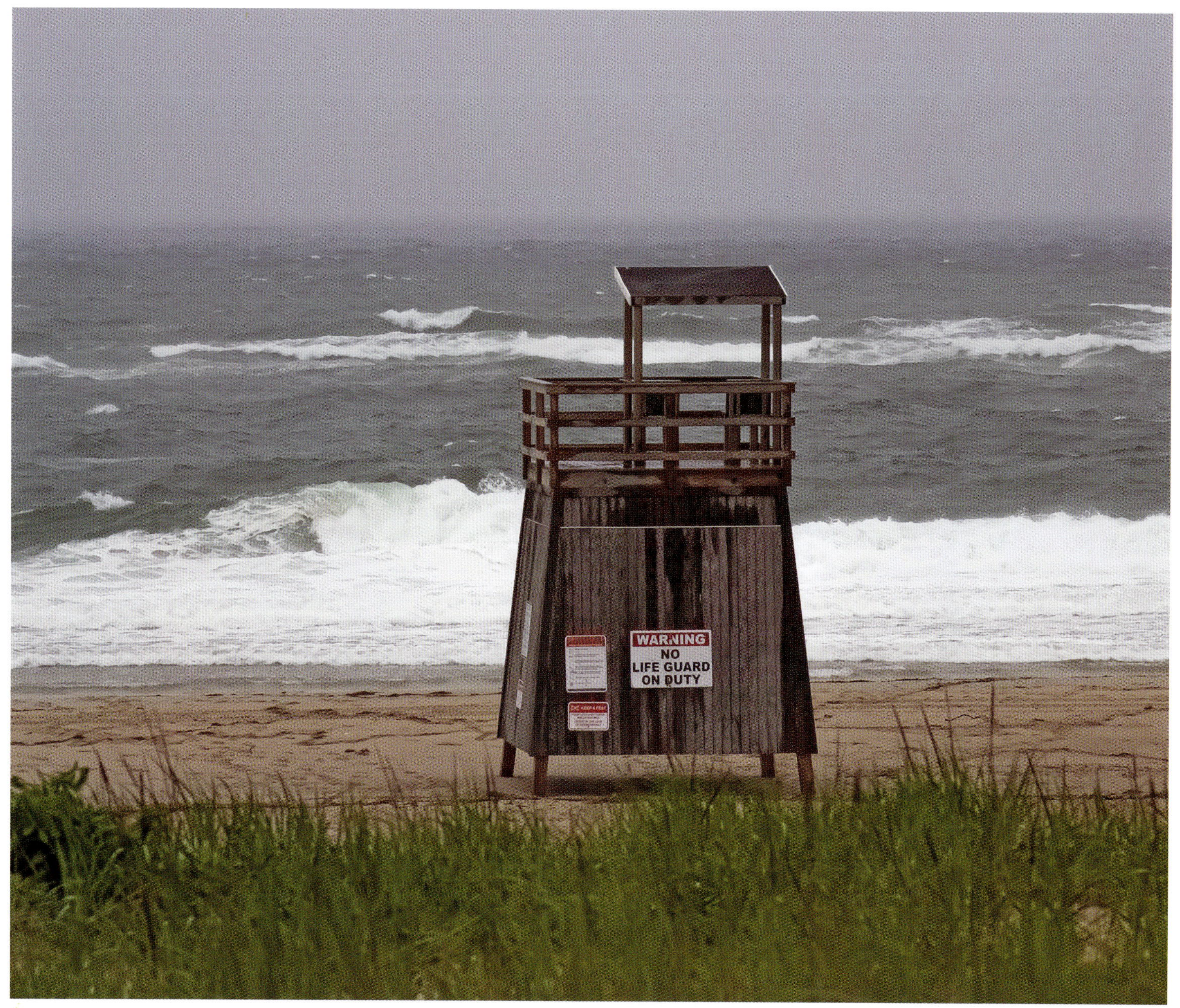

With a cold ocean before it and still-cold sand below, an empty lifeguard chair suggests warmer days to come.

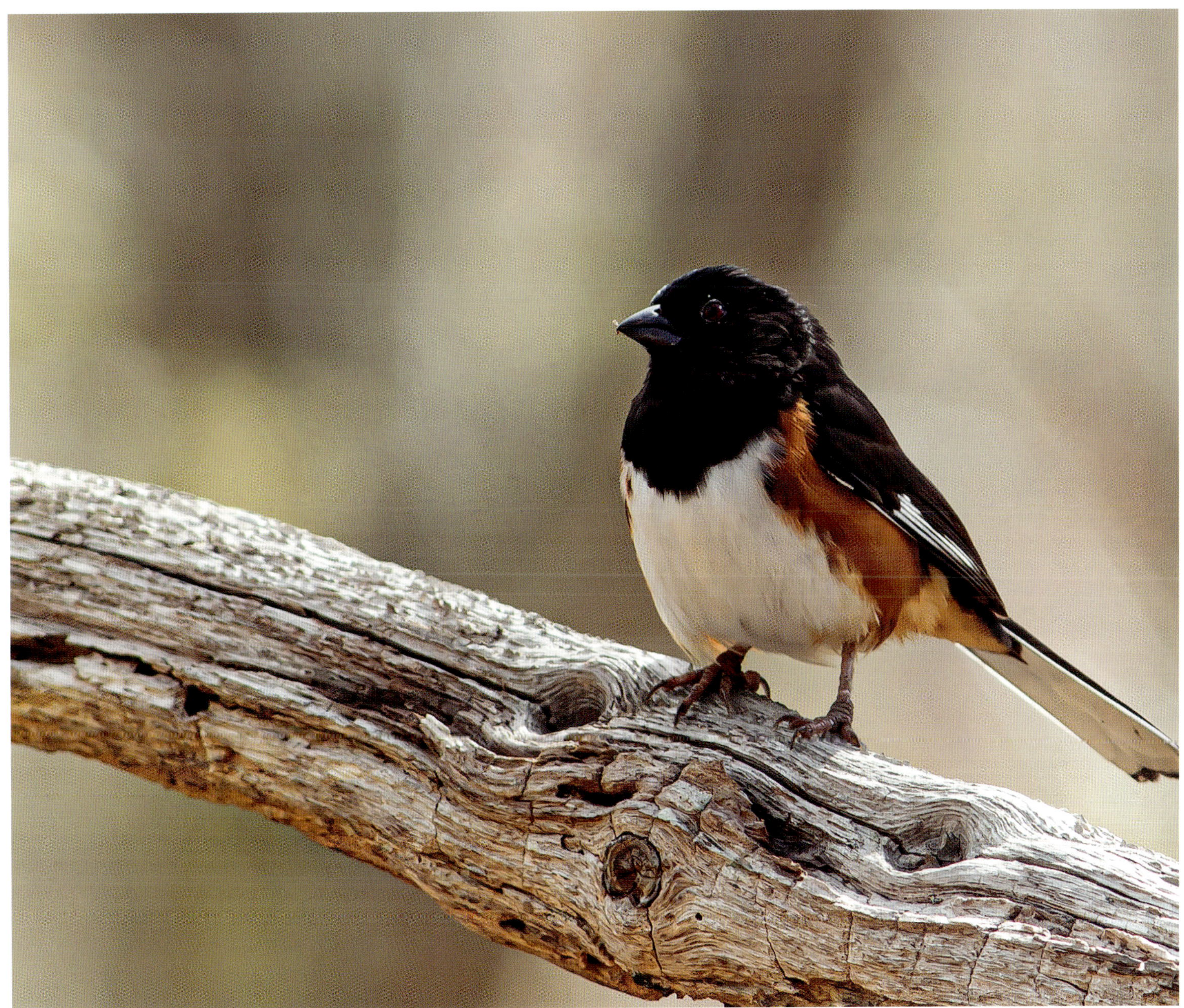

We wait in early May for the *chewink* sounds of the eastern towhee, a ground-nesting woodland songbird.

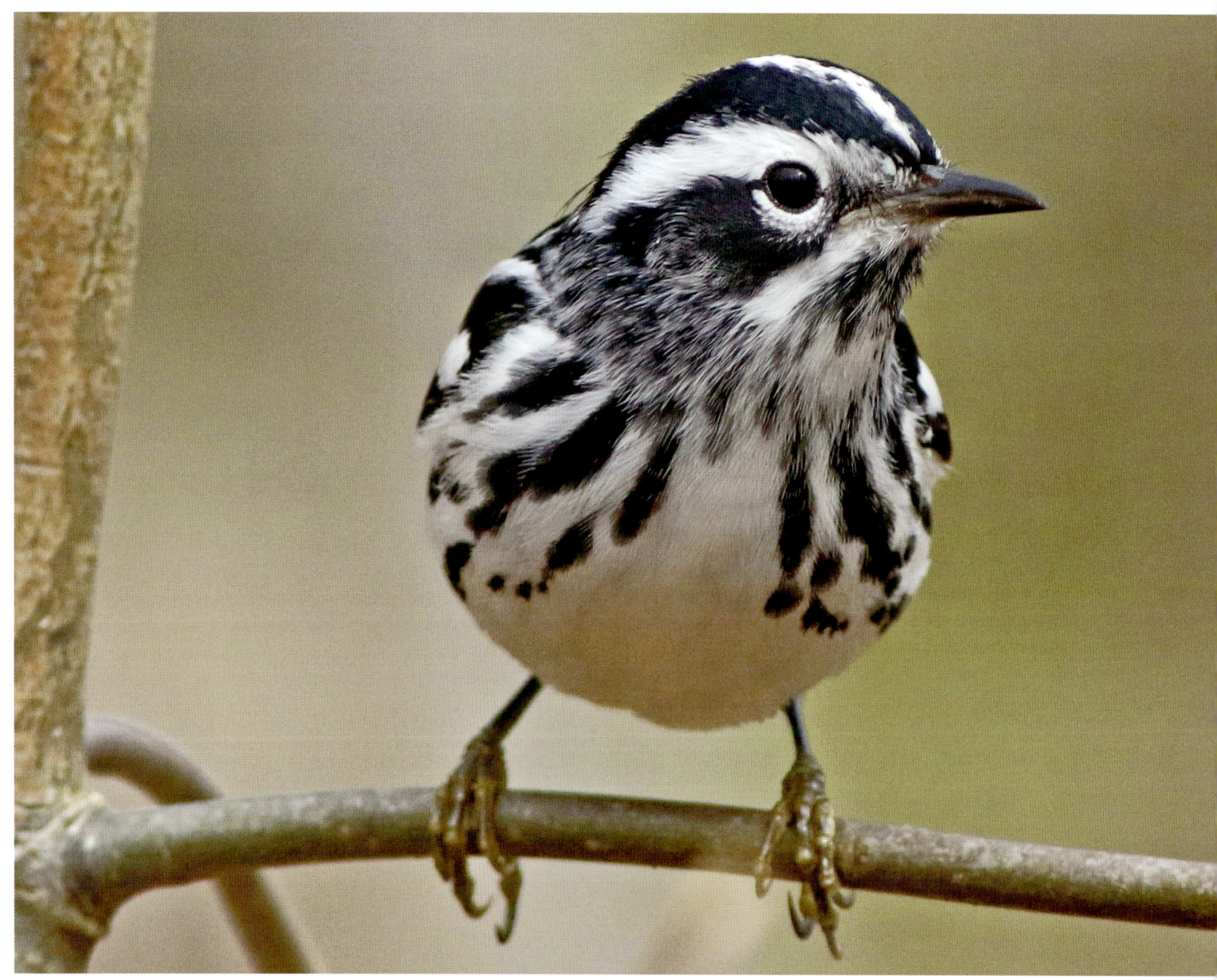

Three woodland warblers just passing through. The black-and-white warbler (*above*), northern parula (*top right*), and chestnut-sided warbler (*bottom right*) are tiny woodland sprites that migrate through the woodlands in May.

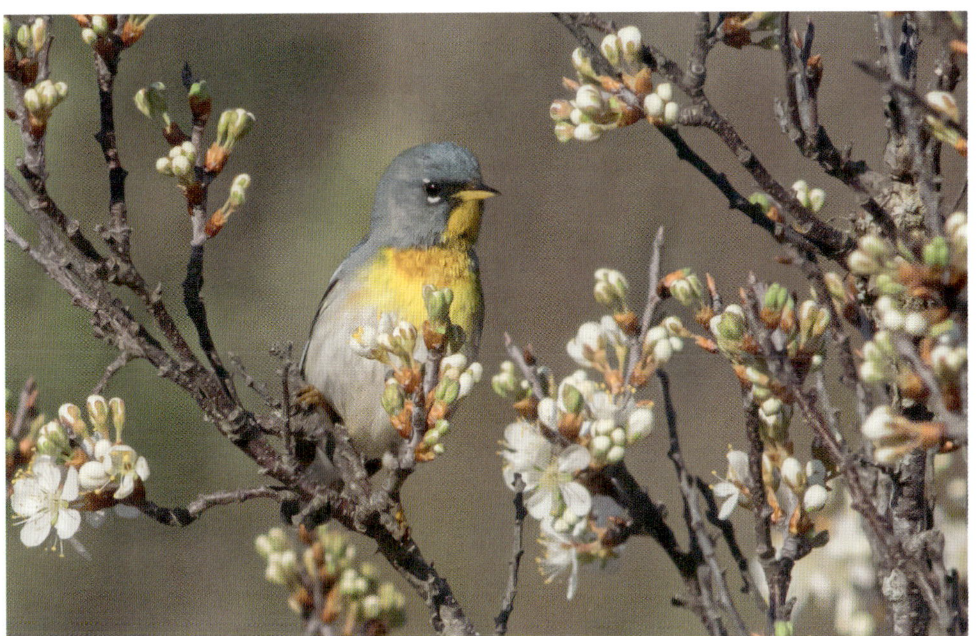
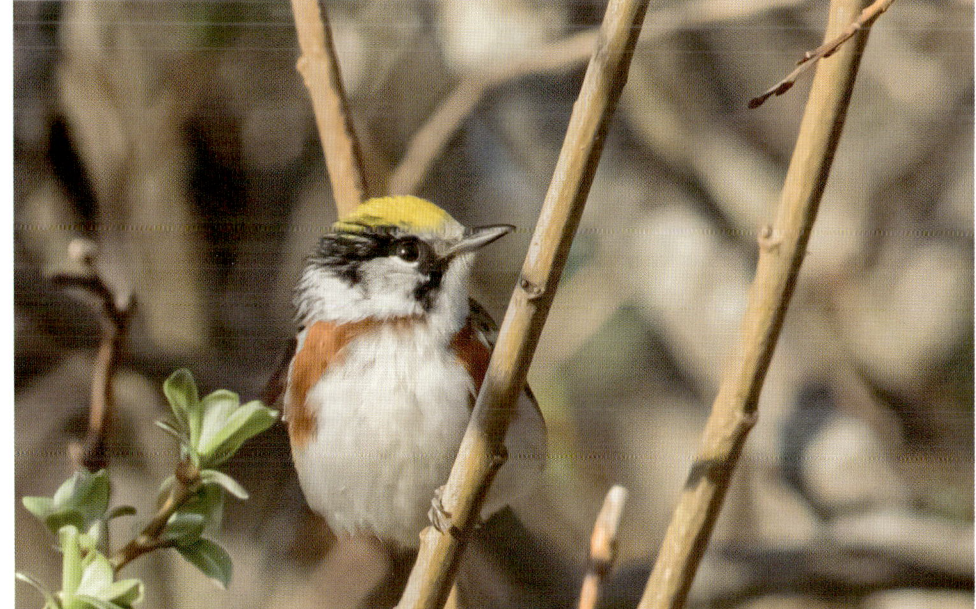

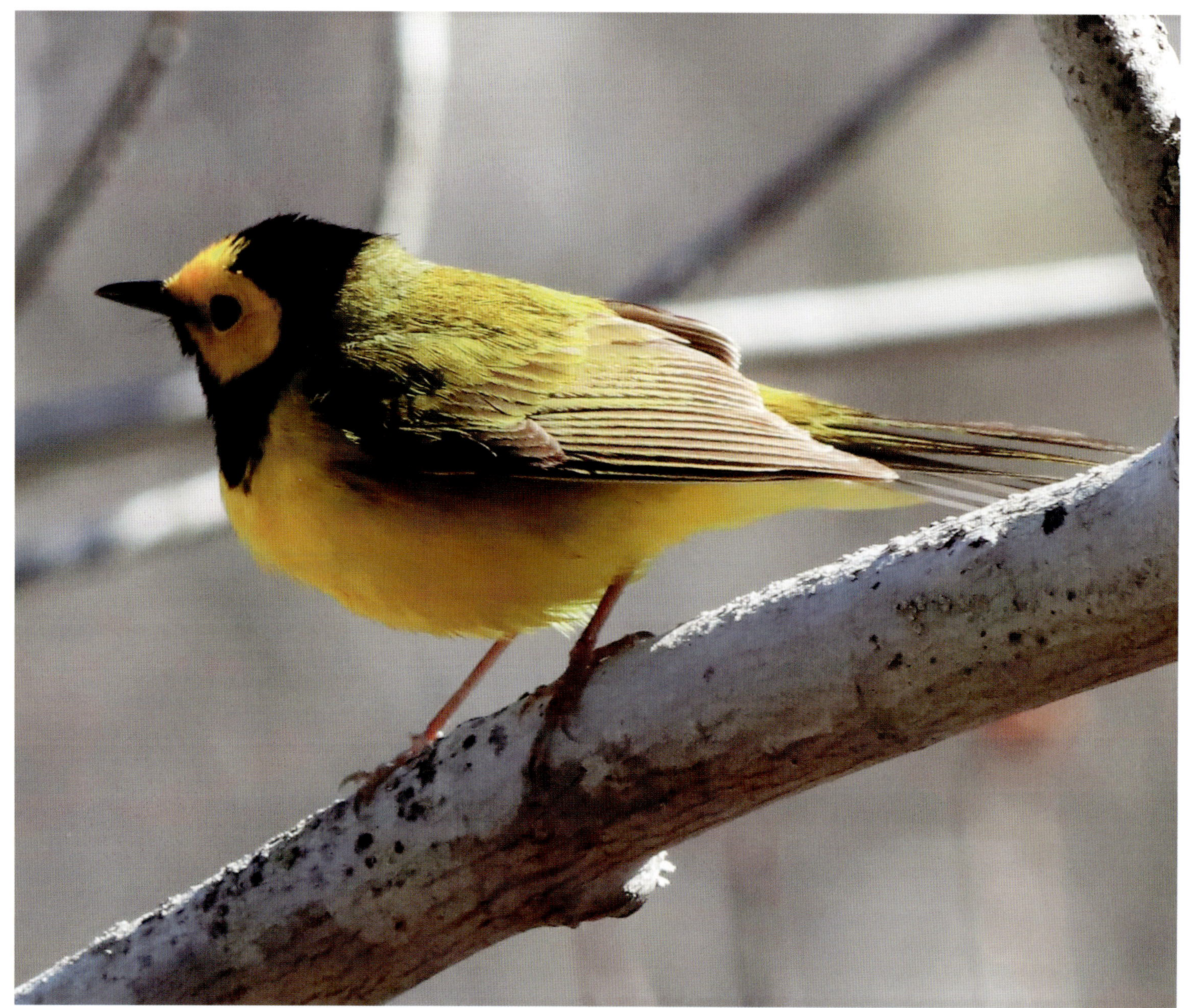

This hooded warbler is a rarity at this time of year. A bird found south of Cape Cod has overshot its spring migration, giving birders a real thrill!

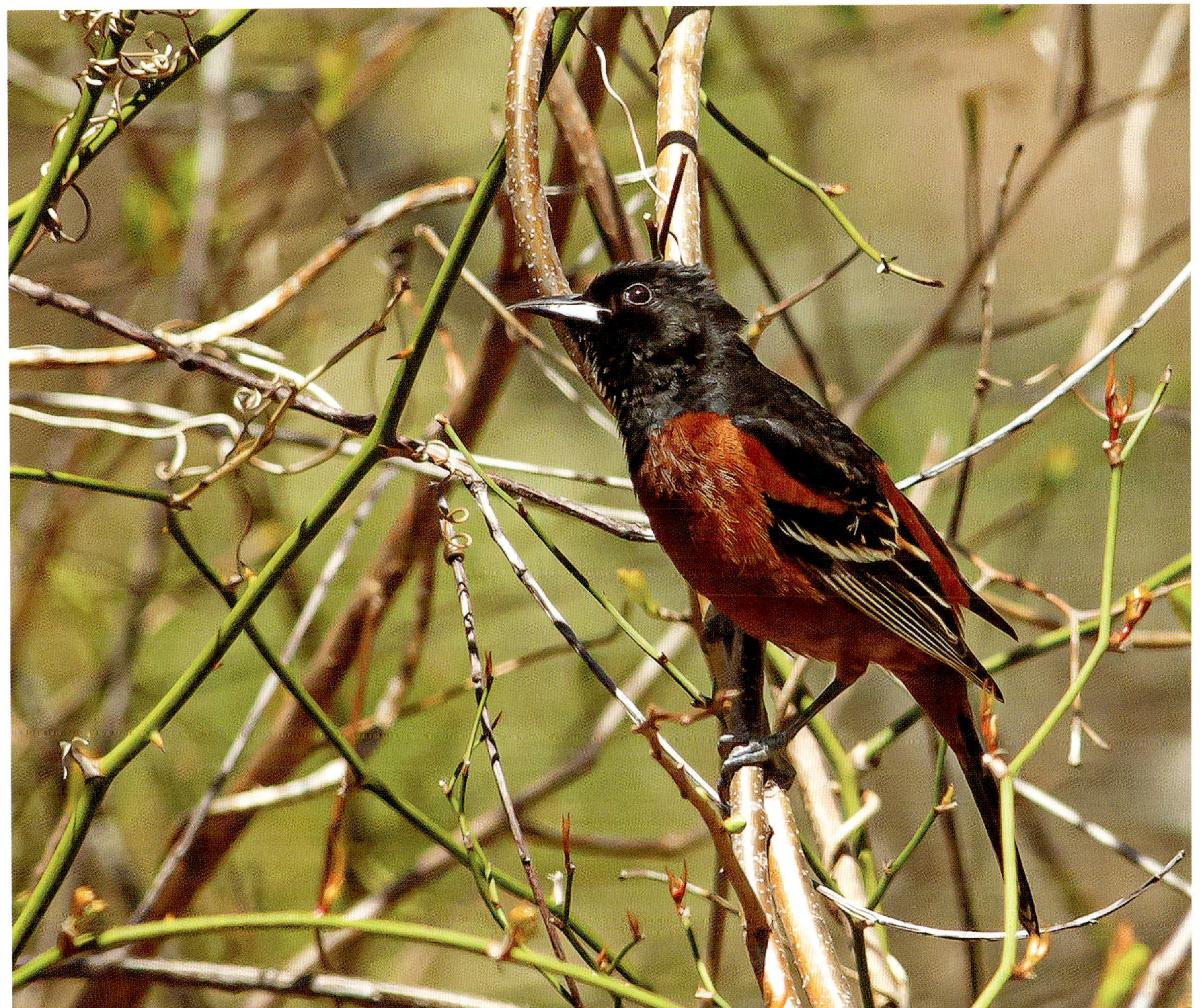

The brick-red orchard oriole nests on Cape Cod, but it is less conspicuous than its bright relative, the Baltimore oriole.

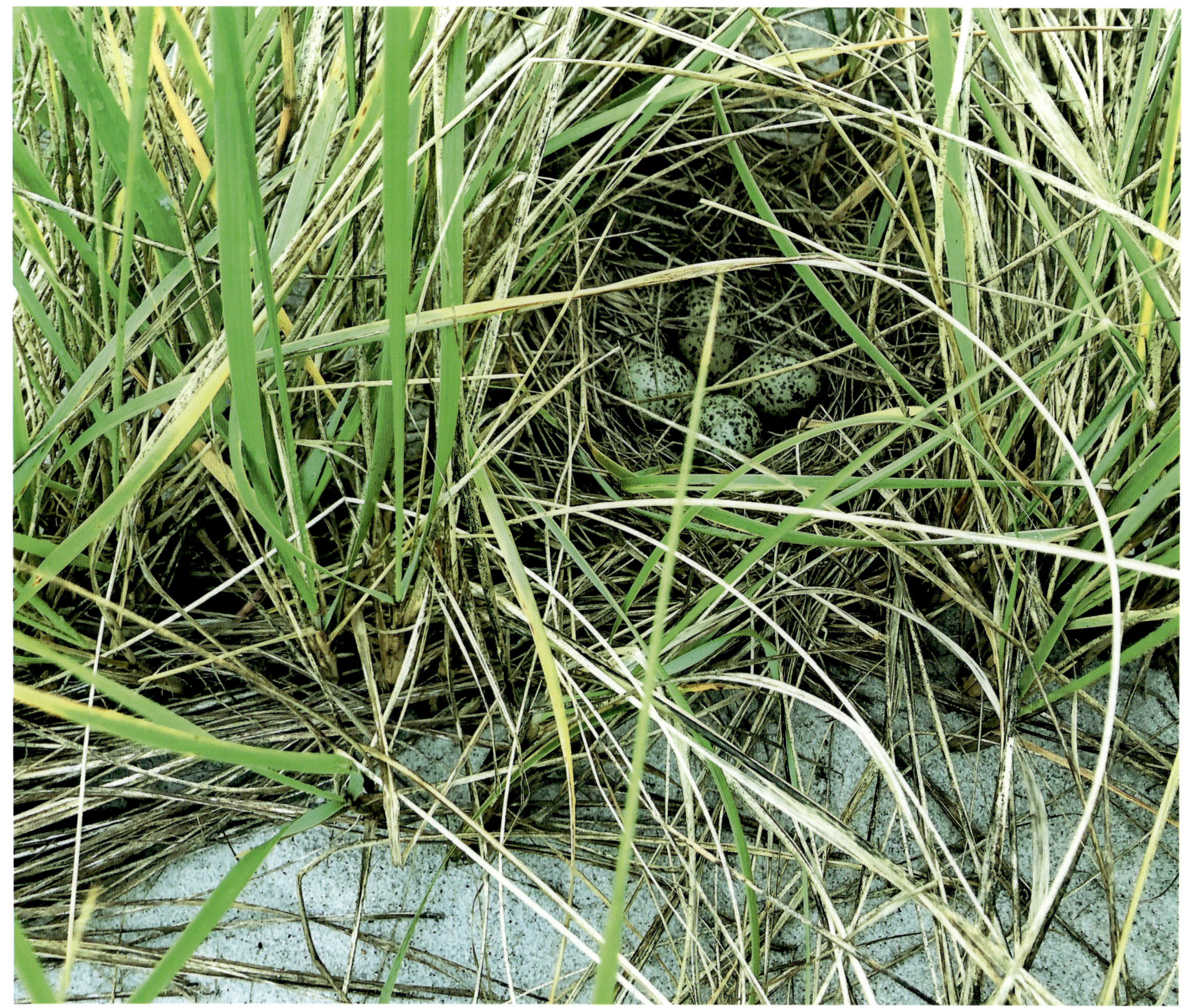

The nest of a large sandpiper, the eastern willet, is well hidden in the grassy edge of a dune and salt marsh. This nest contains four eggs, which is typical.

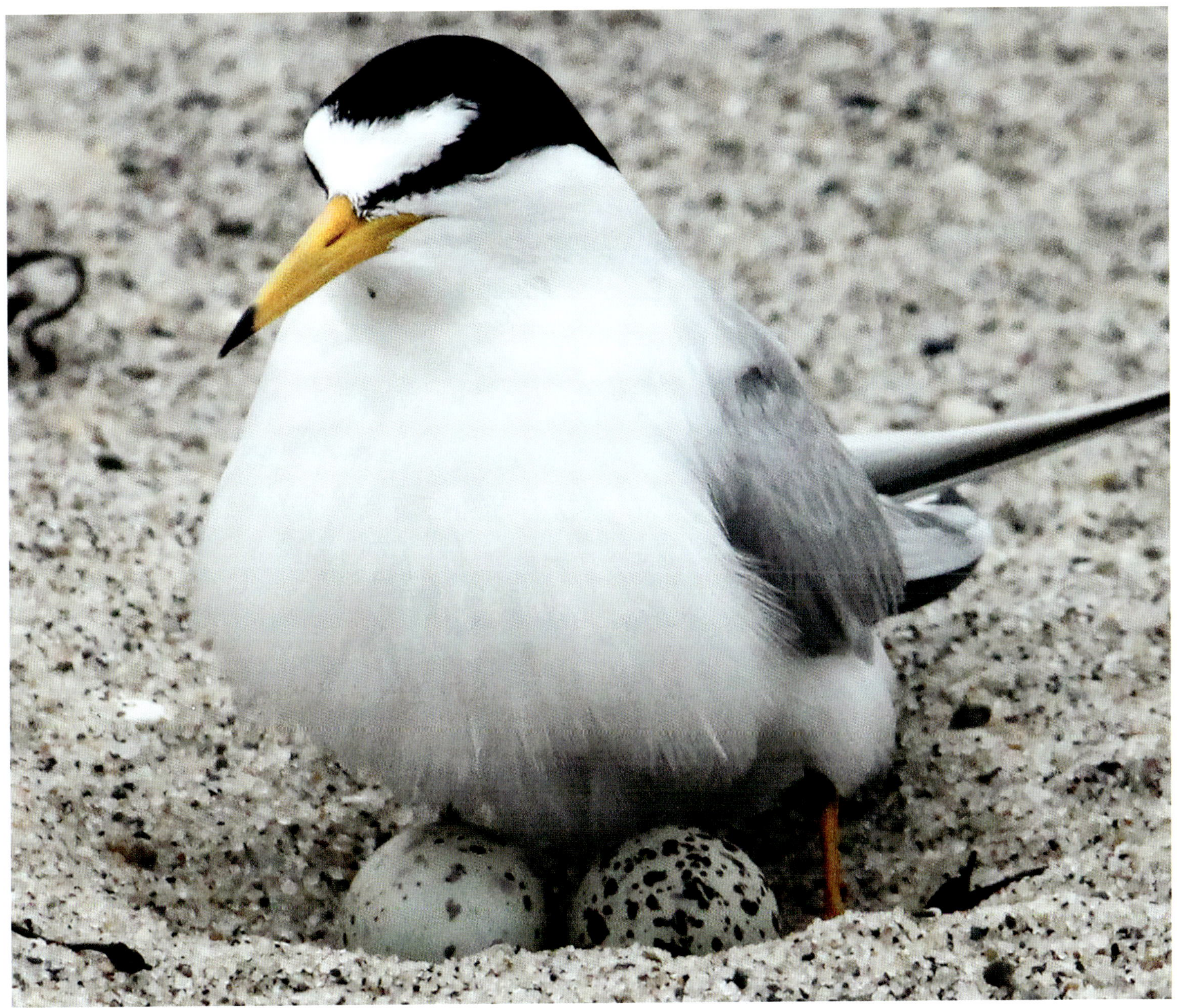

The least tern, smallest of our beach-nesting terns, prepares to incubate its two-egg clutch.

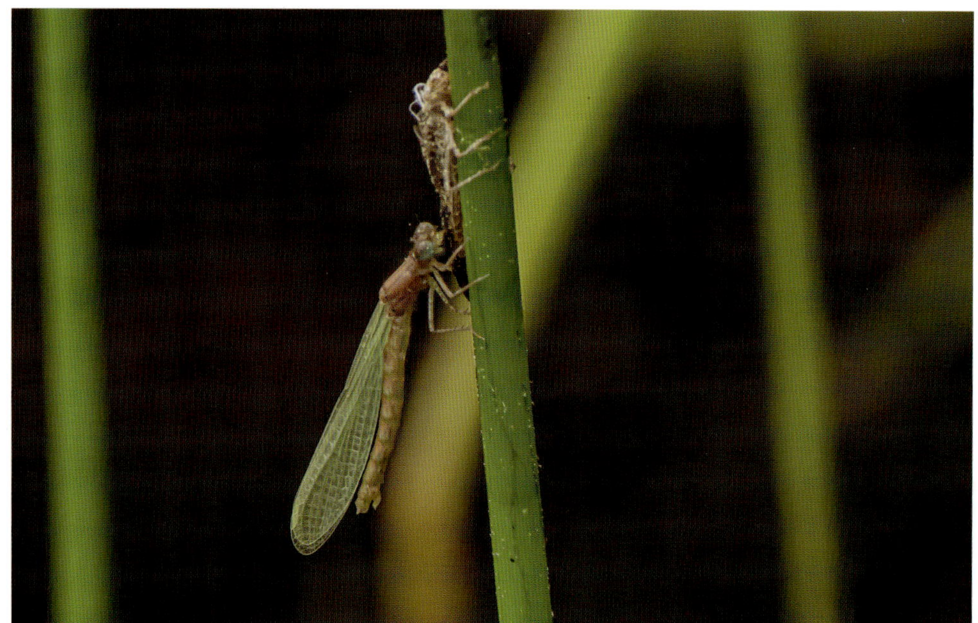

This damselfly has just emerged, transitioning from the larval to the adult stage of its development. In the form of what is now a dried exoskeleton (*top*), called an exuviae, the insect had lived for a year or more on the pond bottom as an aquatic predator before emerging as this soon-to-be-colorful adult.

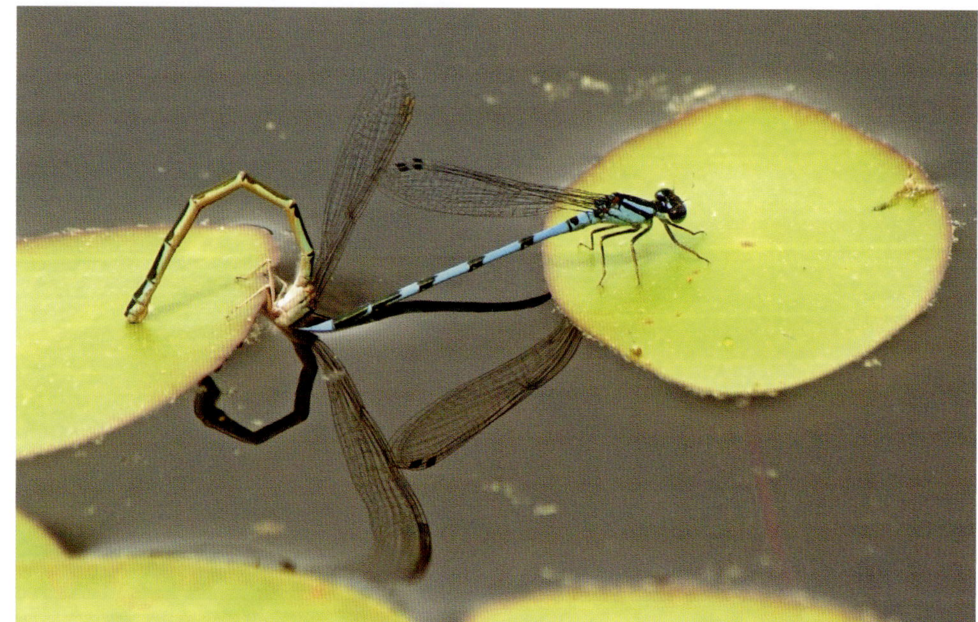

A male pine barrens bluet clasps a female behind her head as she scrambles to get above the lily pad. The female will tuck her abdomen (ovipositor) beneath the pad and lay eggs on the underside.

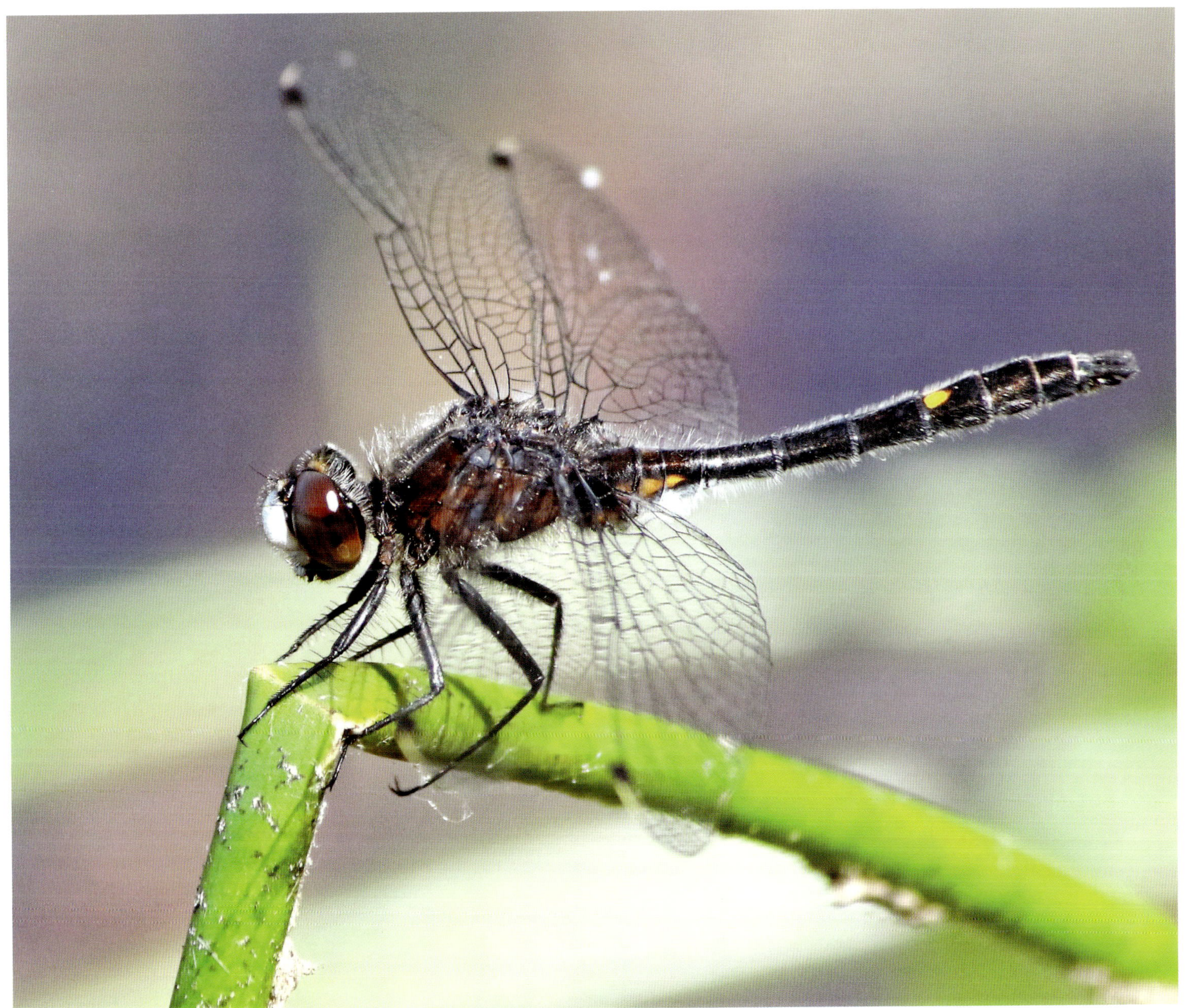

Dot-tailed white face, an appropriately named dragonfly.

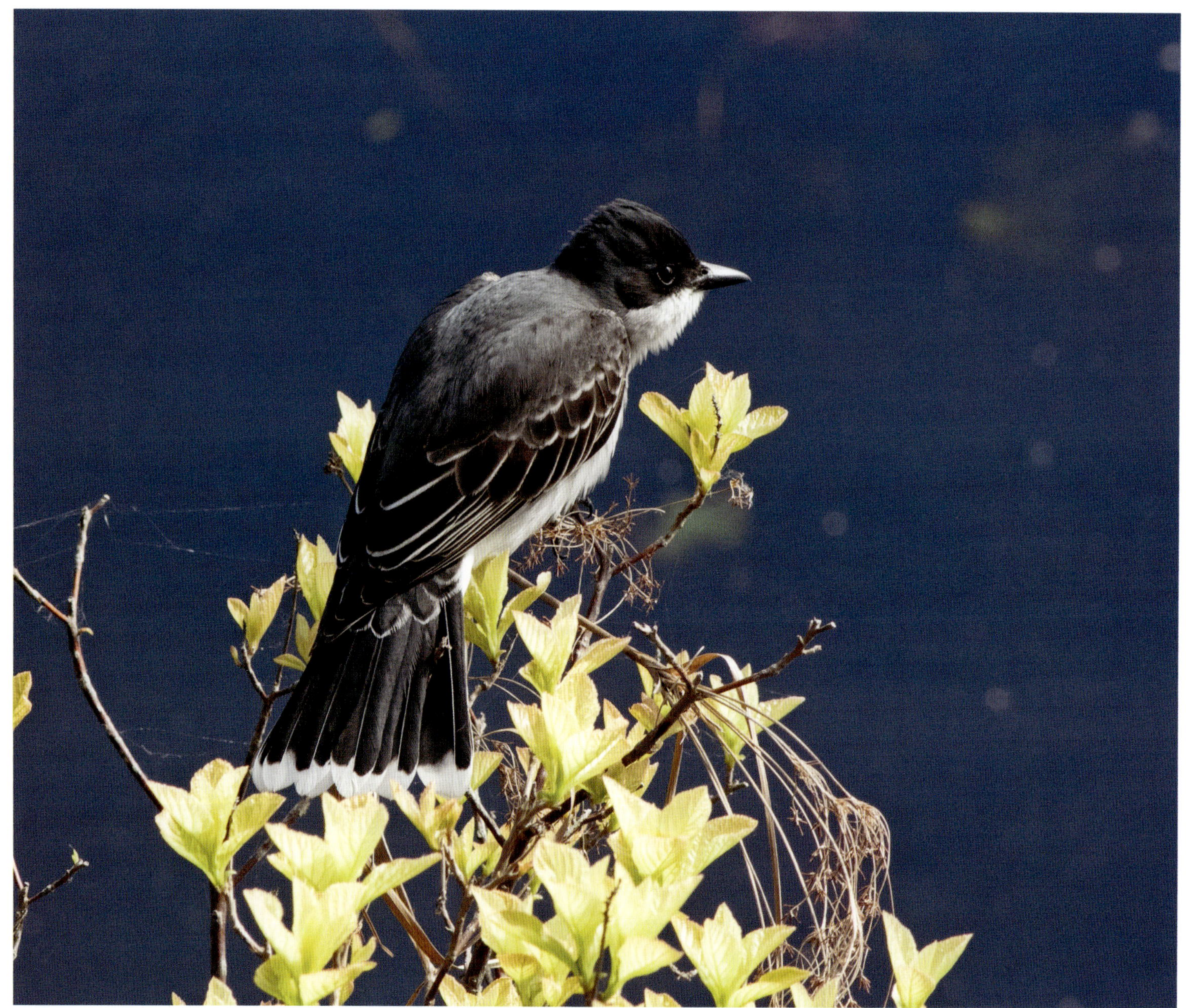

Eastern kingbird is a predator of these dragons and damsels. From a perch, it swoops out over the pond and lilies and grabs its prey.

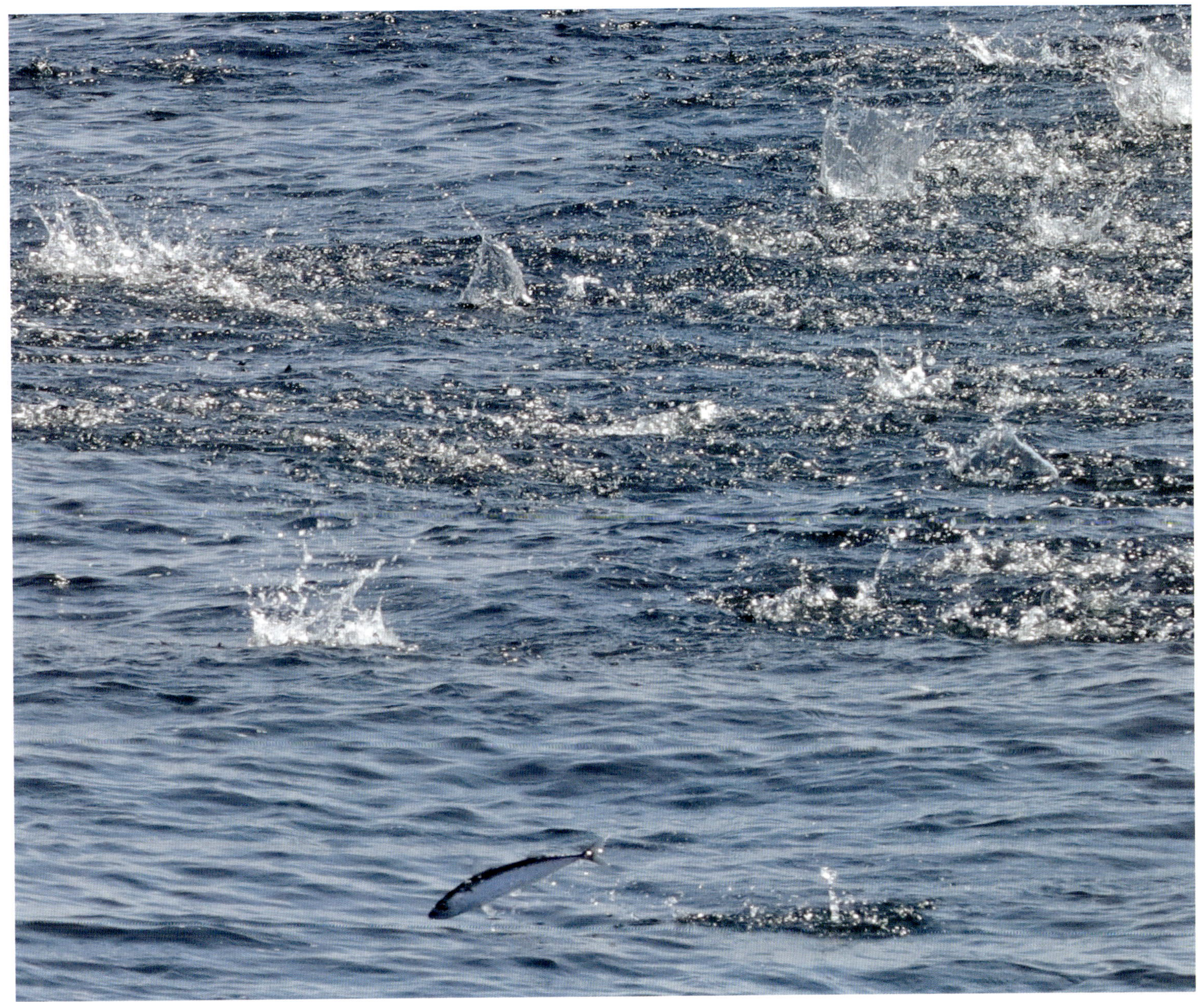

As we head offshore, the waters east of Chatham splash and froth as millions of mackerel slash through a school of sand eels. The predatory mackerel often leave the water as they frantically burst through the school of smaller fish.

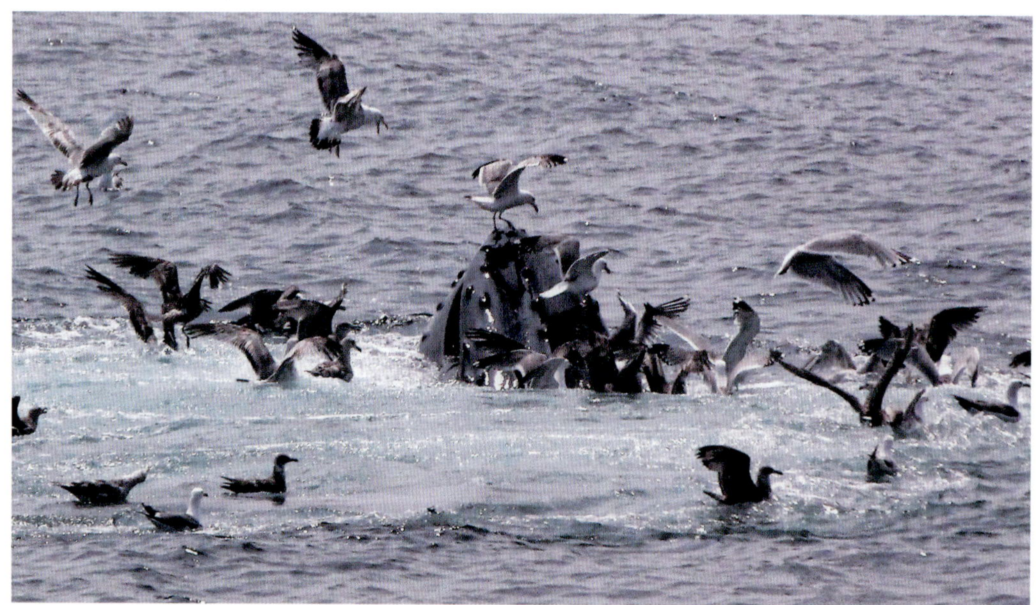

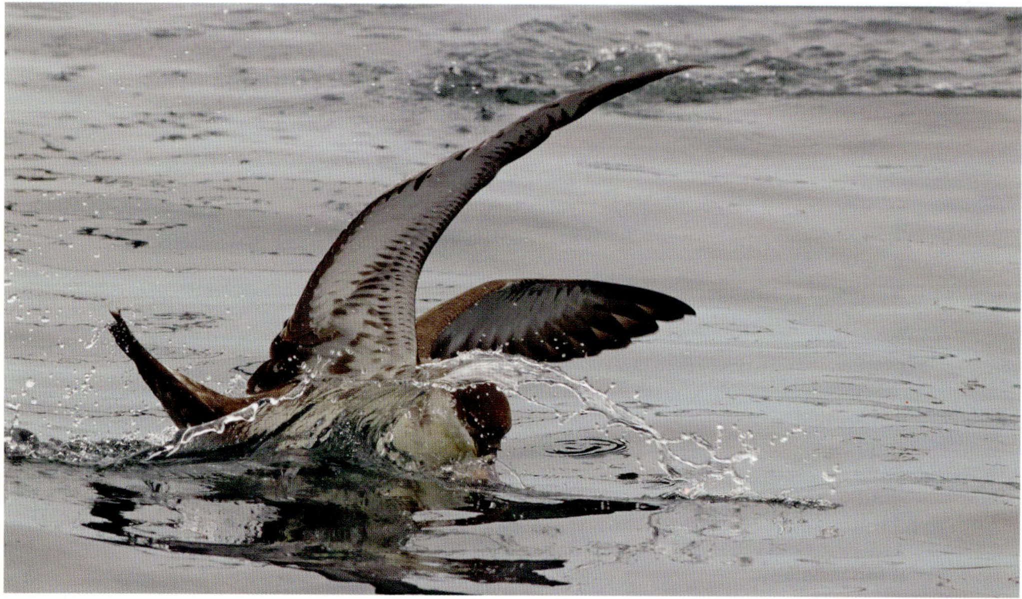

Higher on the food chain, a humpback whale surfaces after gorging itself with the abundant mackerel, while the gluttonous great shearwaters and gulls feed on the leftovers.

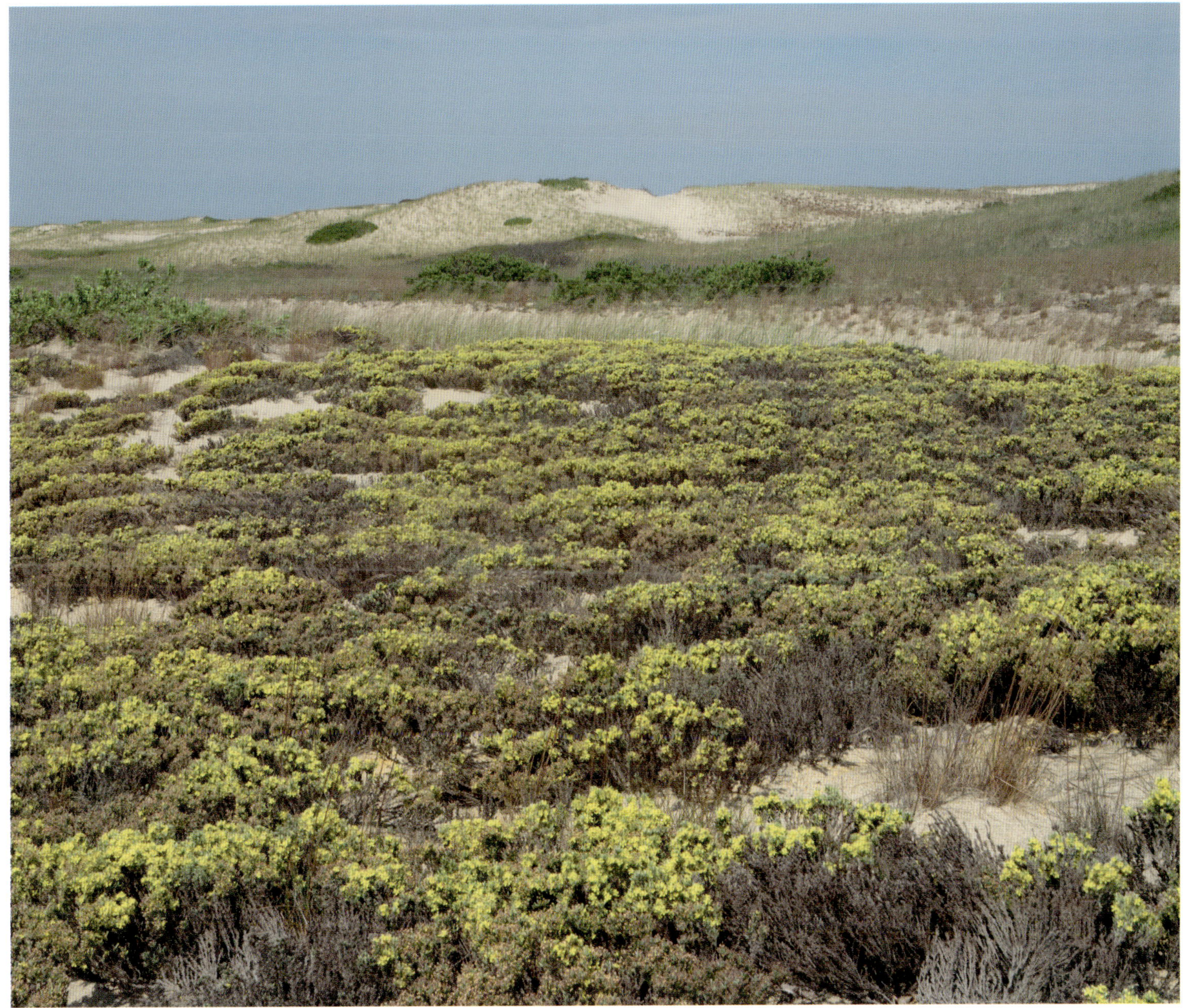

Poverty grass, *Hudsonia tomentosa*, carpets the dunes with beautiful yellow flowers through the month of June.

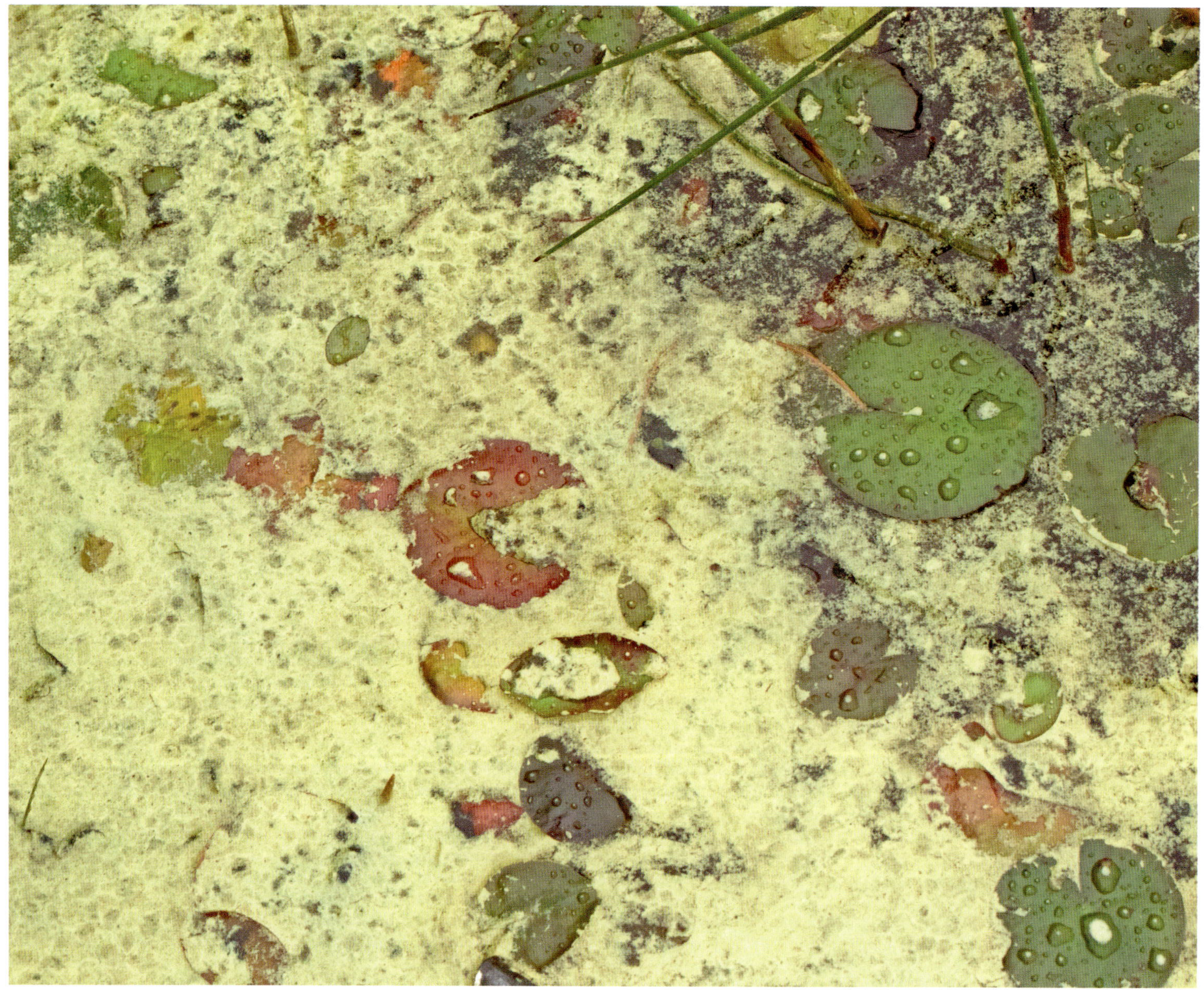

Every Cape Codder dreads the ubiquitous yellow carpet of pine pollen that blankets cars, walkways, and even the furniture in our homes during June. Here, the pond edge and plants are covered.

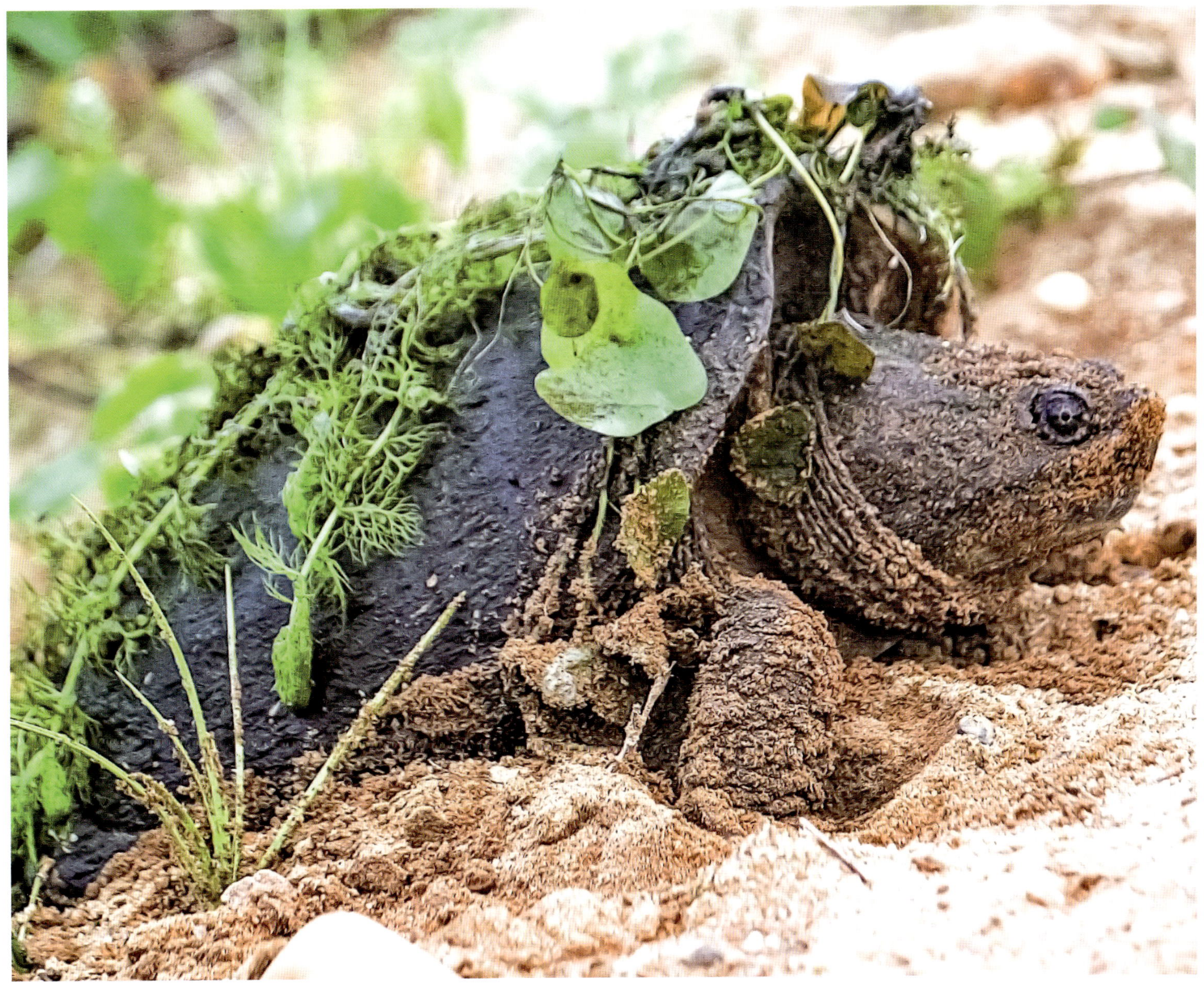

A female snapping turtle emerges from her pond. She will dig a hole and deposit her eggs in the sandy substrate. Eggs typically hatch in ninety days, early September, but may winter over and hatch out in April. The babies will quickly clamor back to the pond, where they may live for more than eighty years. Northern snapping turtles reach sexual maturity at twelve to fourteen years of age.

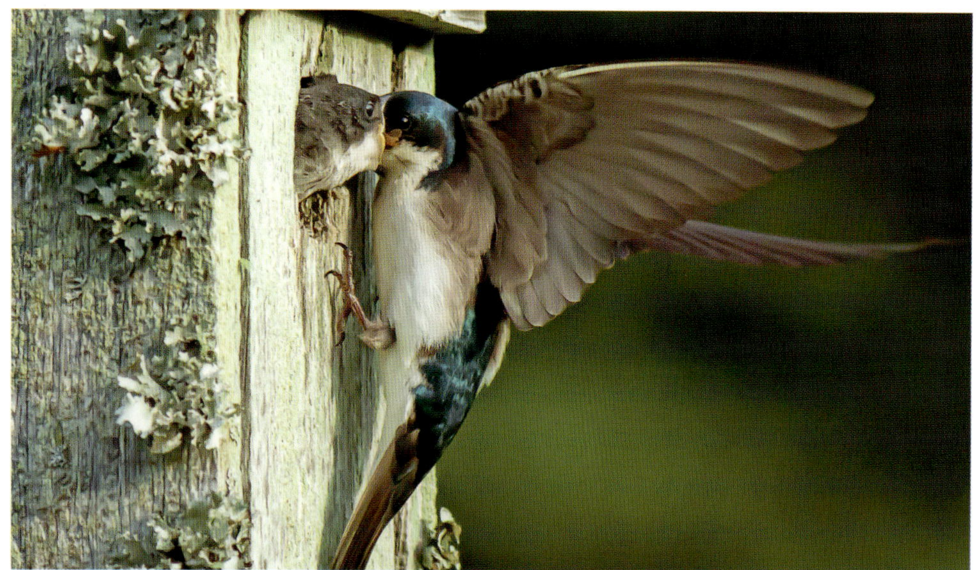

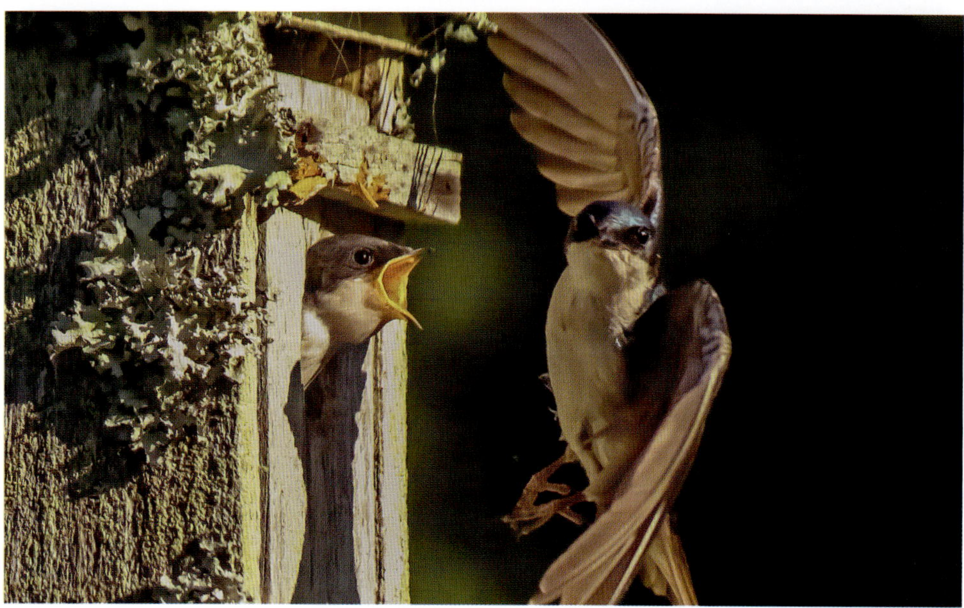

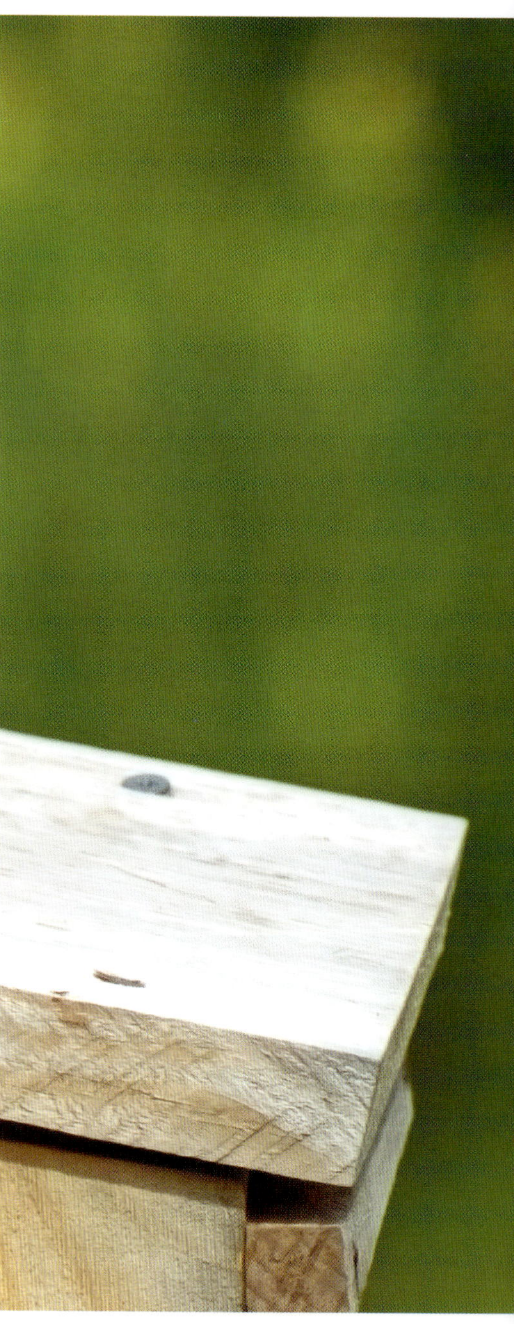

Tree swallows and eastern bluebirds take readily to nest boxes. Here, a tree swallow jams food into its chick's throat (*top*) and later flies off to collect food (*above*) as its chick begs, "More! More!" A female eastern bluebird comes in with a meal (*right*).

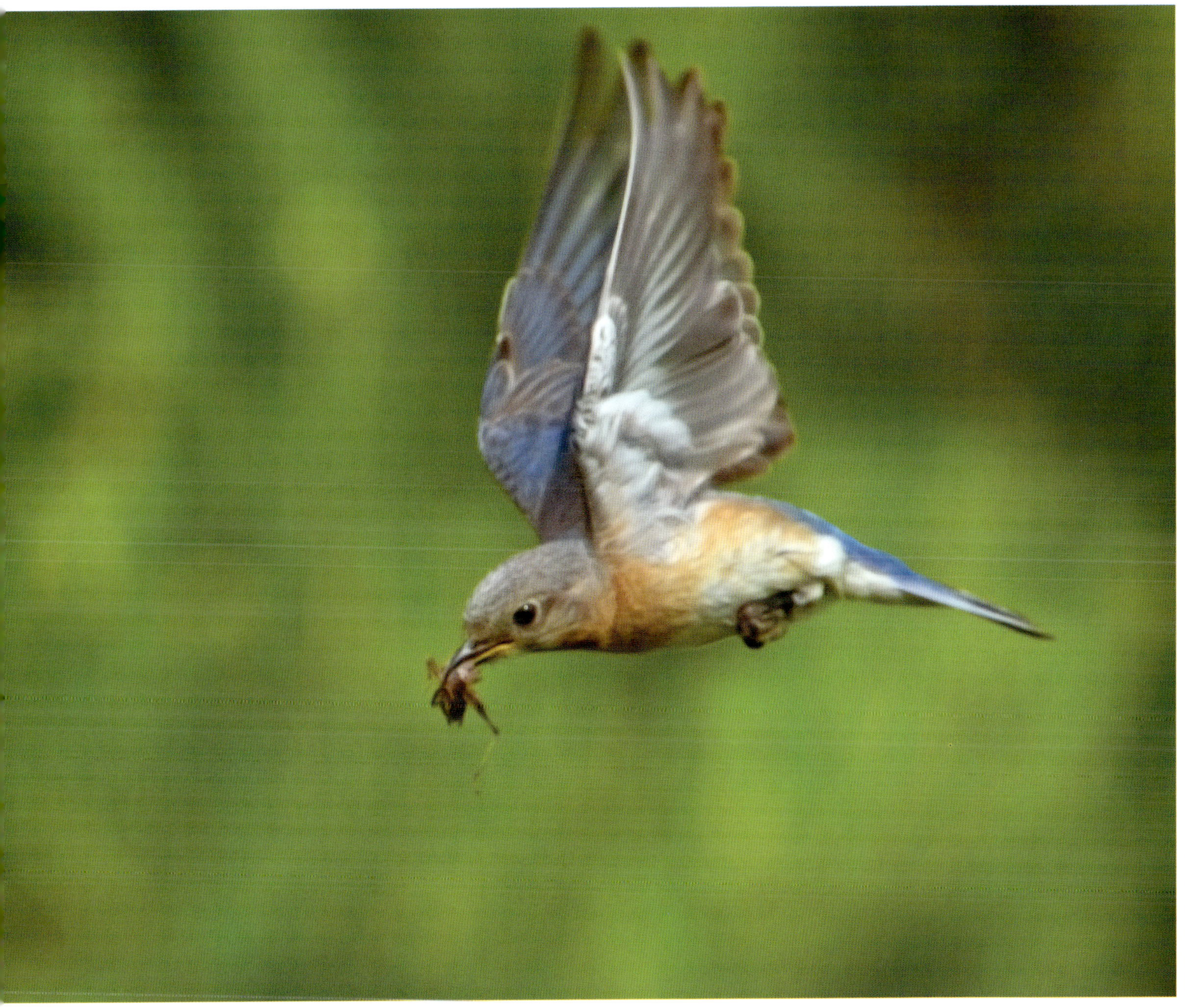

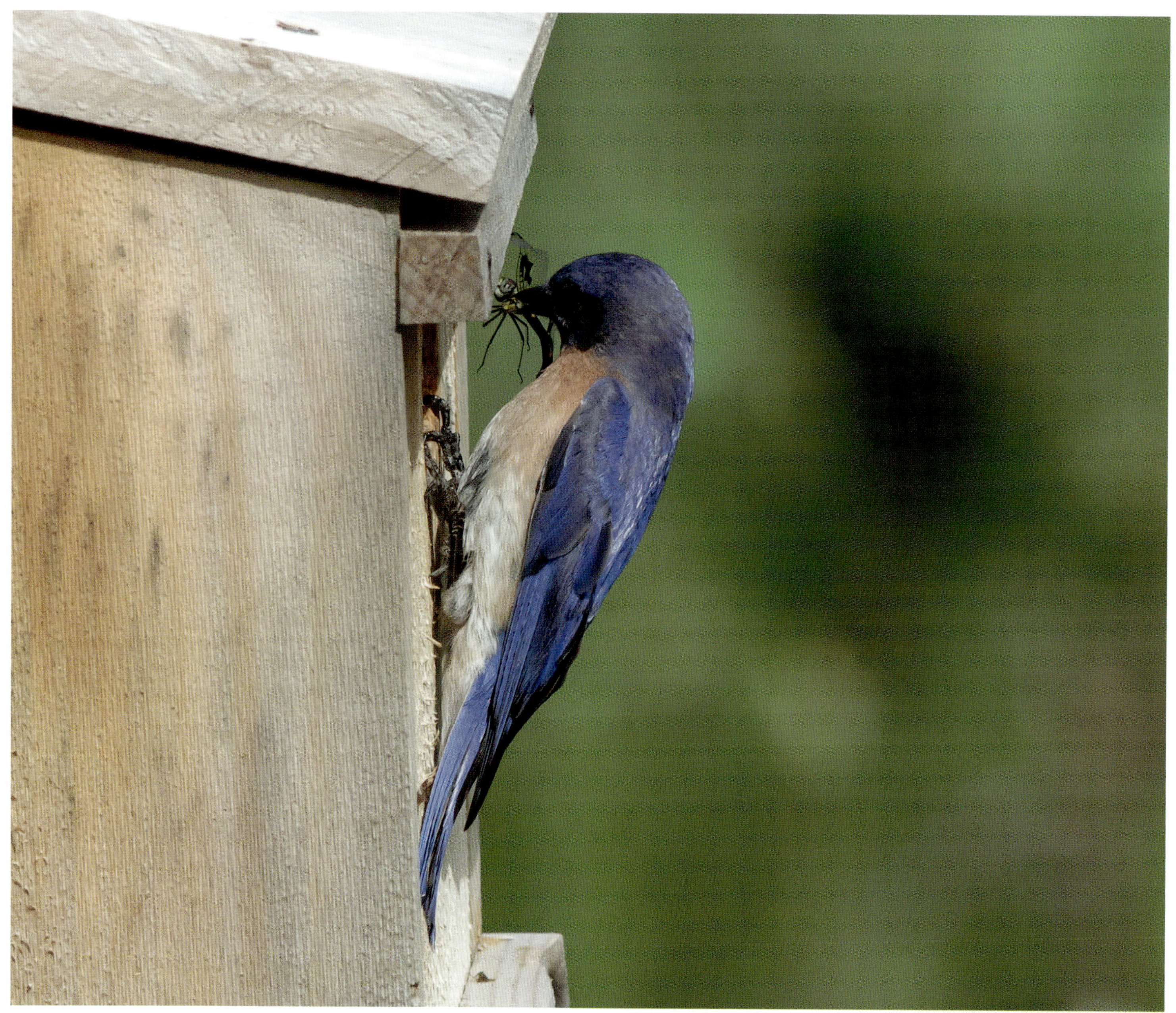

A male eastern bluebird returns to feed one of its chicks a dragonfly.

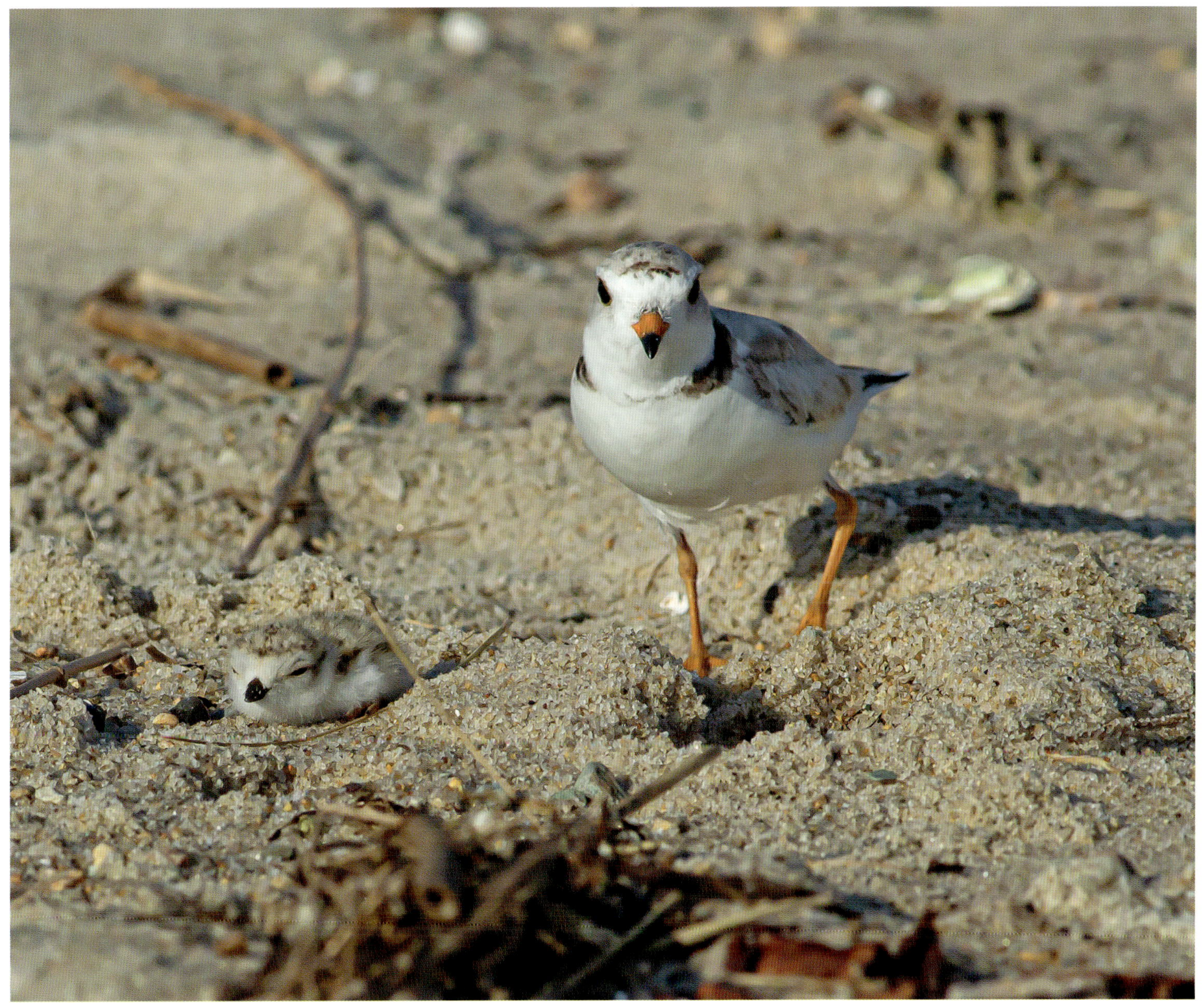

A days-old piping plover chick hunkers down next to its parent. The tiny, cryptic chick is virtually impossible for casual observers and avian predators to see against the sand.

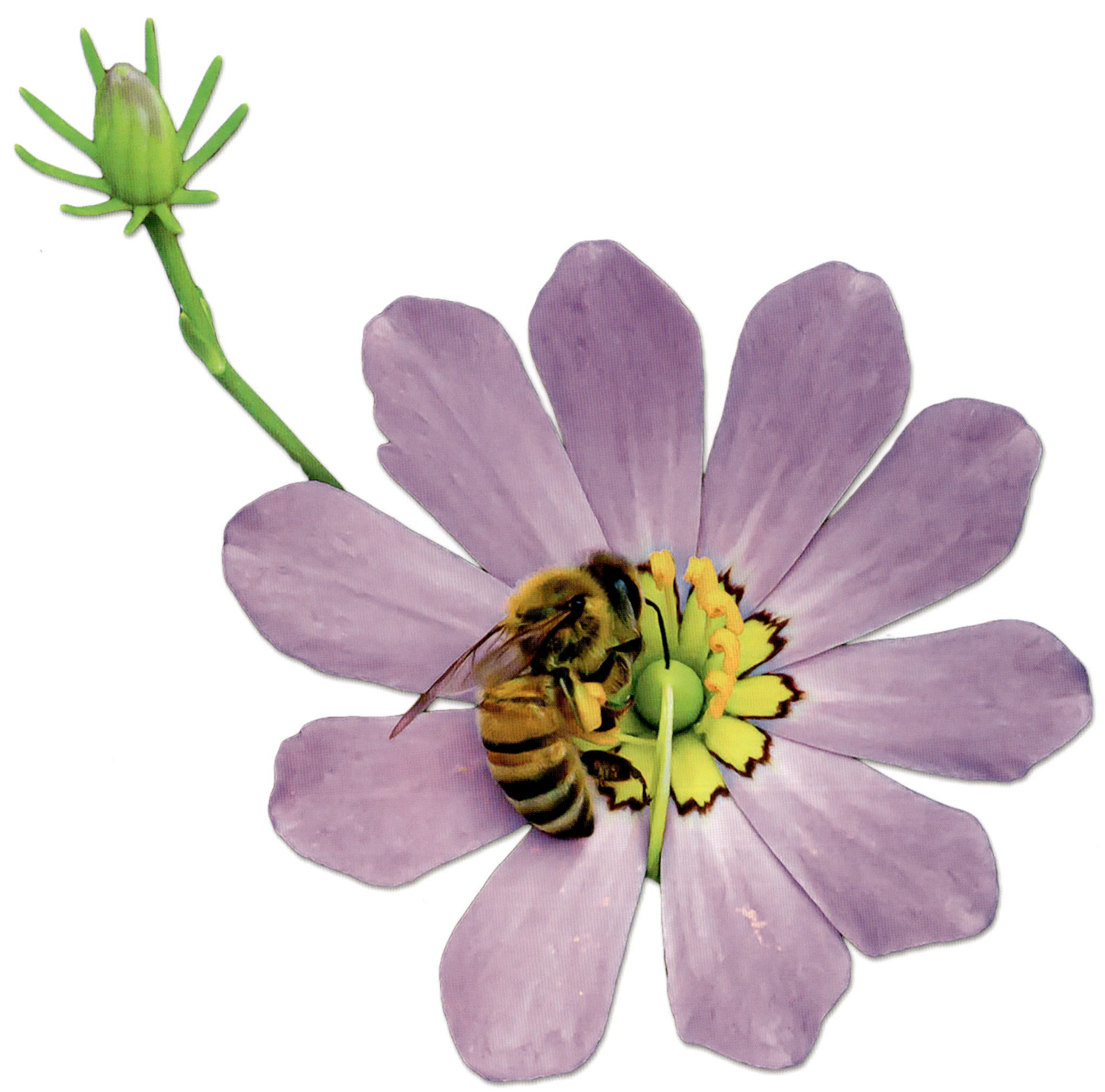

JULY AND AUGUST
Shorter Days Foreshadow Autumn

These are the months that cape residents and tourists consider the height of summer. Indeed, they are the two hottest months of the year, with the days averaging 78 degrees and 77 degrees, respectively. July and August are the most crowded months on Cape Cod, with millions of people enjoying the summer sun, beaches, and activities. But hold on. With the summer solstice weeks past, the days are getting shorter by mid-July and especially August. The incontrovertible realization is that in the realm of nature, these two months represent early autumn.

By July 10, thousands of sandpipers and plovers have left their Arctic tundra breeding grounds and are migrating south to their wintering quarters in South America. Cape Cod is a rich and bountiful feeding area for these birds. The tidal flats, beaches, and salt marshes are teeming with insects and marine invertebrates. On any given day in July or August, the flats are covered with a diversity of south-moving shorebirds. The sea is warm and warming up during these two months, with several species of whales, predominantly humpback and finback whales, just offshore, and common dolphins often seen among them.

Marine birds, such as the great shearwater and Wilson's storm petrel, can be seen on whale-watching or fishing trips. These two species, Antarctic nesters, are here on their wintering grounds. Because the Northern and Southern Hemispheres have opposite seasons, these oceanic wanderers nest during our winter and make a transequatorial migration north in the austral autumn. We see them in July and August.

Perhaps the most diverse and exciting haunts for a curious naturalist are around—and waist-deep in—any of the hundreds of coastal-plain ponds, or exploring the wild meadows found over the entire cape. Nature's calendar is booked with events around the ponds and meadows. Pond creatures are easy to observe; turtles and frogs are abundant to the keen observer; dragonflies and their petite cousins, the damselflies, grace the pond edges like jewels in the rim of a crown. Grab a net and get wet! Birds exploit the hatches of insects, whether on the wing or plucking them from twig tips. The beaches are rich in rose hips, and, of course, the sandpipers and plovers have arrived in large numbers. It's early fall and soon September.

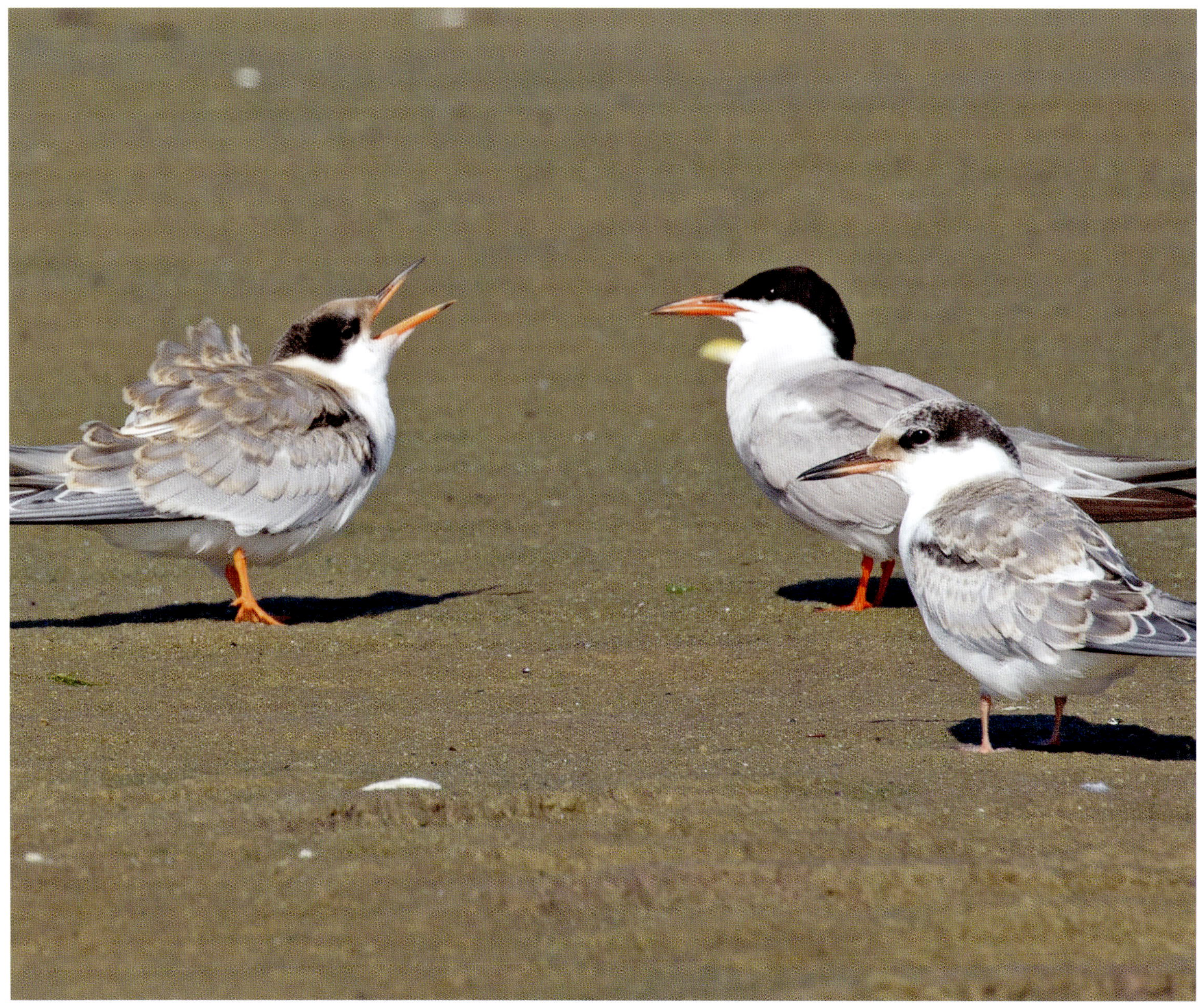

By early July, common tern chicks are fledged and flying but have not yet perfected their fishing habits. As one fledged chick stands contentedly, its sibling begs frantically for the parent to go and get more food!

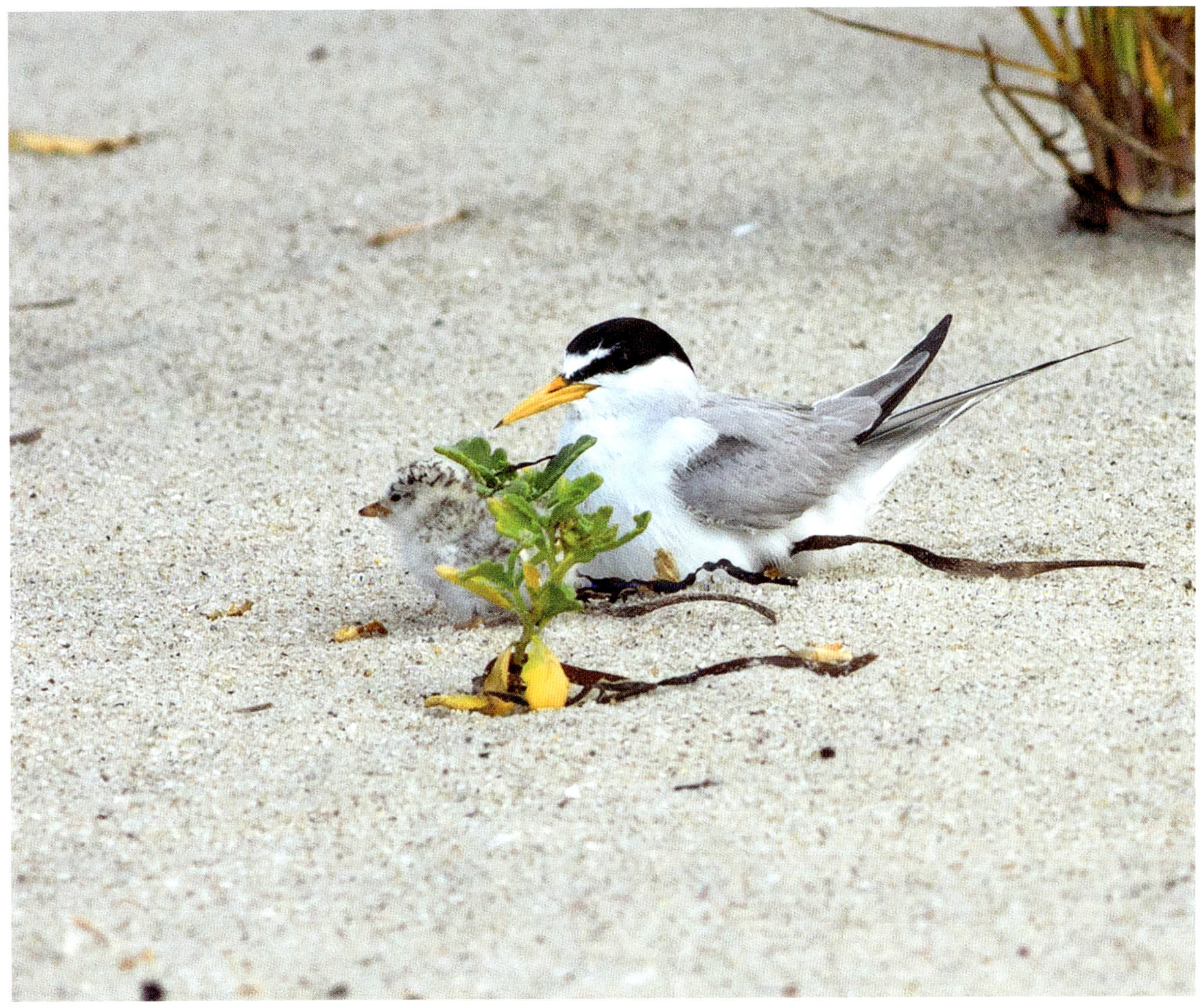

Least terns nest along the beachfront, which makes their nests vulnerable to high tides and storm overwash. They frequently lose their eggs and must renest. Here, a days-old chick from a second nesting attempt sits close to a parent.

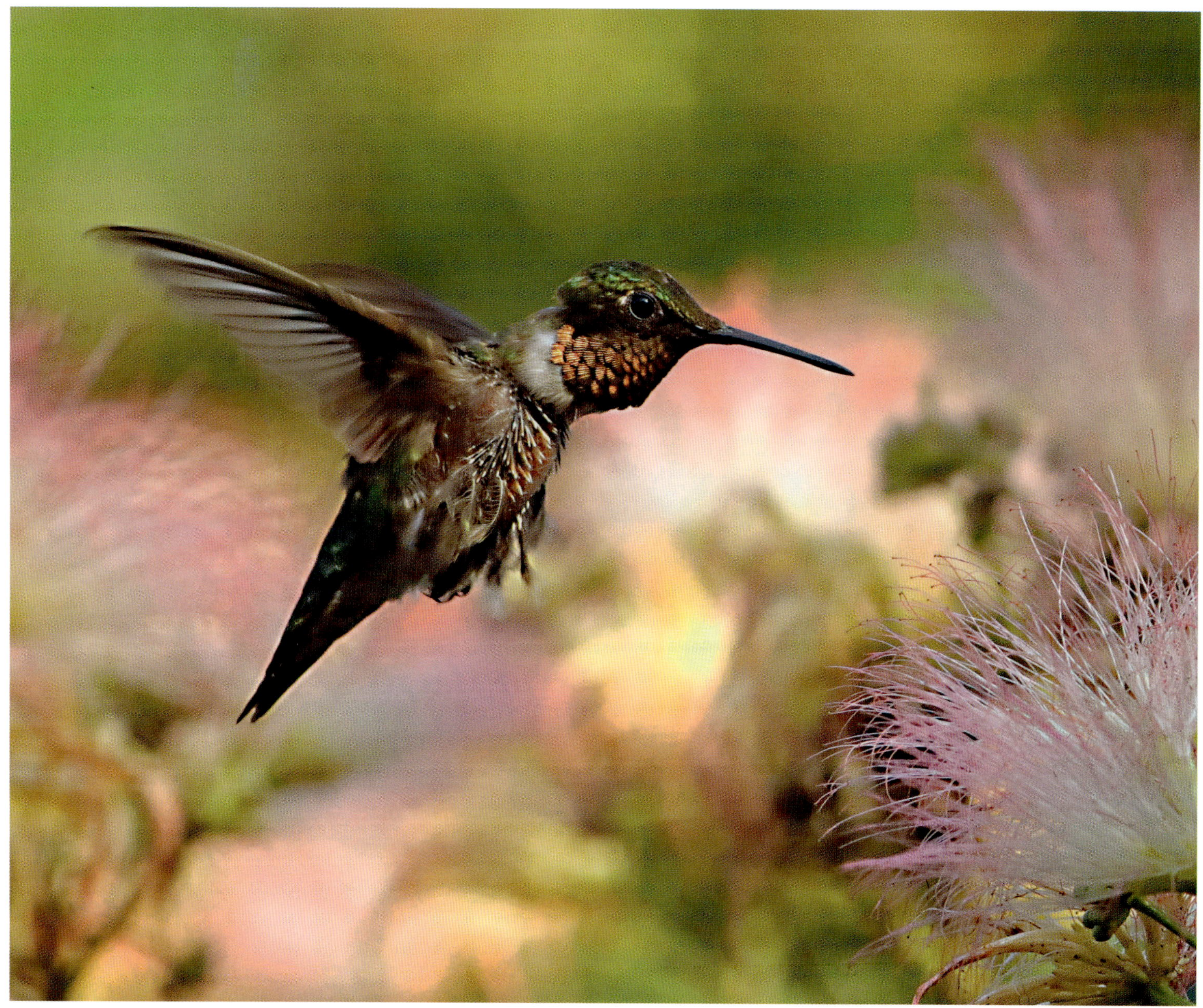

This ruby-throated hummingbird appears to have lost its breast feathers and is growing them back. This species usually molts on the wintering grounds, so the loss of the feathers and the appearance of these new pinfeathers growing in is a mystery. If only we could hear the story this tiny bird has to tell.

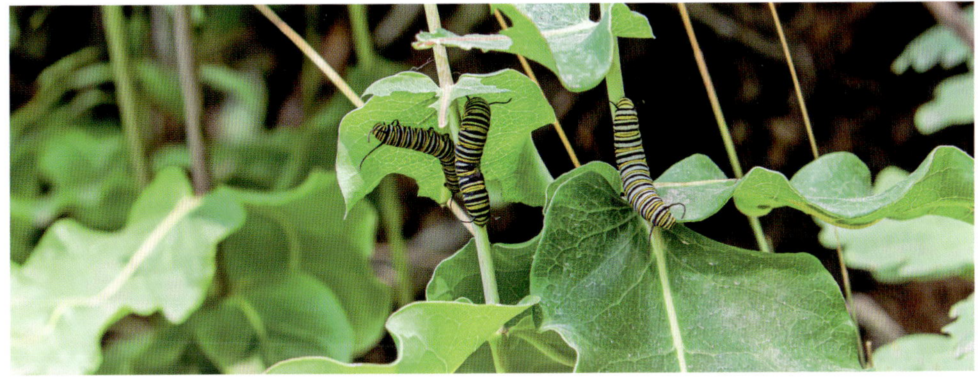

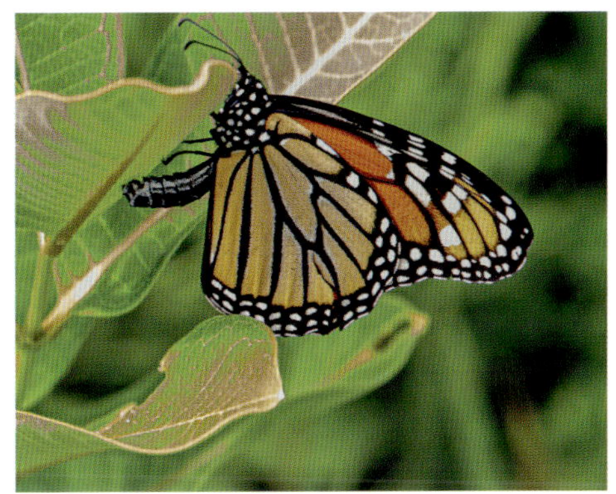

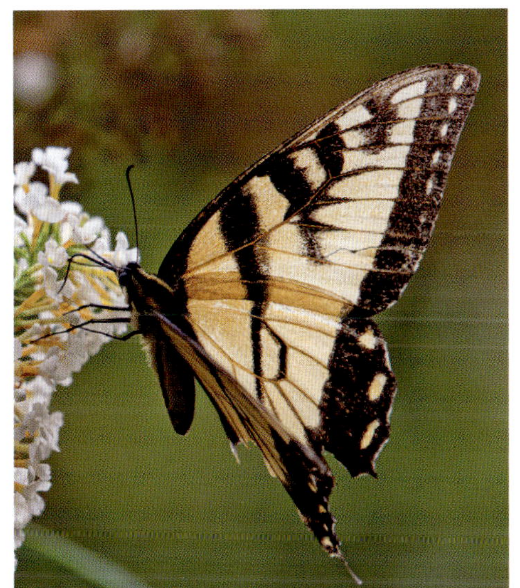

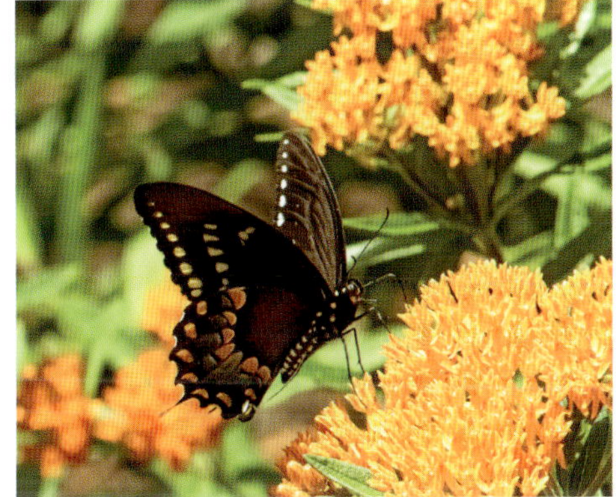

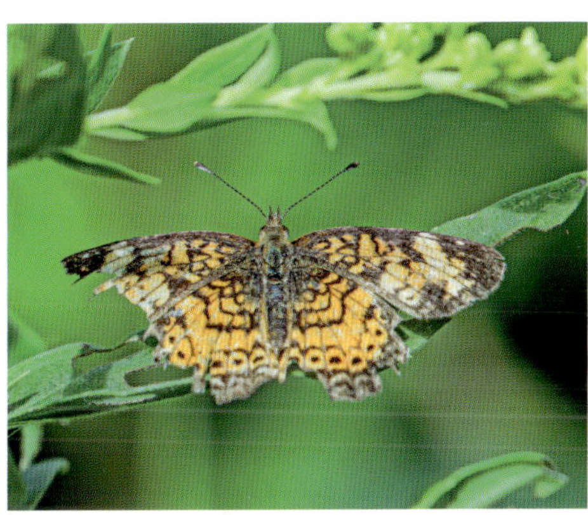

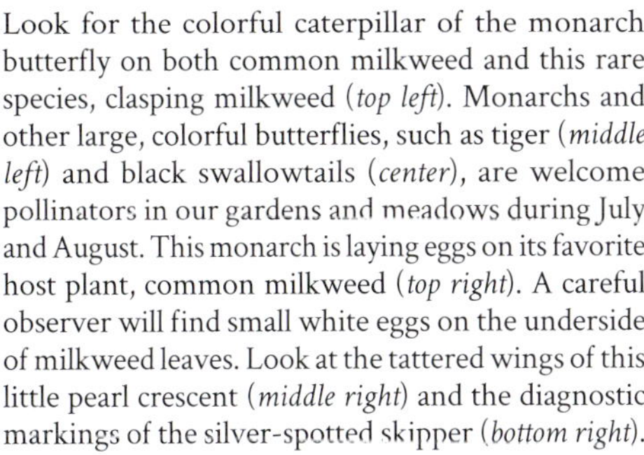

Look for the colorful caterpillar of the monarch butterfly on both common milkweed and this rare species, clasping milkweed (*top left*). Monarchs and other large, colorful butterflies, such as tiger (*middle left*) and black swallowtails (*center*), are welcome pollinators in our gardens and meadows during July and August. This monarch is laying eggs on its favorite host plant, common milkweed (*top right*). A careful observer will find small white eggs on the underside of milkweed leaves. Look at the tattered wings of this little pearl crescent (*middle right*) and the diagnostic markings of the silver-spotted skipper (*bottom right*).

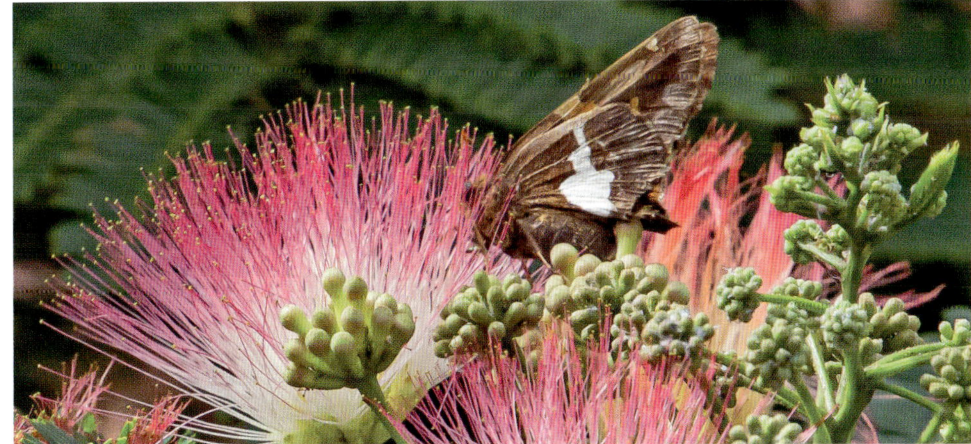

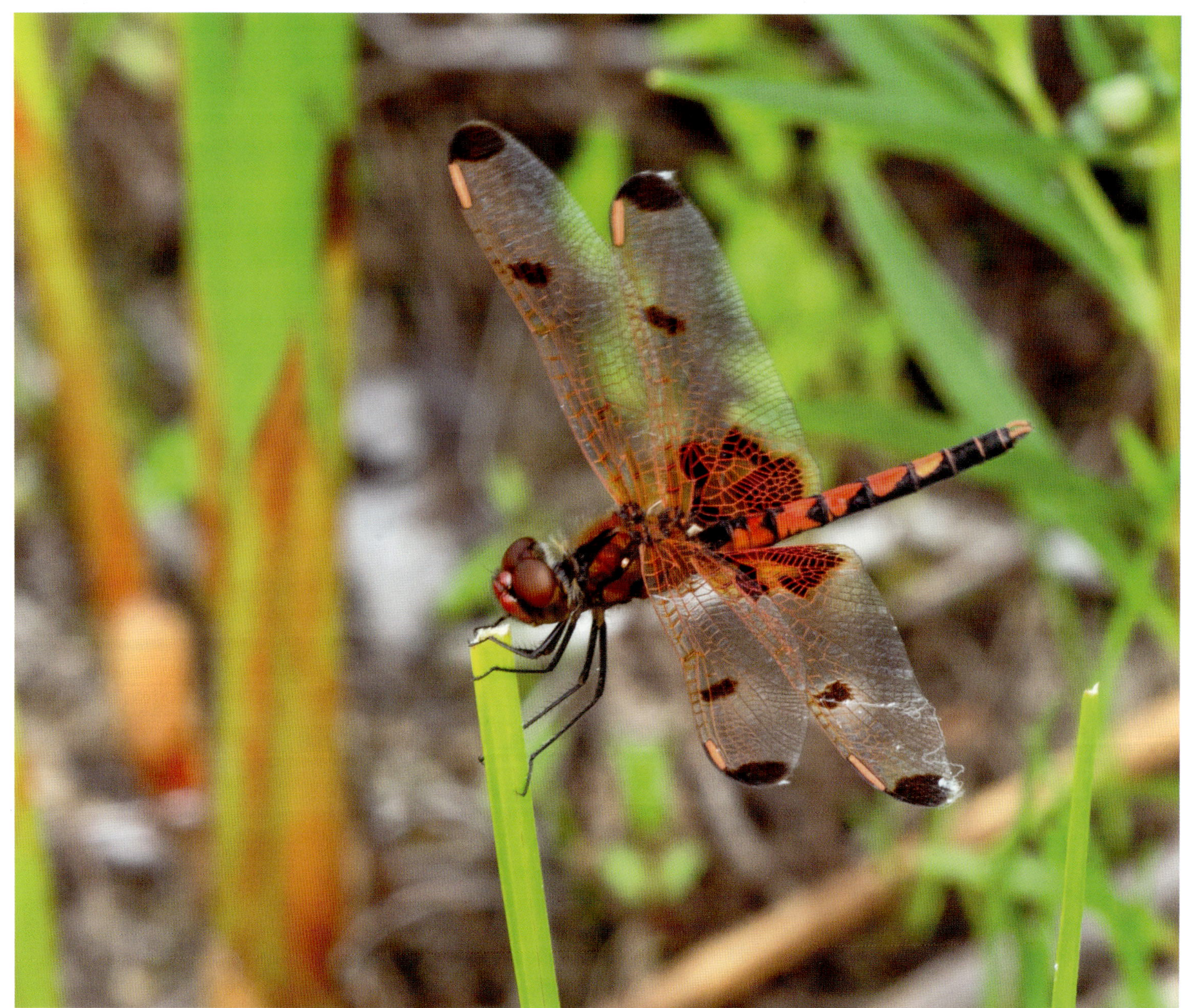

This male calico pennant is a beautiful pondside dragonfly.

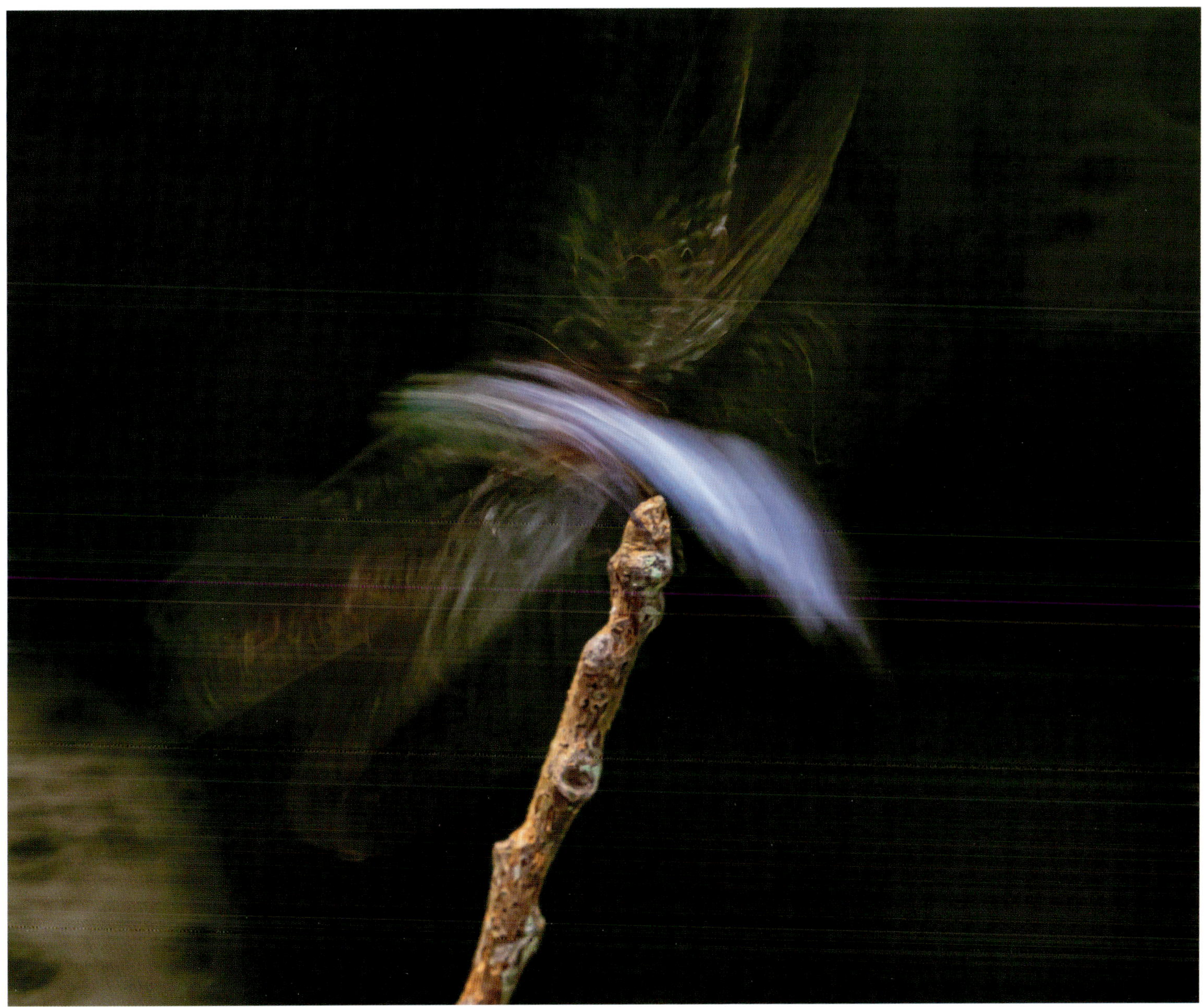

Dragonfly takes flight. In this seemingly abstract image, I was photographing a blue dasher dragonfly with my camera on a tripod at slow shutter speed when it took flight at the moment of shutter release. In my mind, a beautiful "mistake."

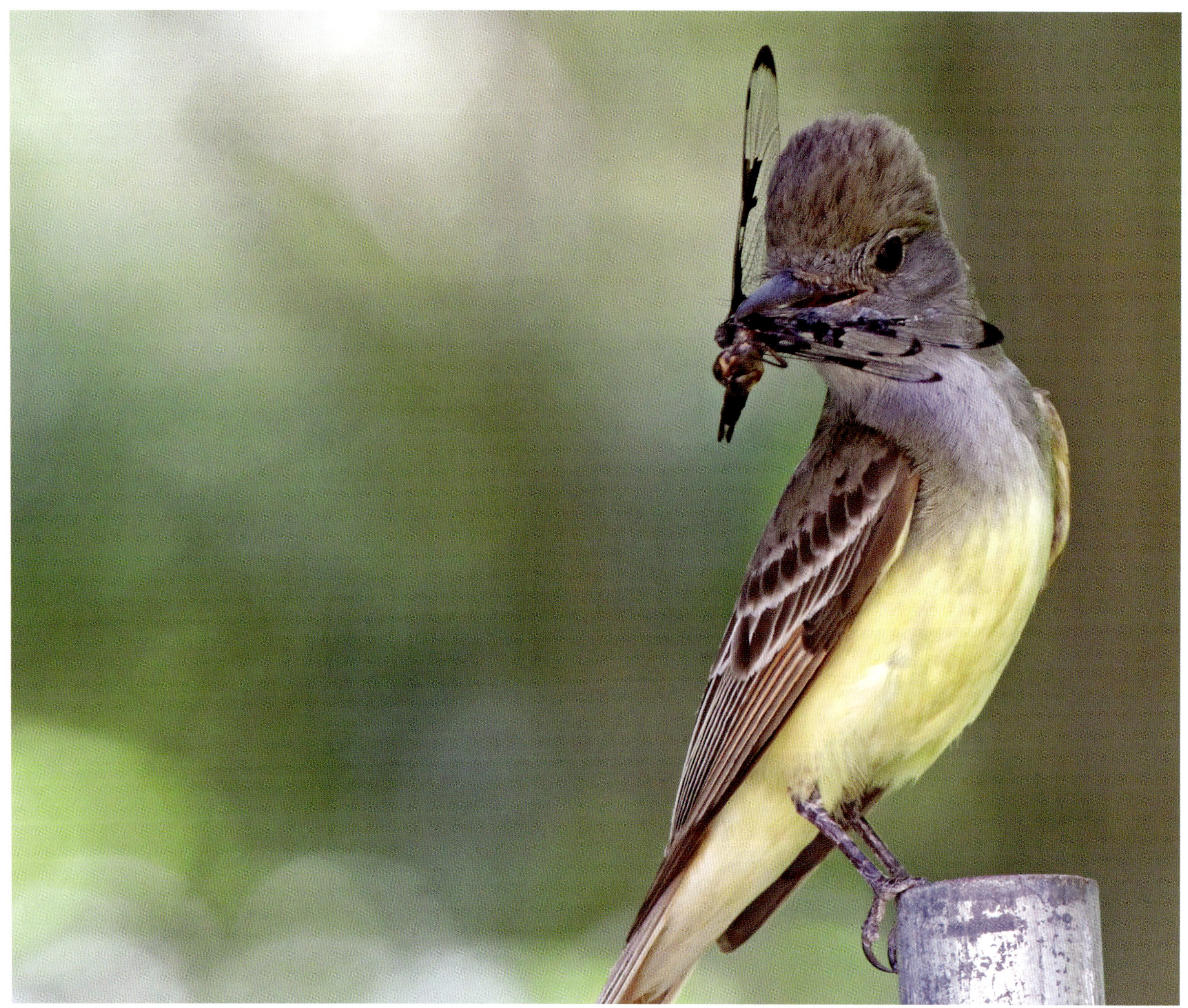

A great-crested flycatcher has captured a dragonfly meal for its young in the nest. This dragon is called a prince baskettail.

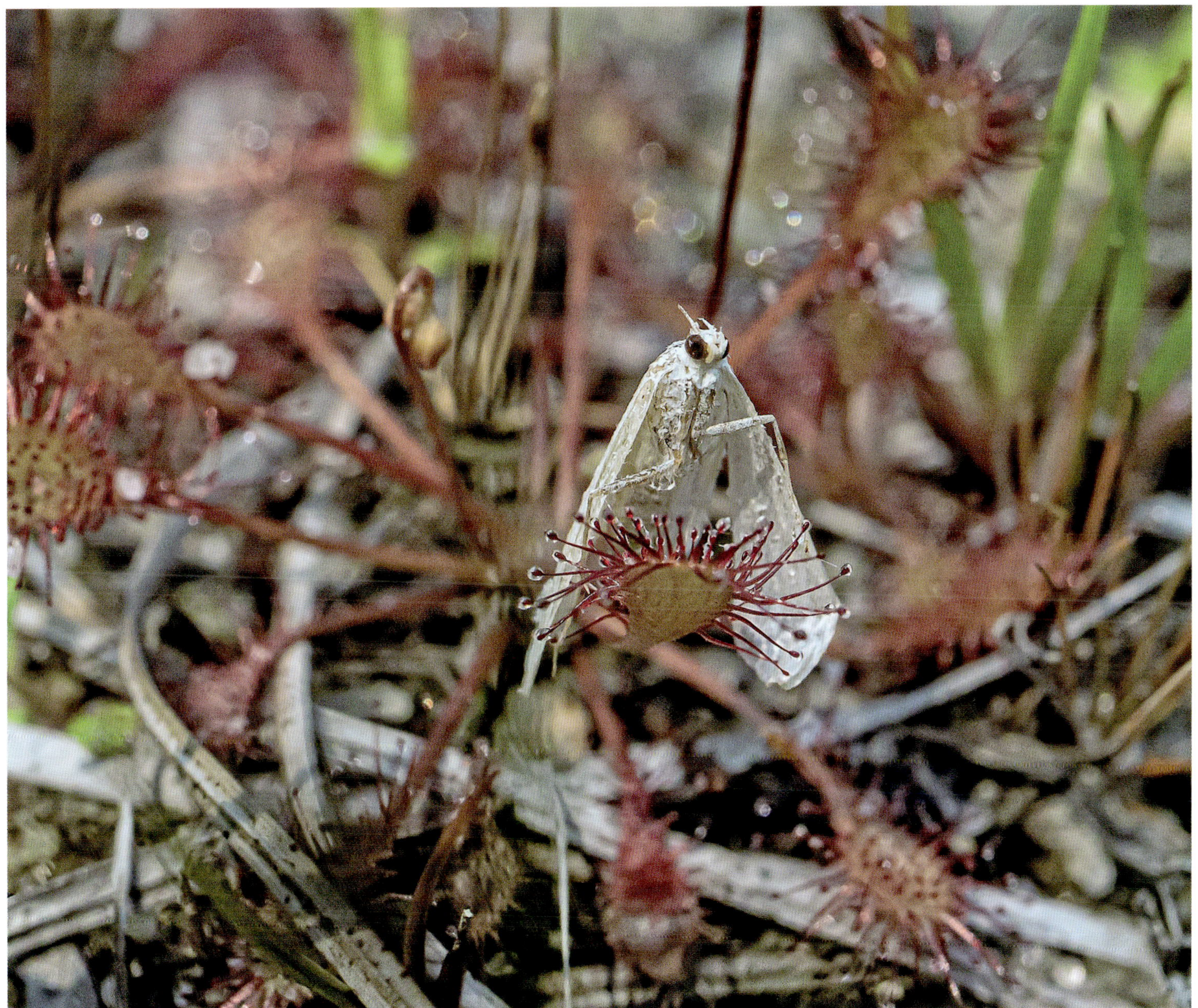

This is likely a pondweed moth of the Crambidae family and has fallen prey to a sticky, carnivorous plant called a sundew.

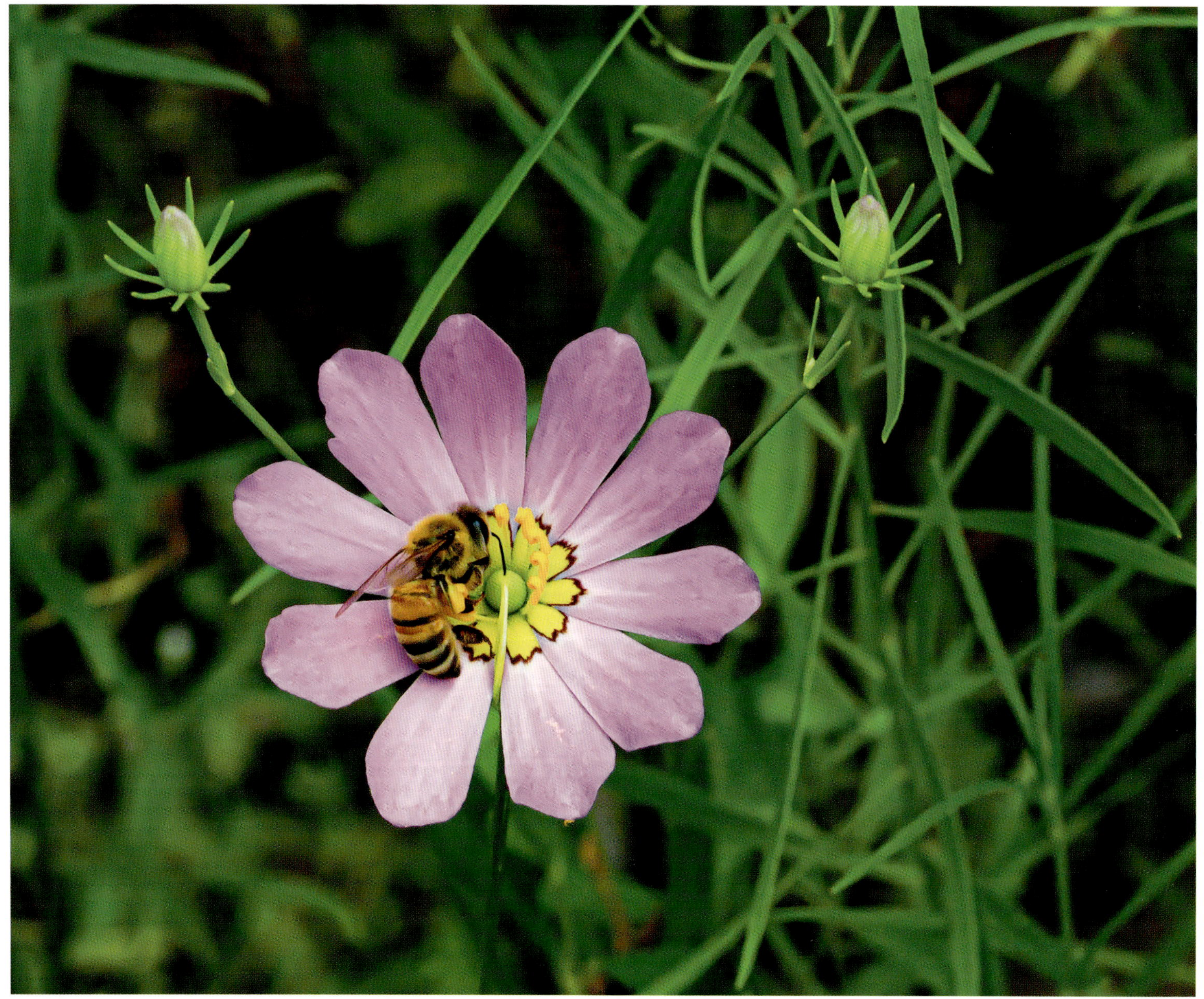

This beautiful wildflower, *Plymouth gentian,* is listed as a species of special concern in Massachusetts and considered globally rare. Found along the sandy shores of coastal-plain ponds here on the cape, it is beloved by humans and honeybees alike.

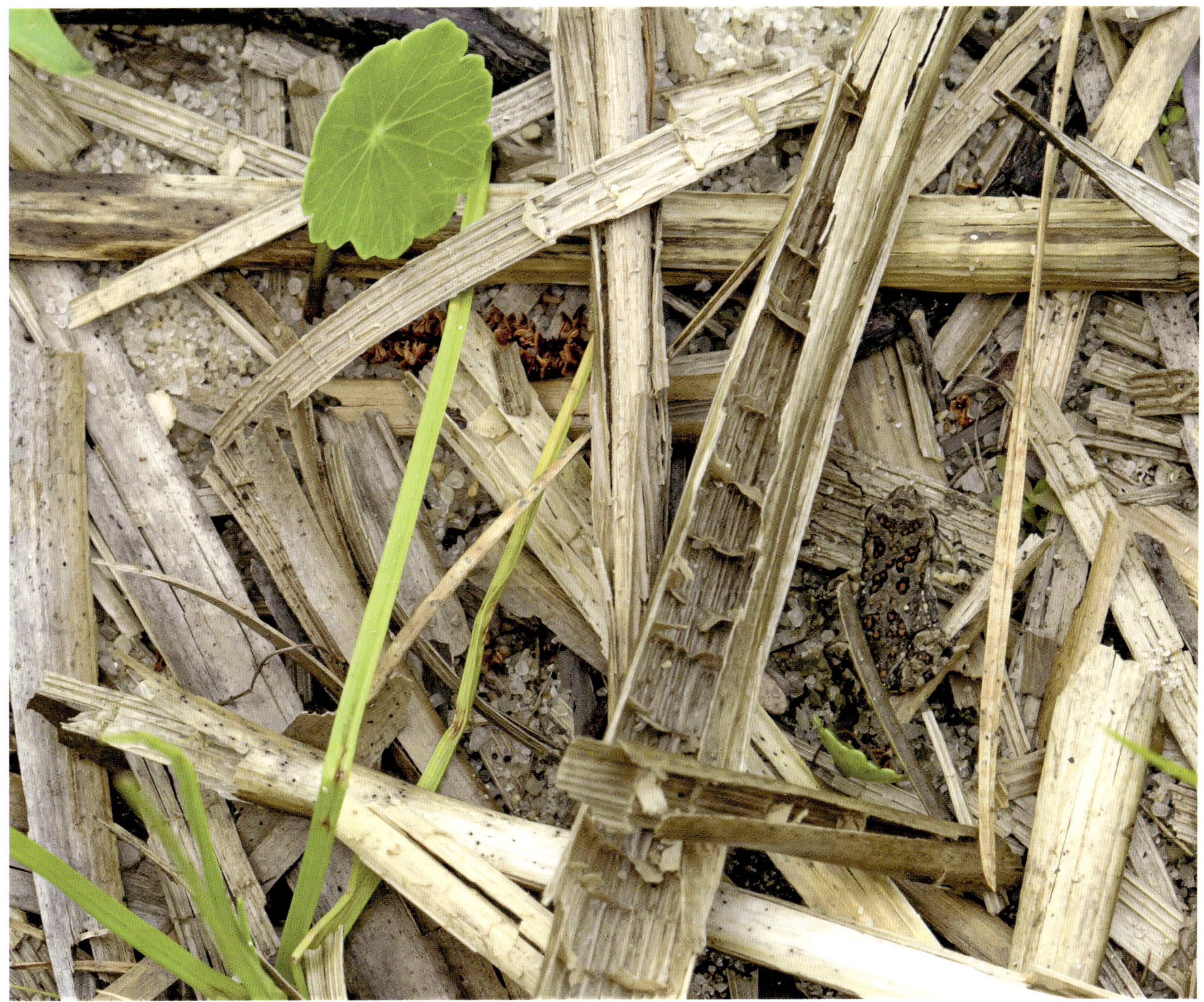

This fowler's toad, barely a centimeter long, has metamorphosed from a tiny black tadpole. A careful observer on any July day may find hundreds of these amphibians hopping along the pond shore.

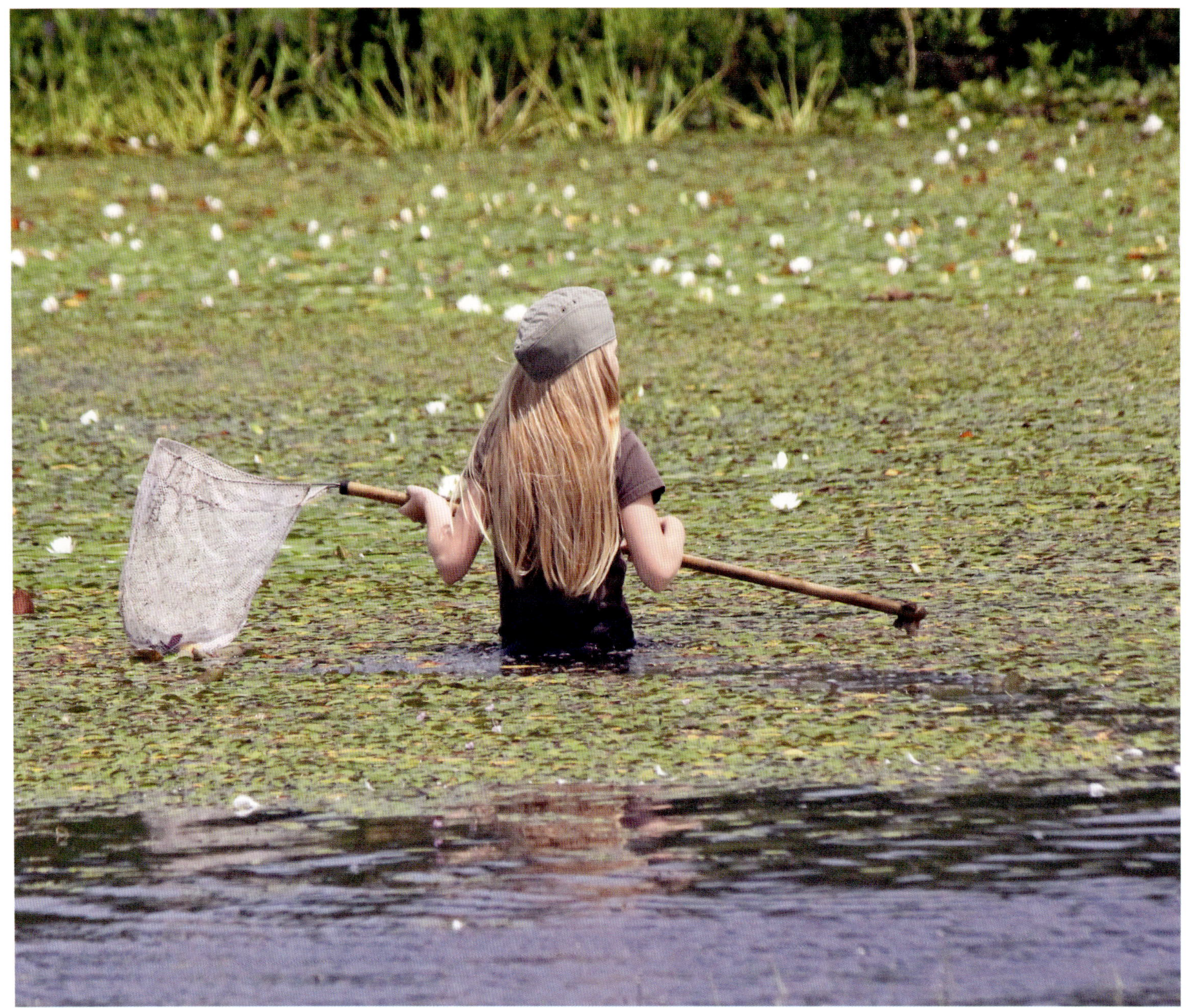

With net ready, a diligent young naturalist can find insects, fish, amphibians, and reptiles on a sunny-day pond adventure.

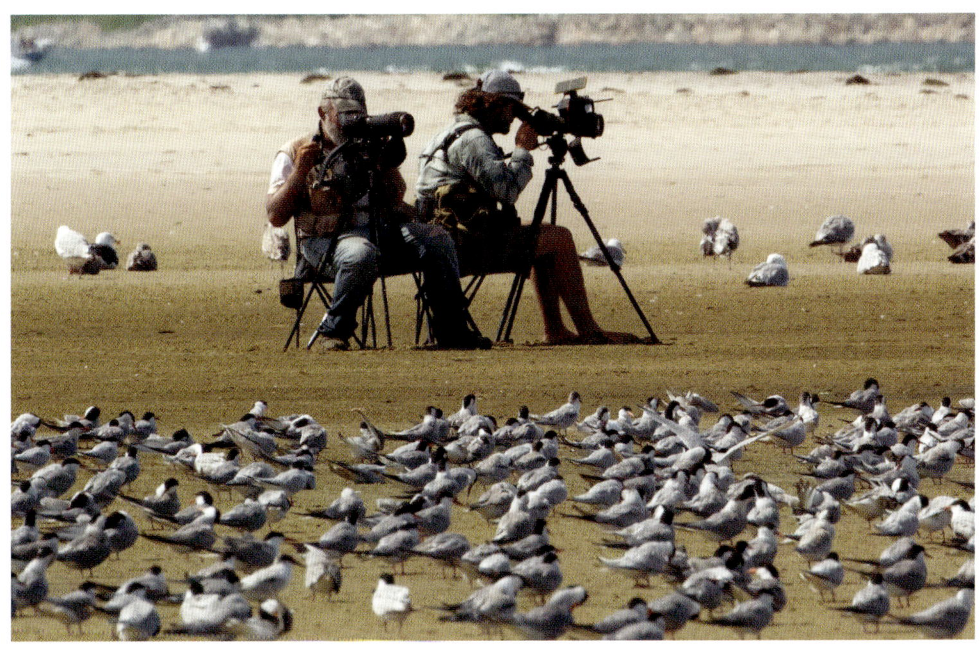

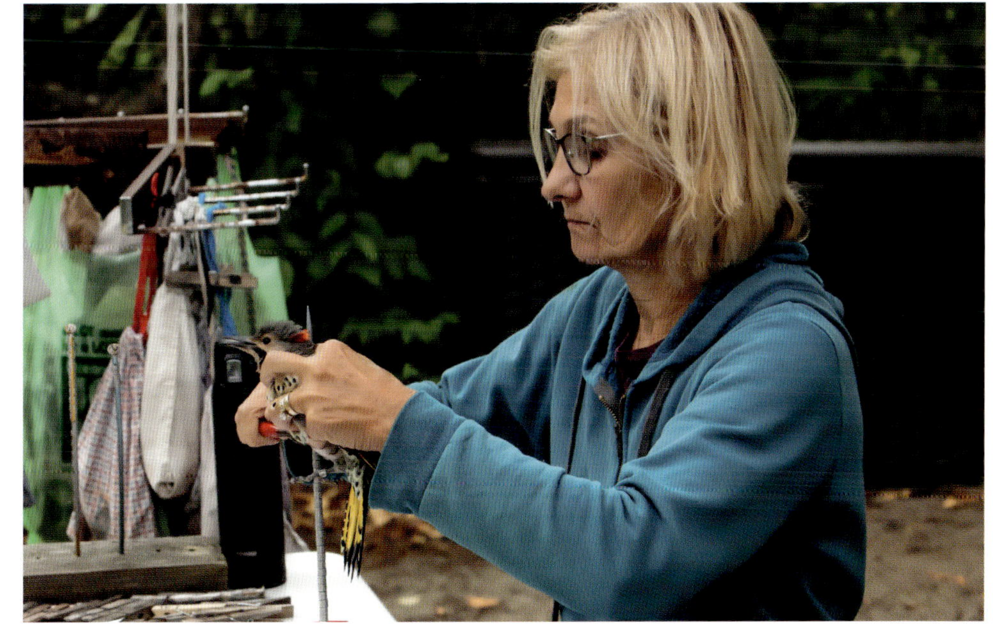

With thousands of migratory birds heading south after the nesting season, researchers spend hours studying flocks of terns and other shorebirds, as well as songbirds, and their progeny moving through the woodlands. Here, Dr. Jeff Spendelow and graduate student Keenan Yakola are using spotting scopes to scan a large flock of common terns and federally endangered roseate terns to identify individual birds with plastic colored, field-readable bands. Keenan is also using a receiving device in the hope of picking up signals from radio-tagged common terns. Master bird-bander Sue Finnegan, hyperfocused at her field station, has just placed a metal band on the leg of a male northern flicker, a large woodpecker. Sue runs the Wing Island Banding Station through the Cape Cod Museum of Natural History.

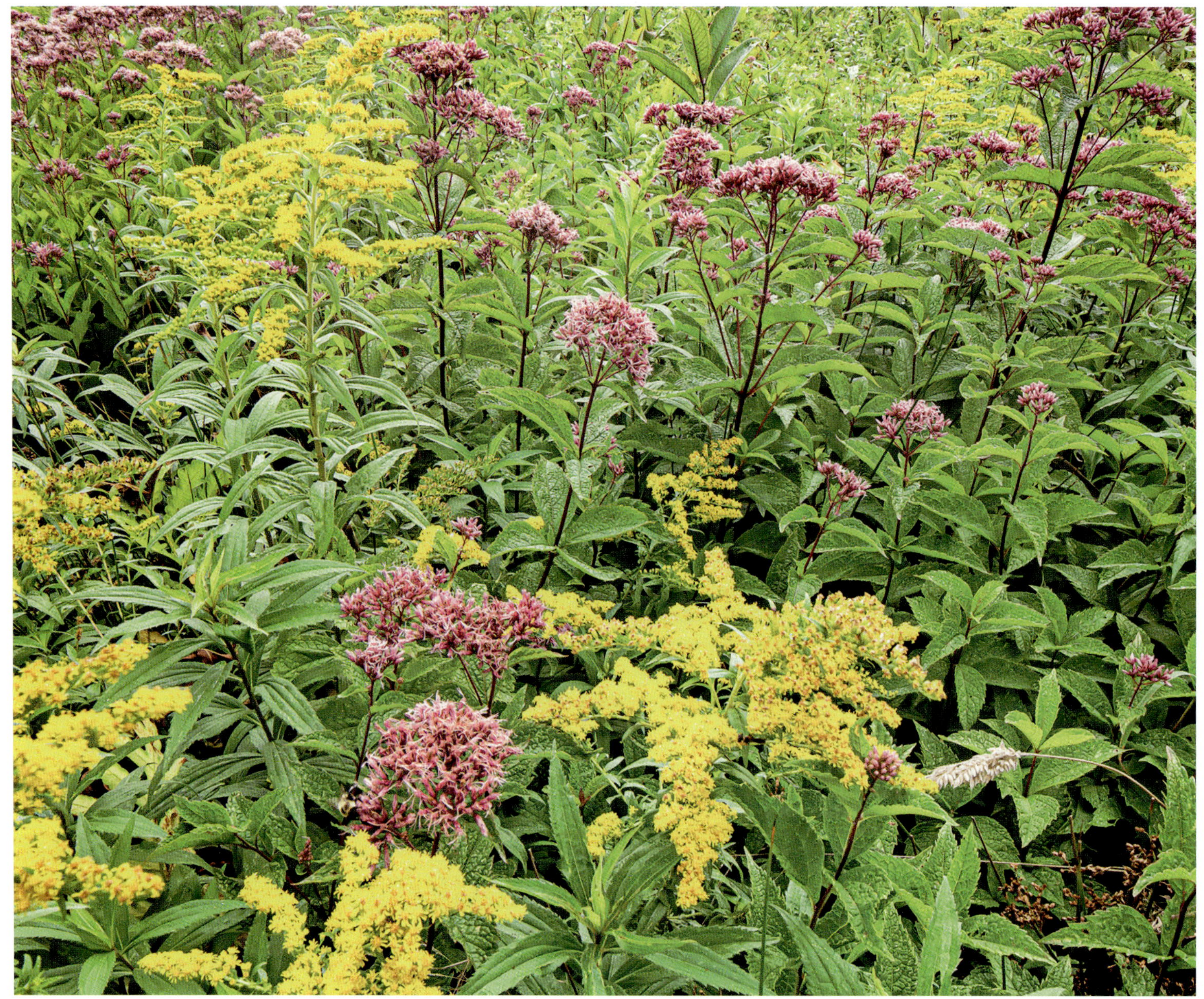

As a boy riding in the back seat of my parents' car on Route 495, I came to know that the stands of purple and yellow flowers, joe-pye weed and goldenrod, clustered along the highway meant summer was ending and autumn was close at hand.

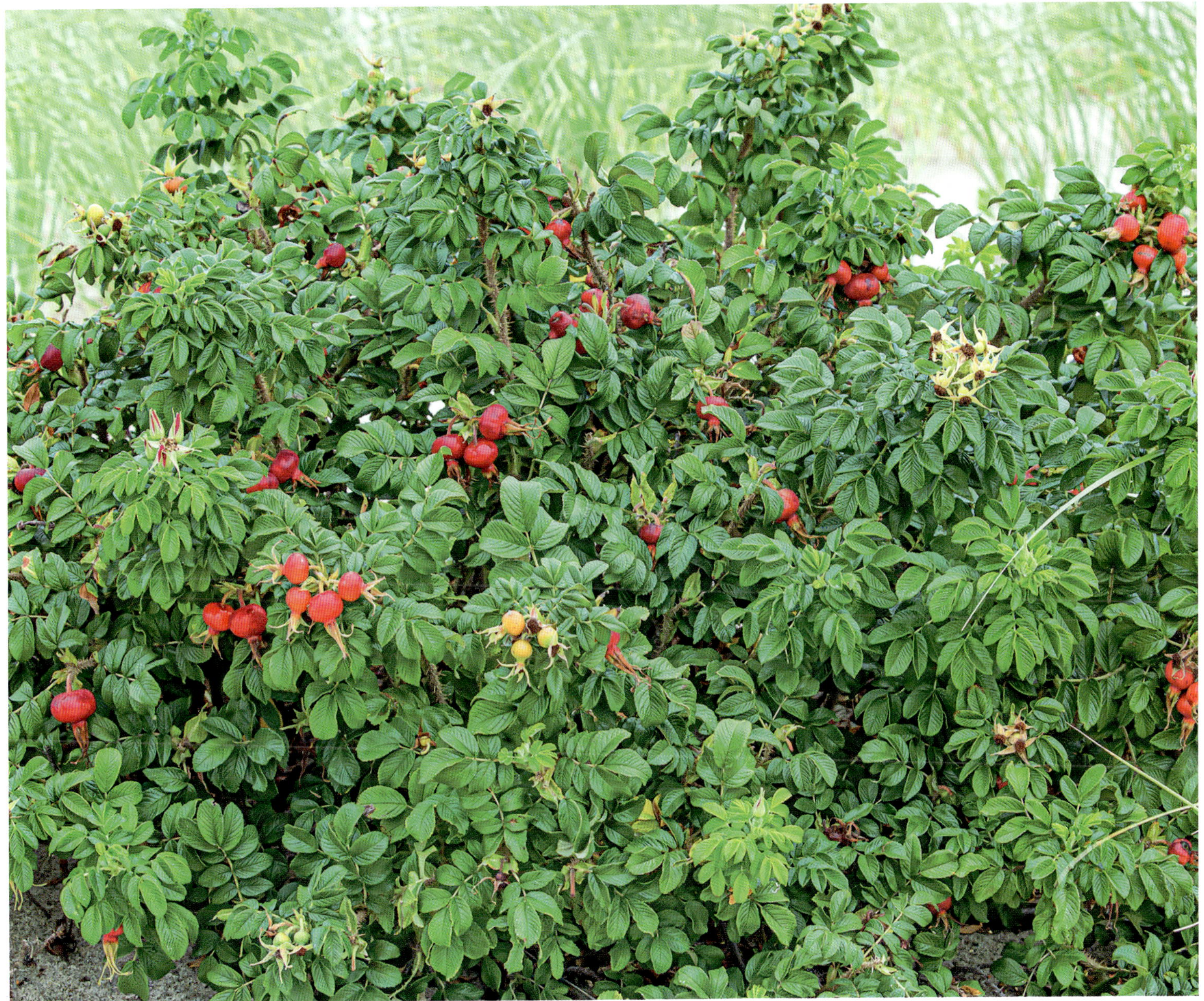

Serenity can be found along the shoreline, away from the crowds. This salt spray rose's fruit is rich in vitamin C. The rose hips can be made into jam or eaten right off the plant.

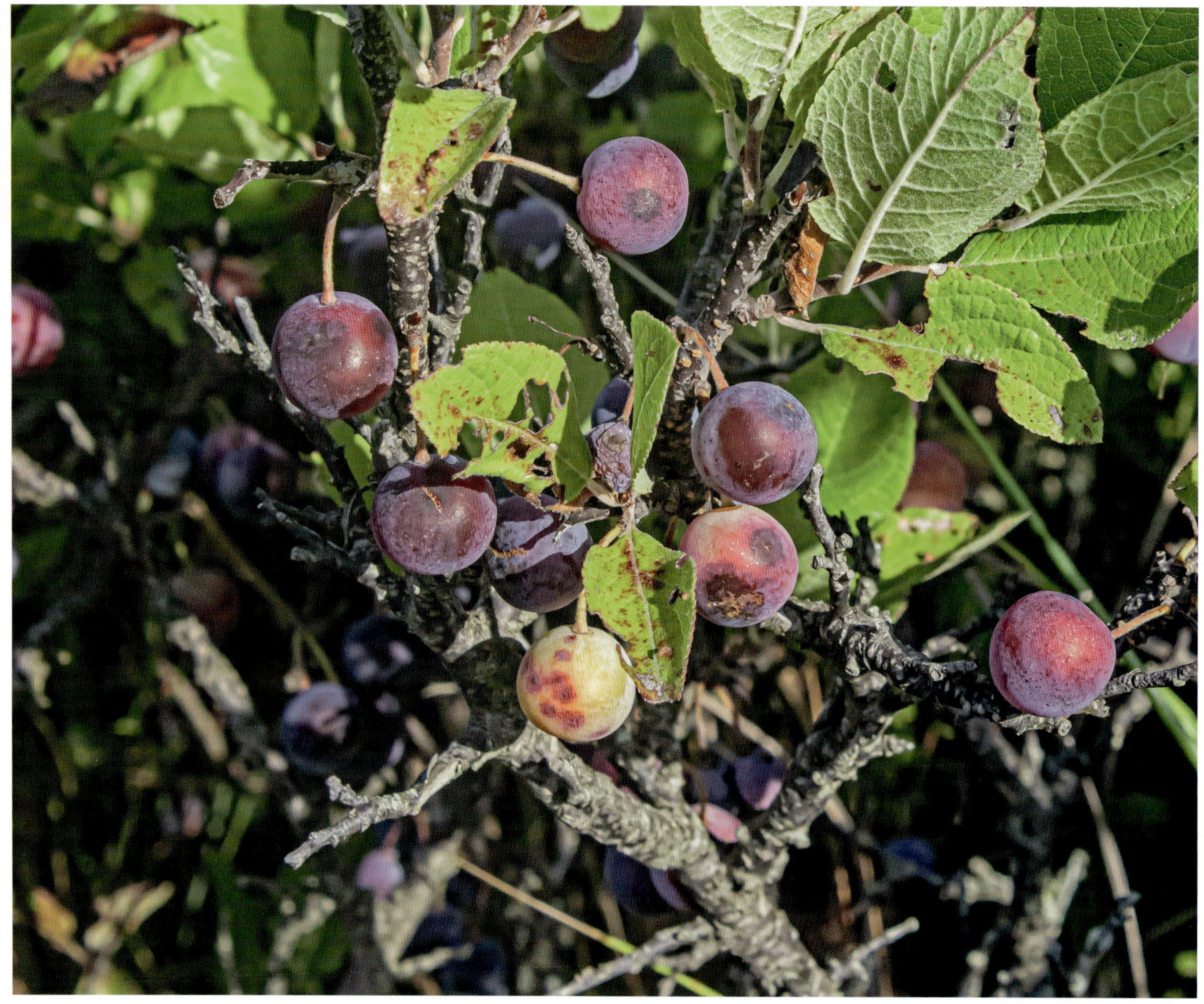

In the dunes and along sandy footpaths, we find wild beach plums growing on low shrubs, easily overlooked by the casual walker. A diligent searcher will fill a bucket of these plump fruits, soon to be made into sweet jam. Most beach plum jam makers I know have their own "secret spot."

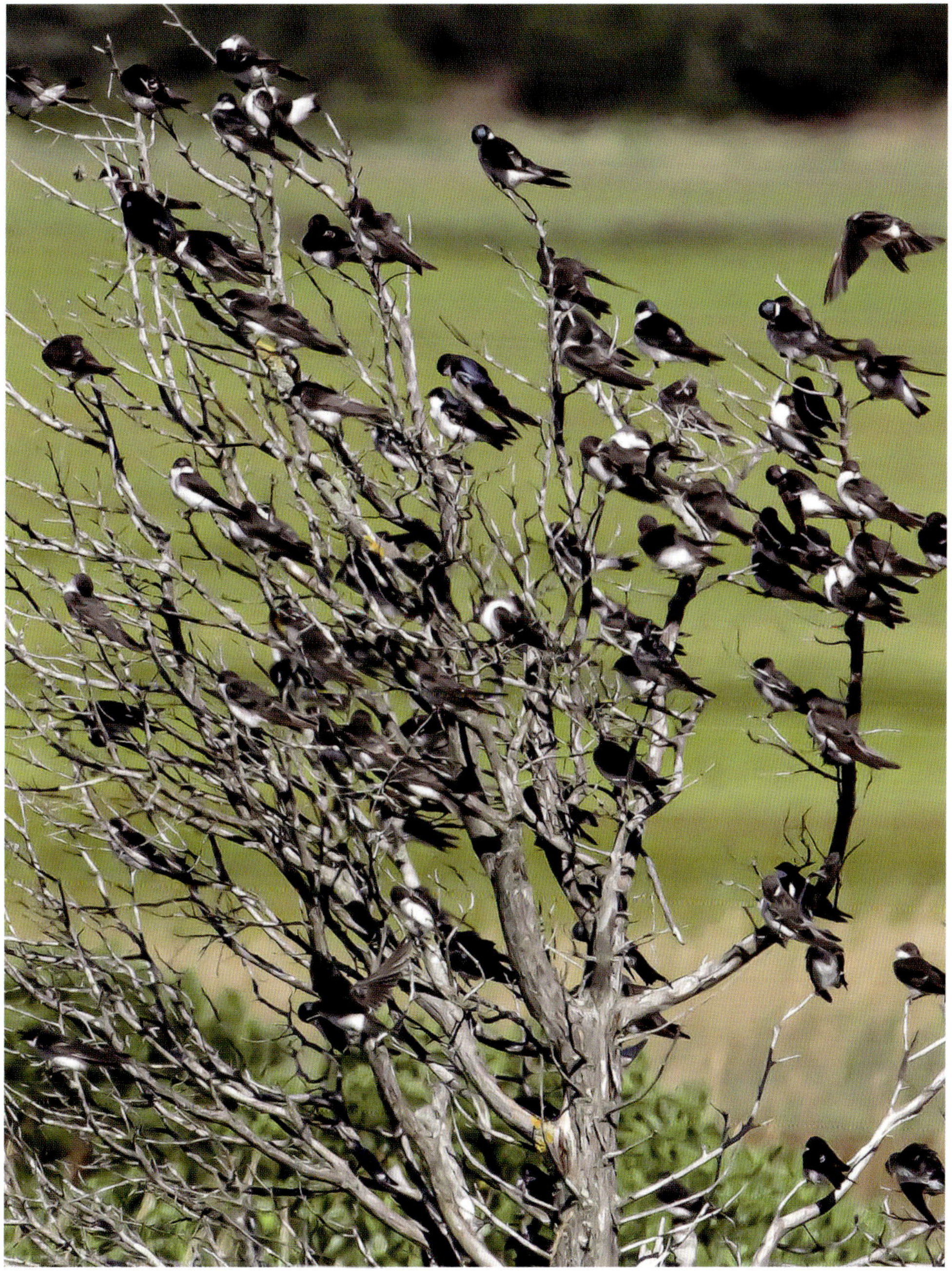

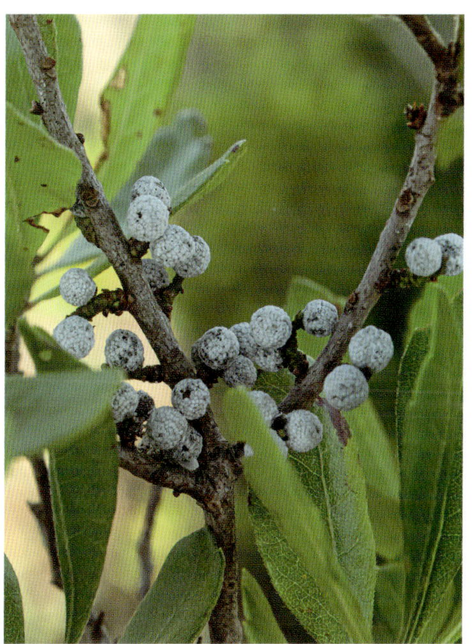

Growing ubiquitously in the dunes from Falmouth to Provincetown, bayberries grow in waxy clusters and are a favorite food of migratory tree swallows. Rich in vitamins and minerals, bayberry bushes are swarmed by tree swallows as the birds migrate south in huge flocks. After gorging themselves, tree swallows rest and digest.

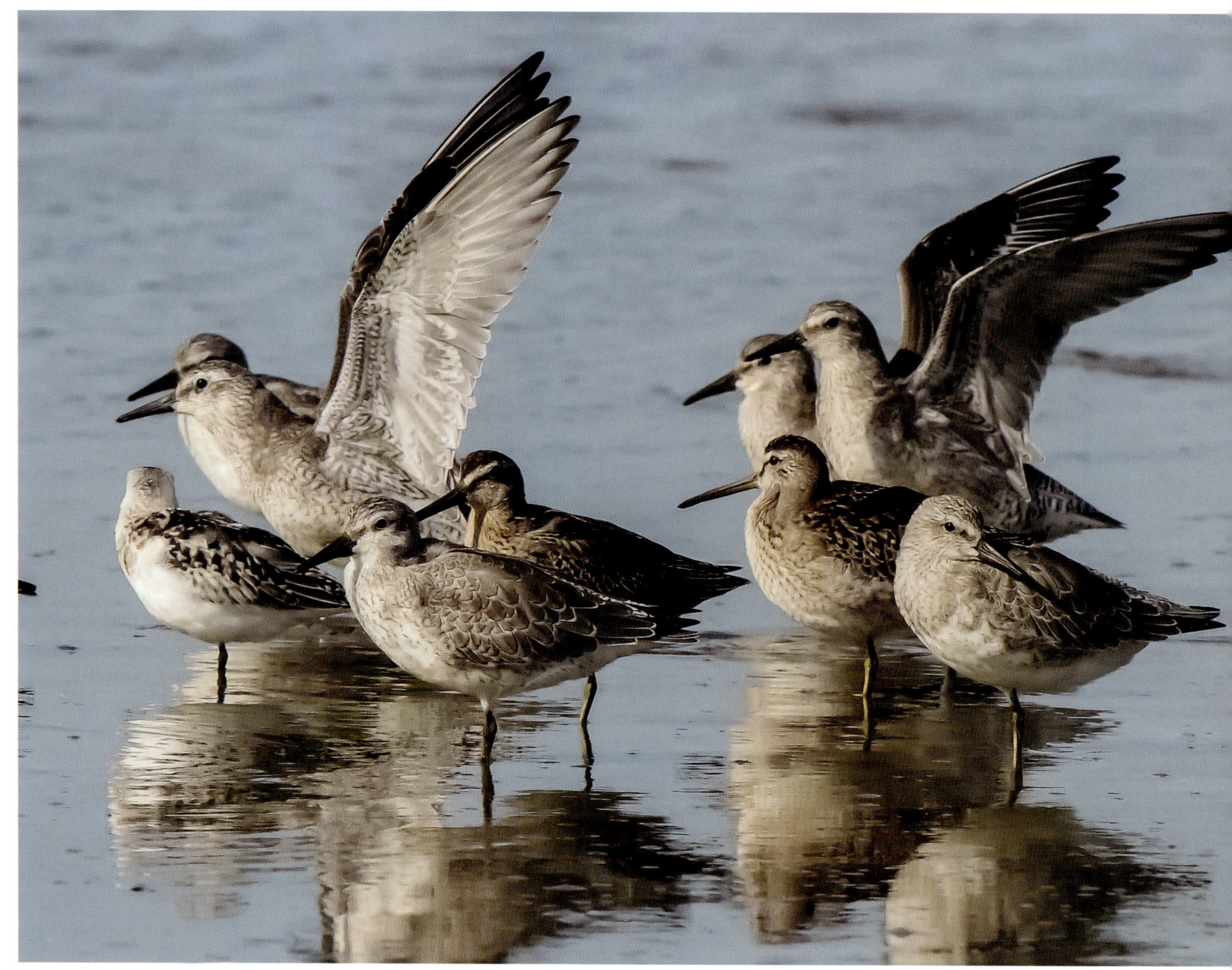

Shorebirds like sandpipers, red knots, and short-billed dowichers, bordered on each side by smaller sanderlings, as well as a ruddy turnstone rest and feed on the beaches and tidal flats. They will probe for worms and crustaceans in the moist, sandy substrate. A ruddy turnstone (*top right*), known for digging and moving objects to find food, takes the method deeper. A dowicher (*bottom right*) probes at sunset.

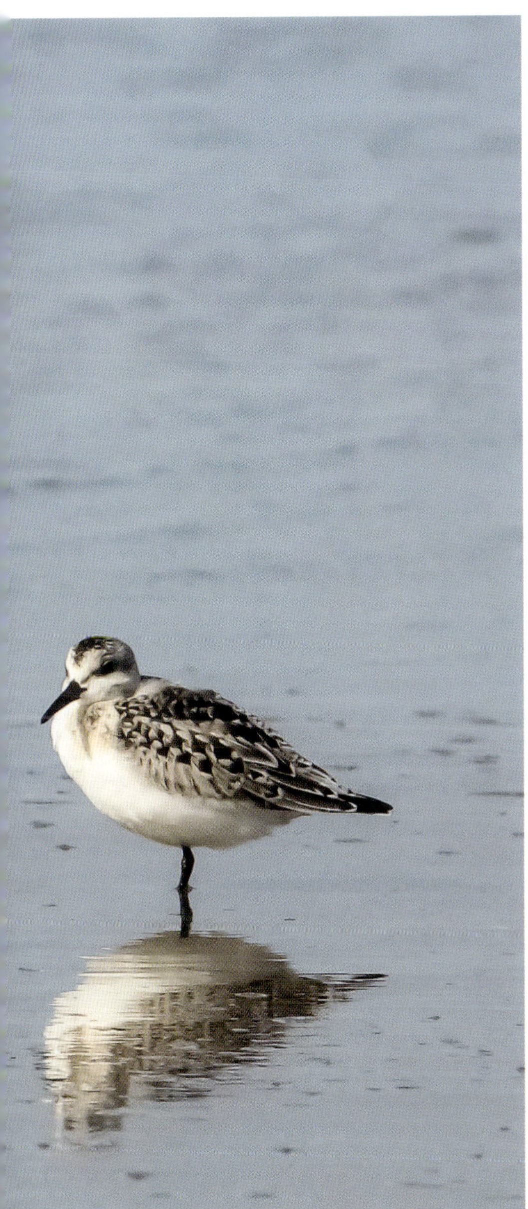

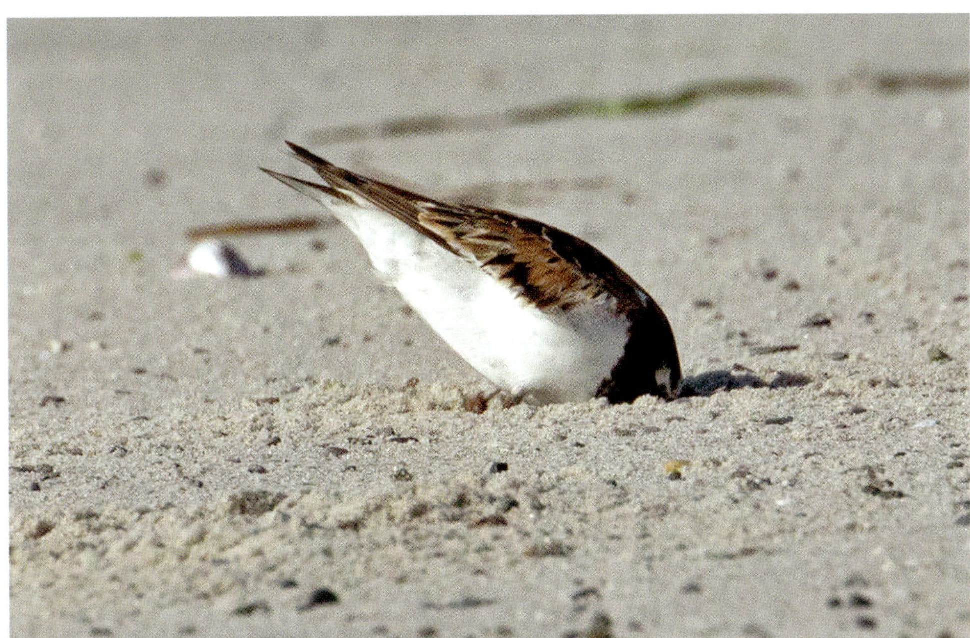

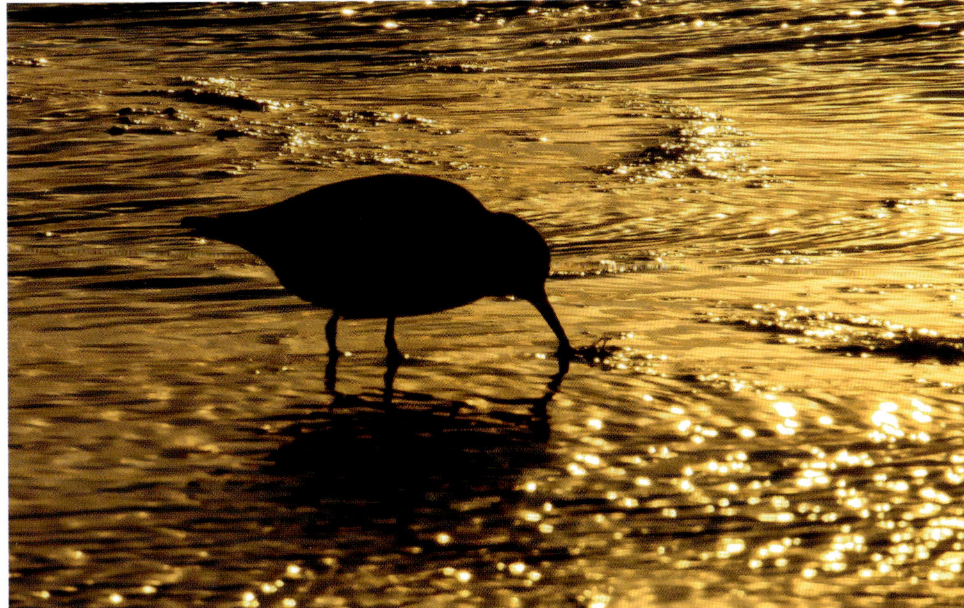

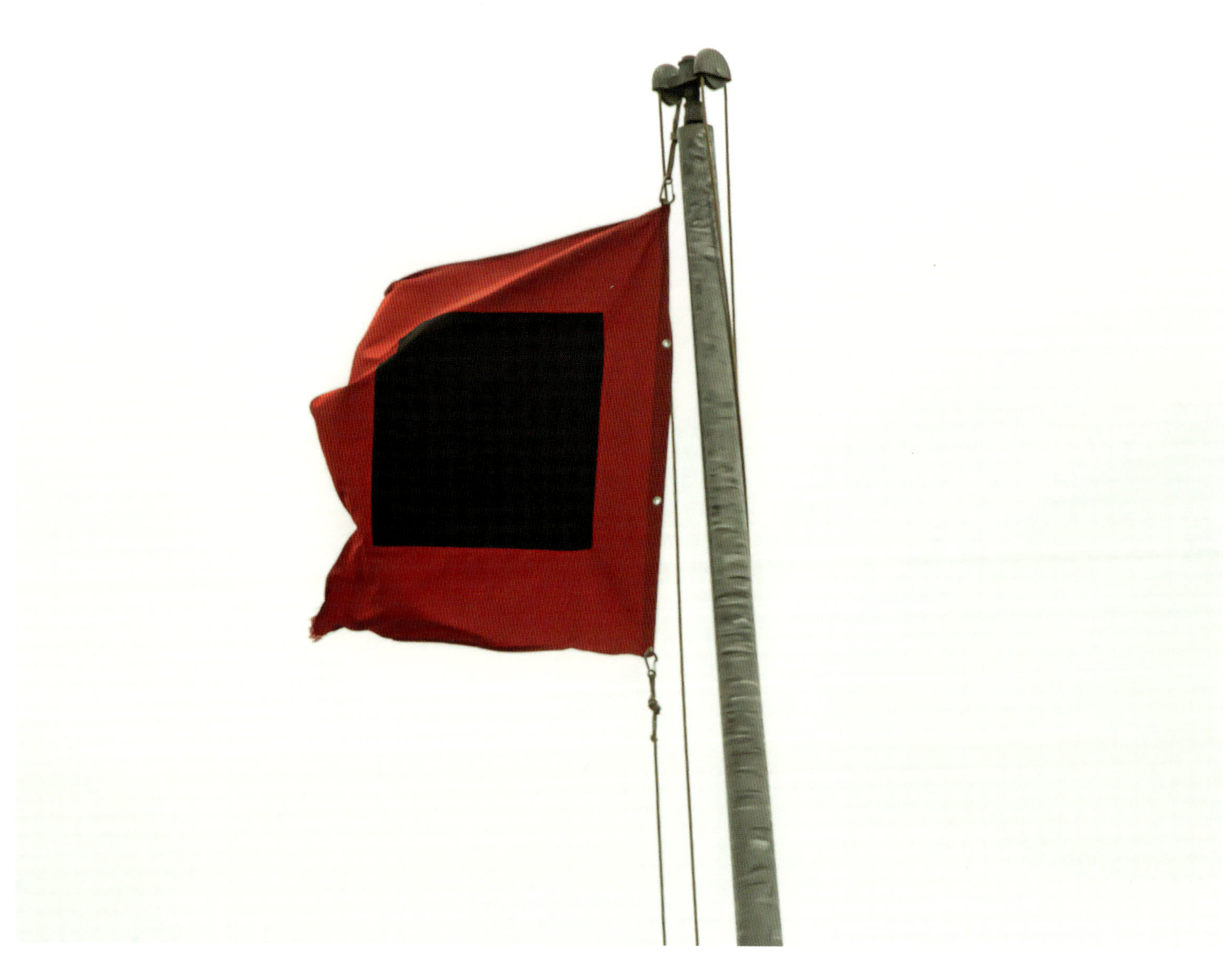

Starting in late August and into September, tropical storms move up the Atlantic coast.

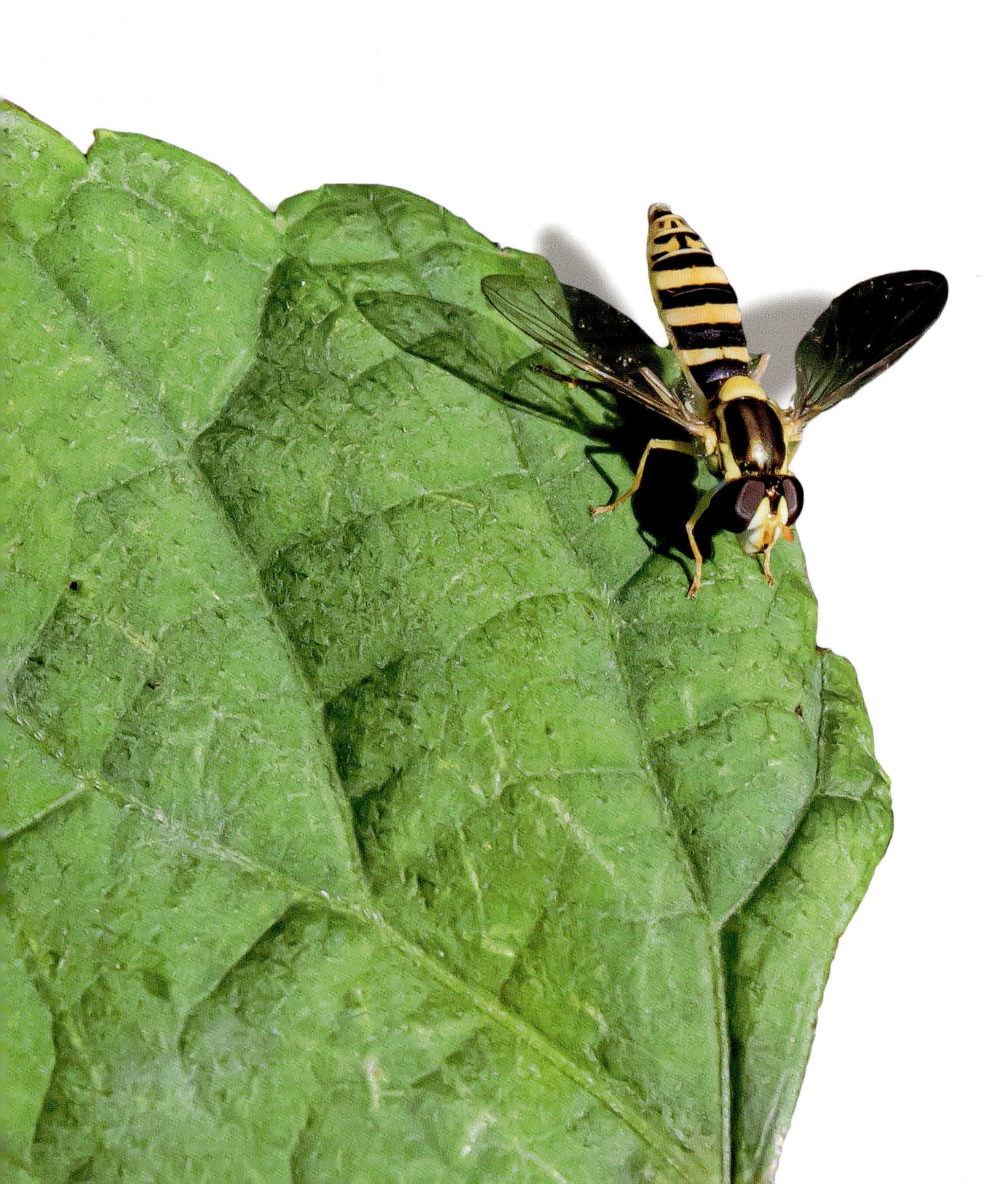

SEPTEMBER AND OCTOBER
A Time of Preparation

It's still warm. The North Atlantic Ocean is keeping temperatures relatively warm, and the low-pressure systems spinning counterclockwise to the west are bringing southern air northward. High-pressure systems off the Carolinas, called Bermuda highs, also bring bright sunshine and warm temperatures in September and October. Autumn colors are everywhere, although they differ dramatically from what most New Englanders think of as fall foliage. Along the beach and in the meadows, we observe bright and bushy goldenrod.

September and October are the months of Nature's changing of the guard. It's been a hot, busy summer for the flora and fauna, but life is about to change. The oaks are turning copper and brown. Tree trunks and storm-torn branches are gray, but we can find some reds and yellows and oranges scattered through different habitats on any cool, sunny autumn walk. The dune grass turns yellow-gold, and the marshes, lit by a dimmer sun, turn down the production of chlorophyll, losing the rich green of summer.

October is cranberry harvest time, and the seemingly dormant bogs become a richer red—indeed, cranberry. Along the shore, birds are busy and on the move, fattening up for winter as they continue on their southern journey. Mammals hunt to put on the necessary fat. The winds of October are sure to move sand and uncover treasures, large or small. The birds are migrating, now heading south to warmer climates as the day shortens. Just offshore, birds and cetaceans are actively feeding as the October gales churn up the sea. November will introduce us to cooler nights and richer sunsets.

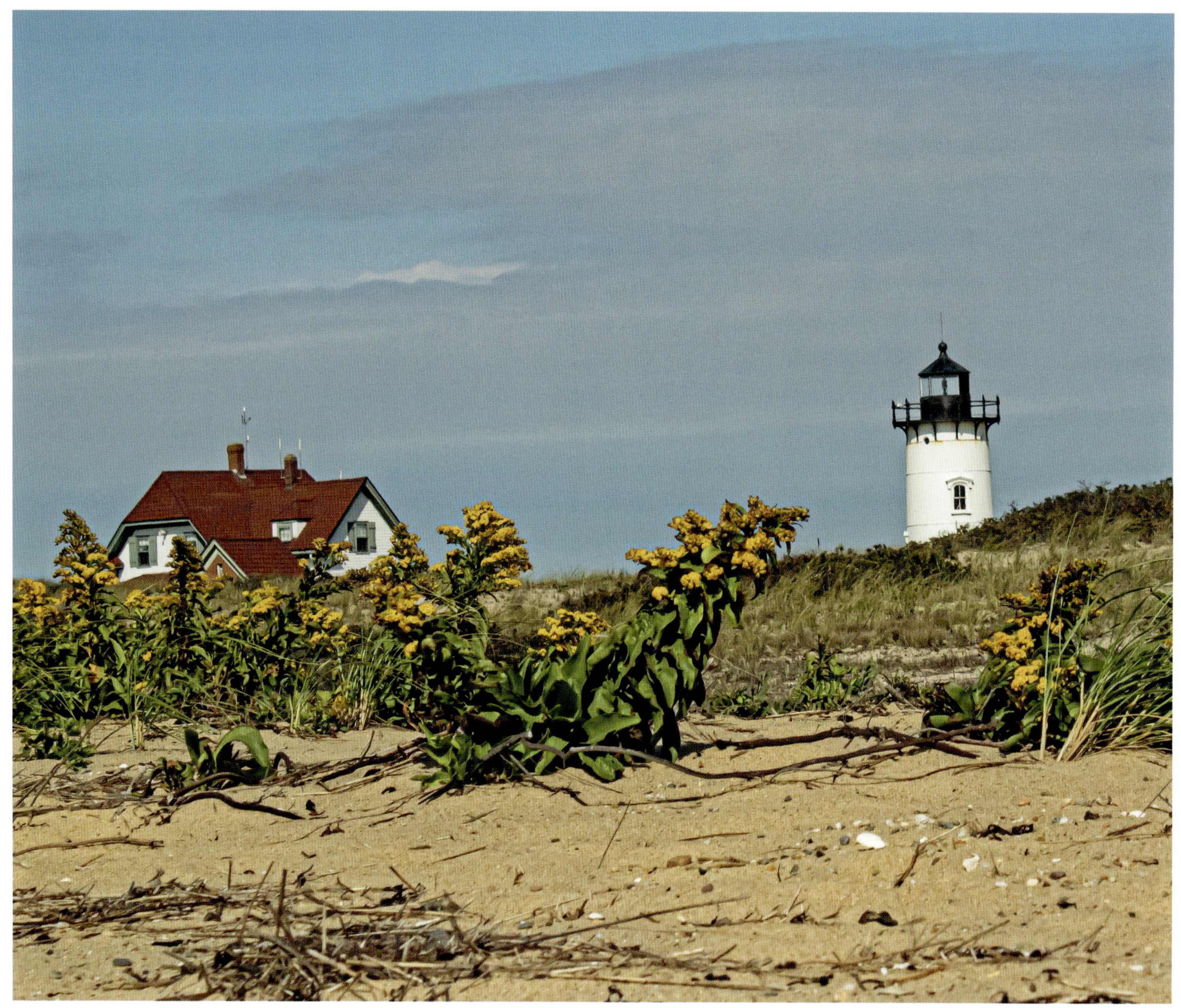

The quintessential bright colors of autumn can be found in scattered habitats around the cape. Golds, yellows, reds, and greens are displayed here at Race Point Light.

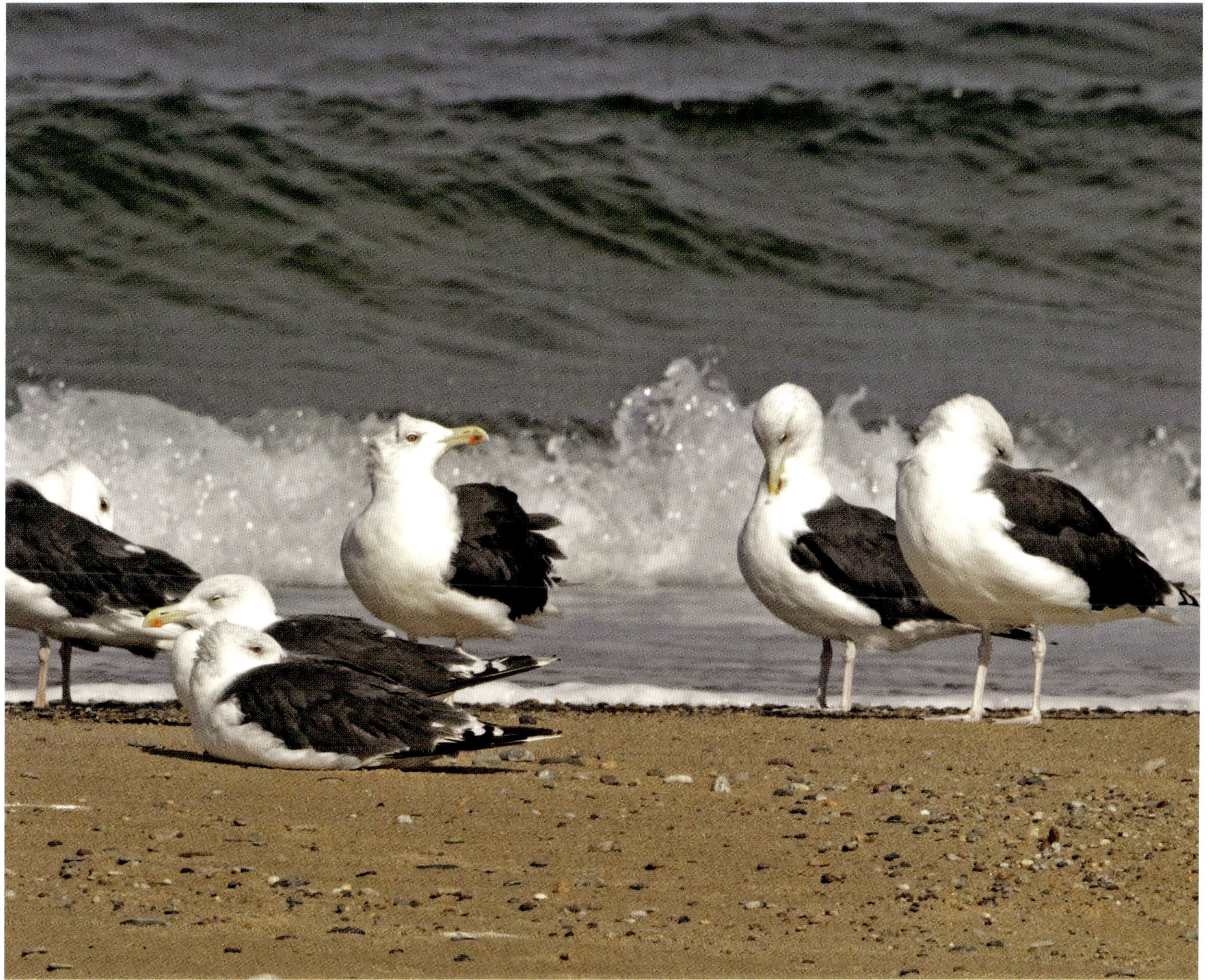

Of course, we know by now that there isn't a bird called a seagull. Yet up to a dozen species of gulls, some rare, may be observed on Cape Cod as the earth travels once around the sun. A diligent birder might observe ten species on the cape in a year. These are the largest of the gulls found on the cape, great black-backed gulls, and if there ever was a "seagull," this would be the bird. Its scientific name is *Larus marinus*, the gull of the sea.

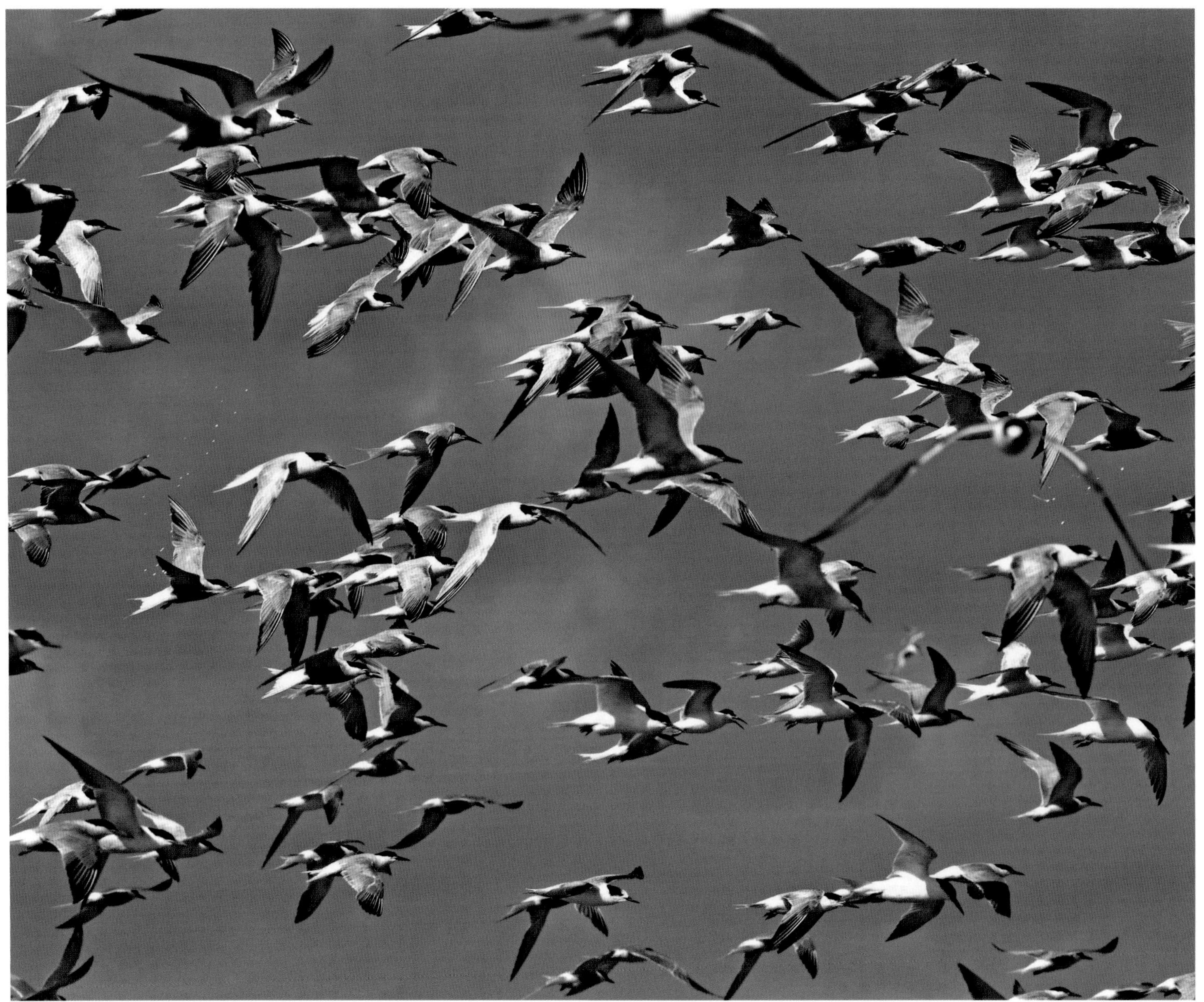

A mixed flock of common and roseate terns take flight, guano flying, as they prepare for a several-thousand-mile migration to the shores of South America, where they'll spend the winter.

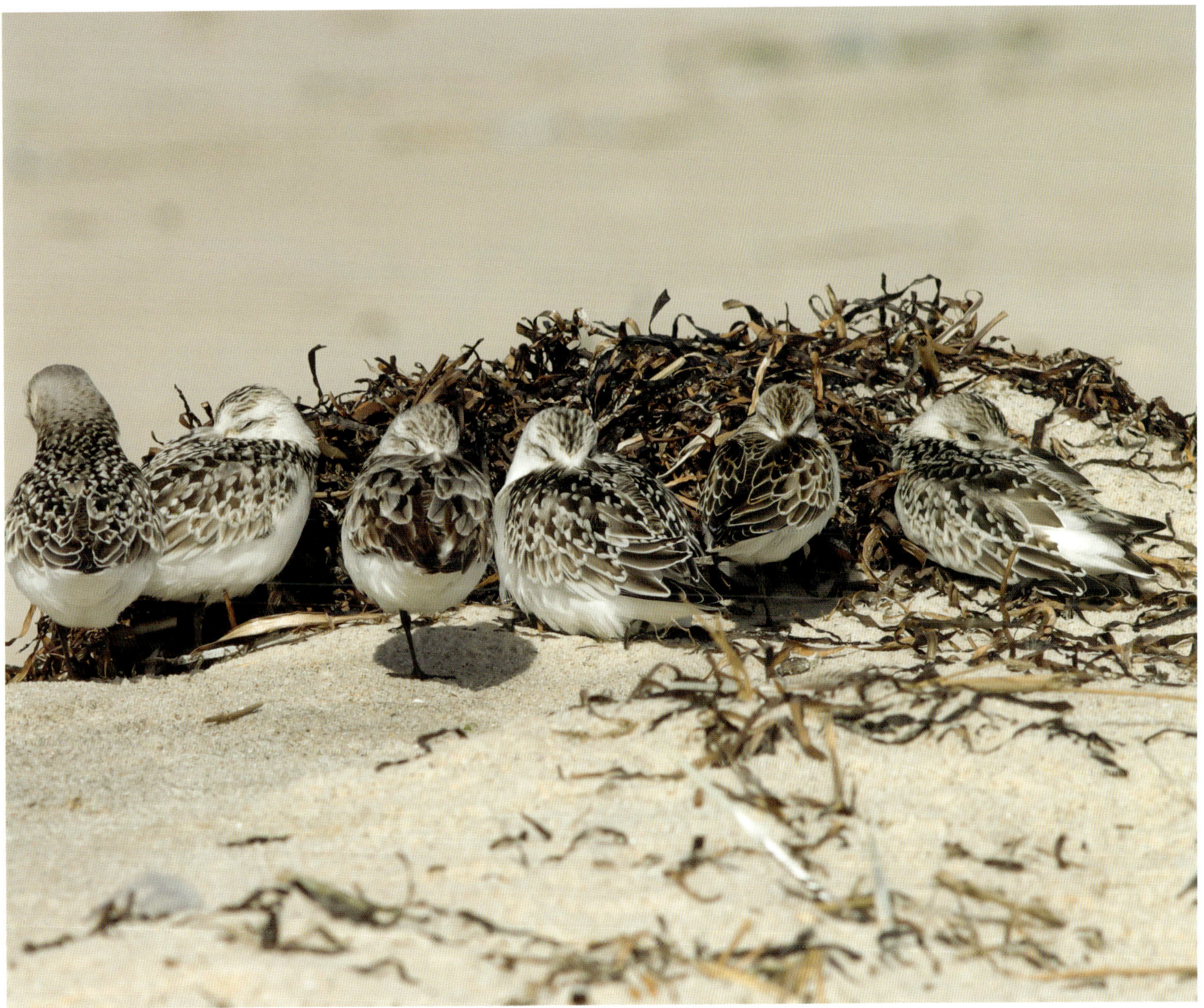

Five sanderlings and a smaller semipalmated sandpiper hunker down to rest before their long migration to the shores of South America. These small birds have already flown several thousand miles from their breeding ground on the Arctic tundra.

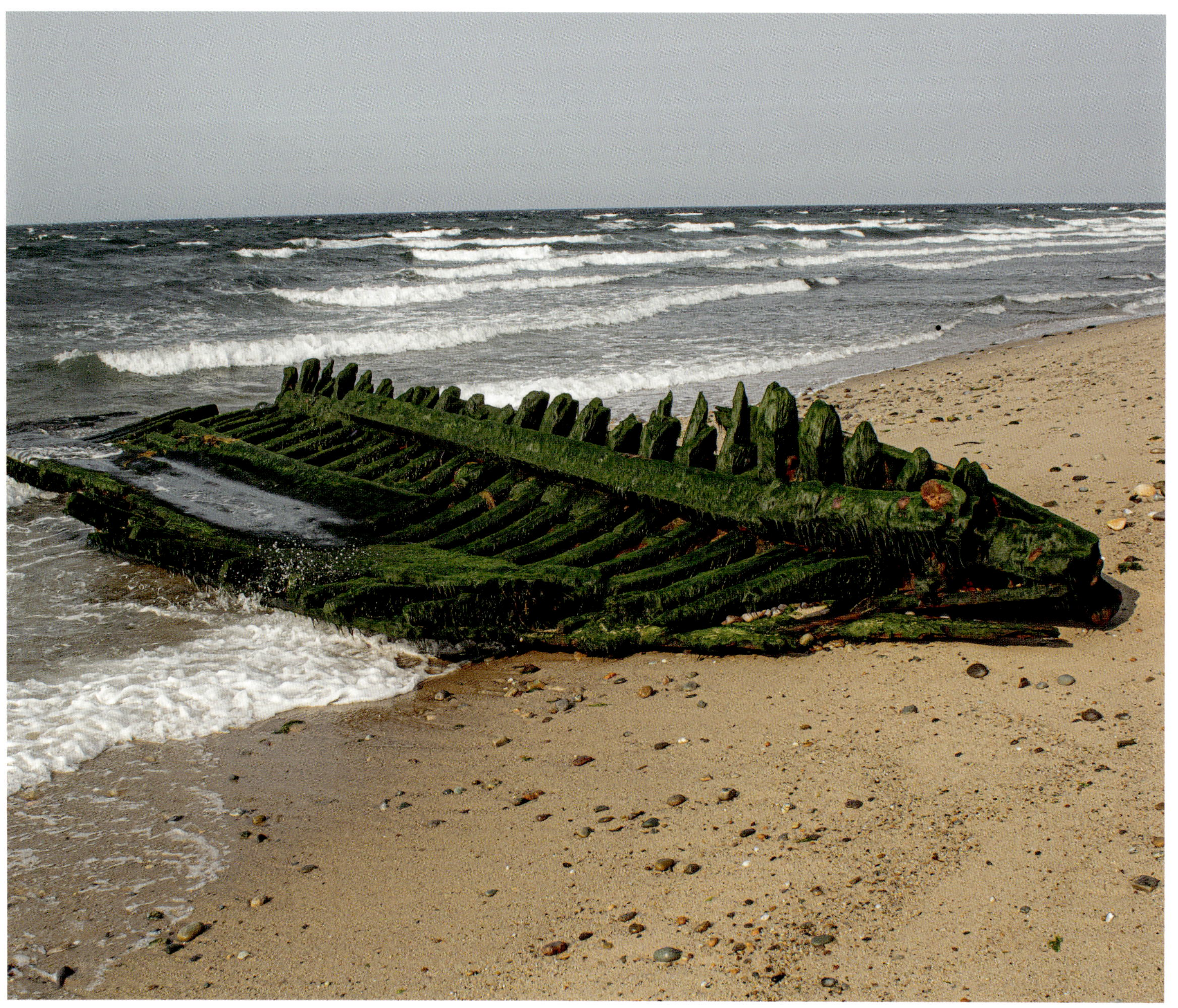

Strong winds and shifting sands uncover ship timbers of bygone days, shown here near Race Point in Provincetown.

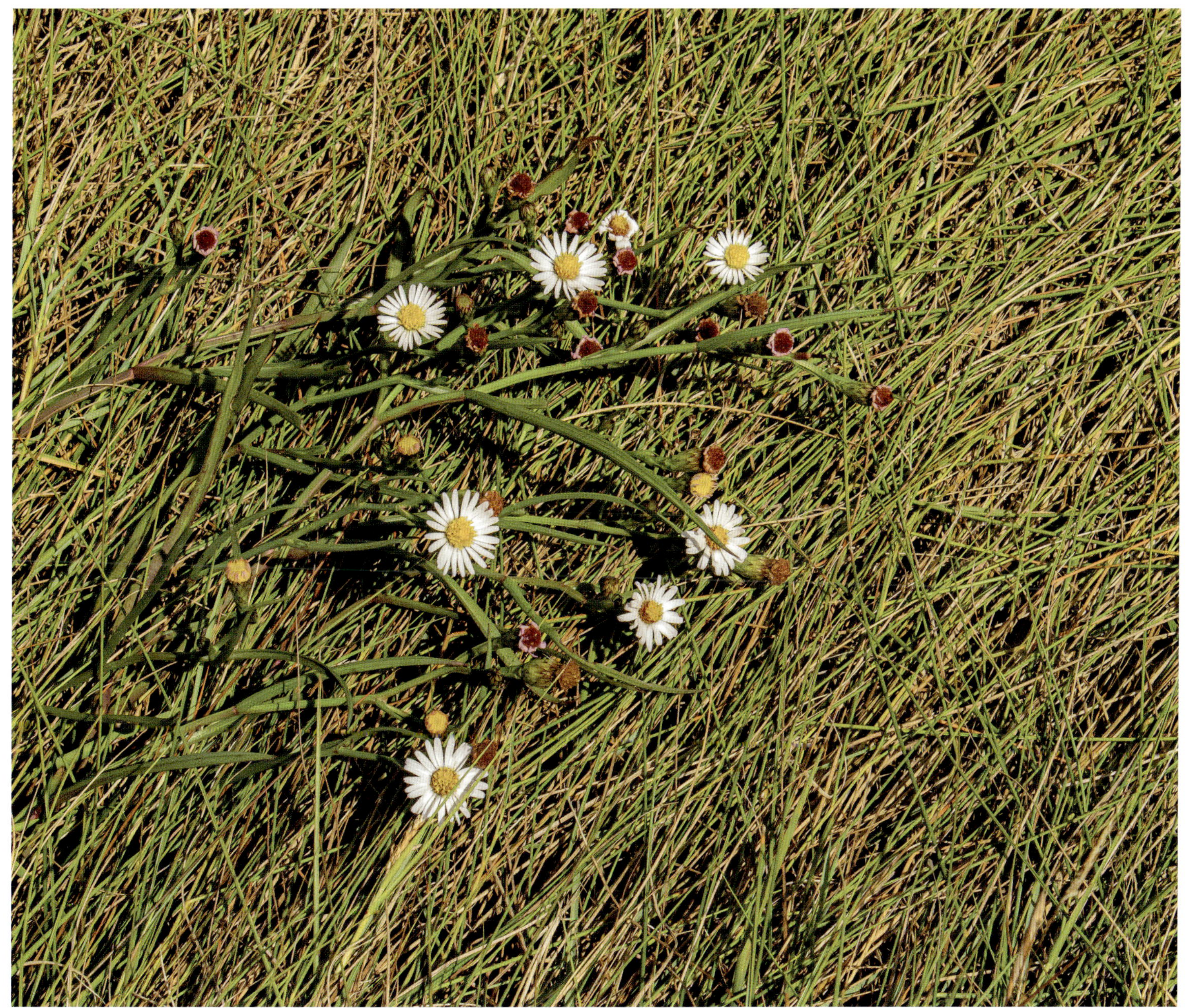

This pretty and petite salt marsh aster enhances the wide expanses of the *Spartina*-rich salt marsh, tolerating salinity that would kill other aster species.

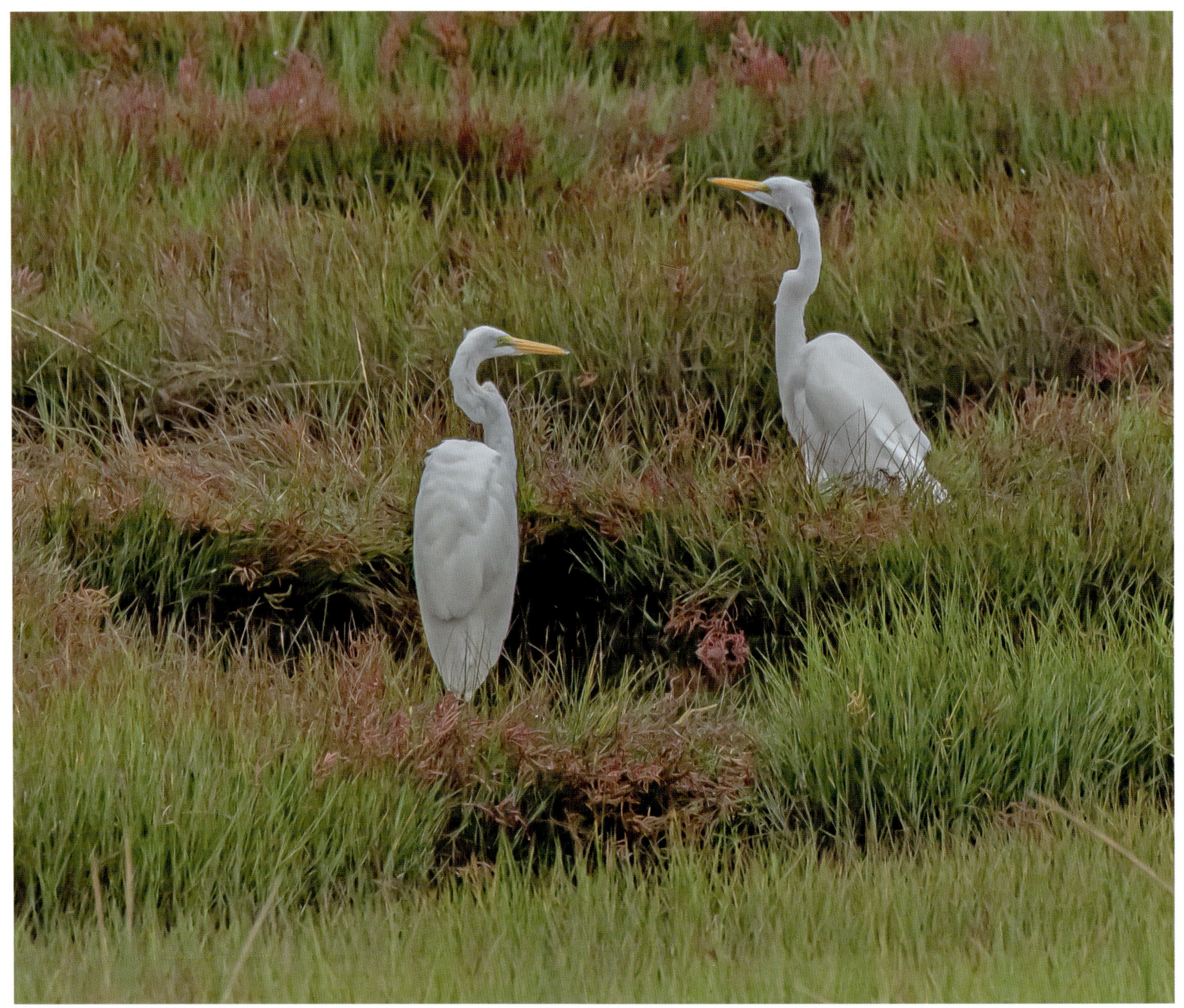

As large as a great blue heron, these pure-white great egrets prey on fish in the salt marsh tidal pools.

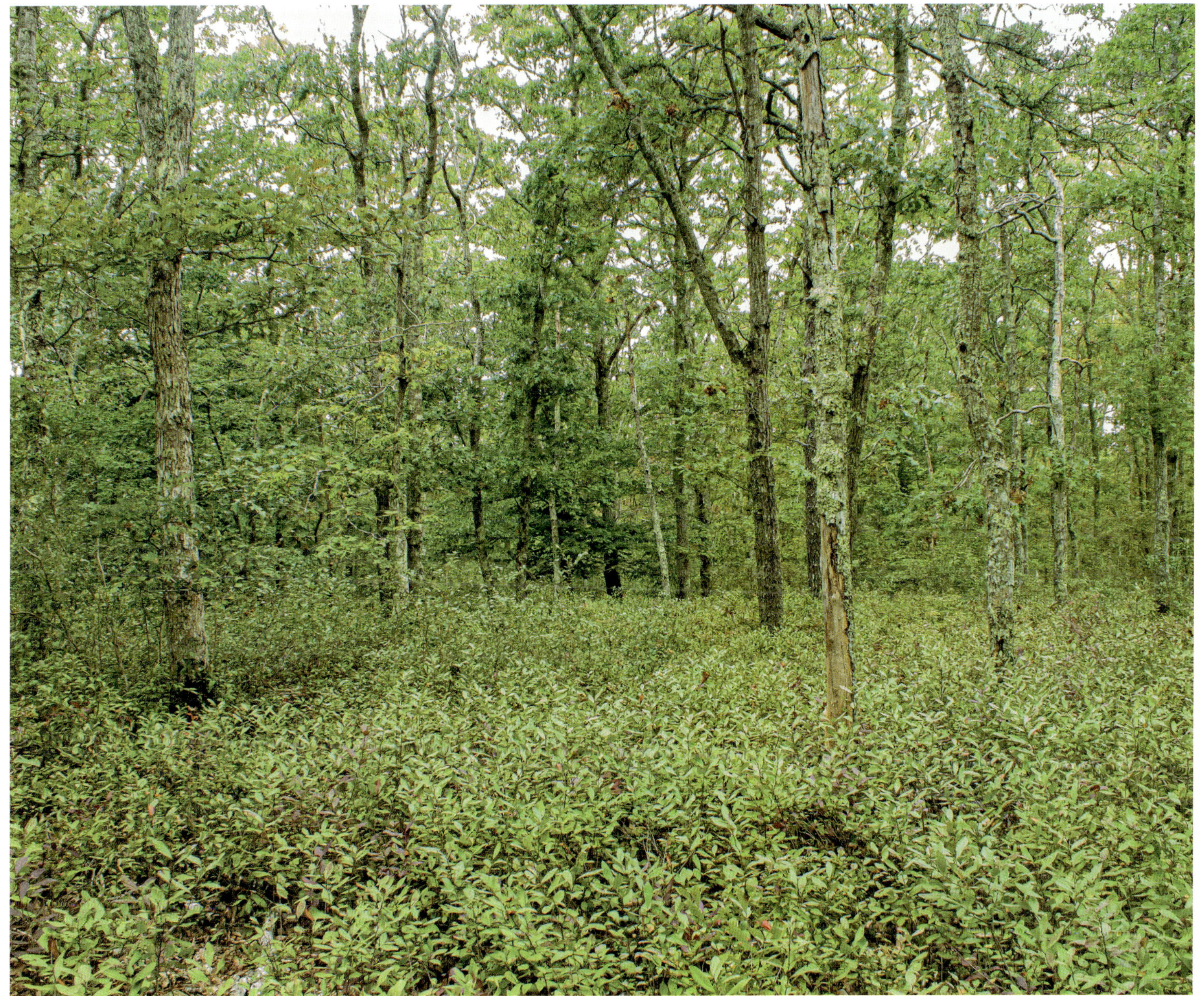

In mid-October, when most people are leaf peeping in New England forests, here the undergrowth of low-bush blueberry, inkberry, oak leaves, and lichen is still bright green.

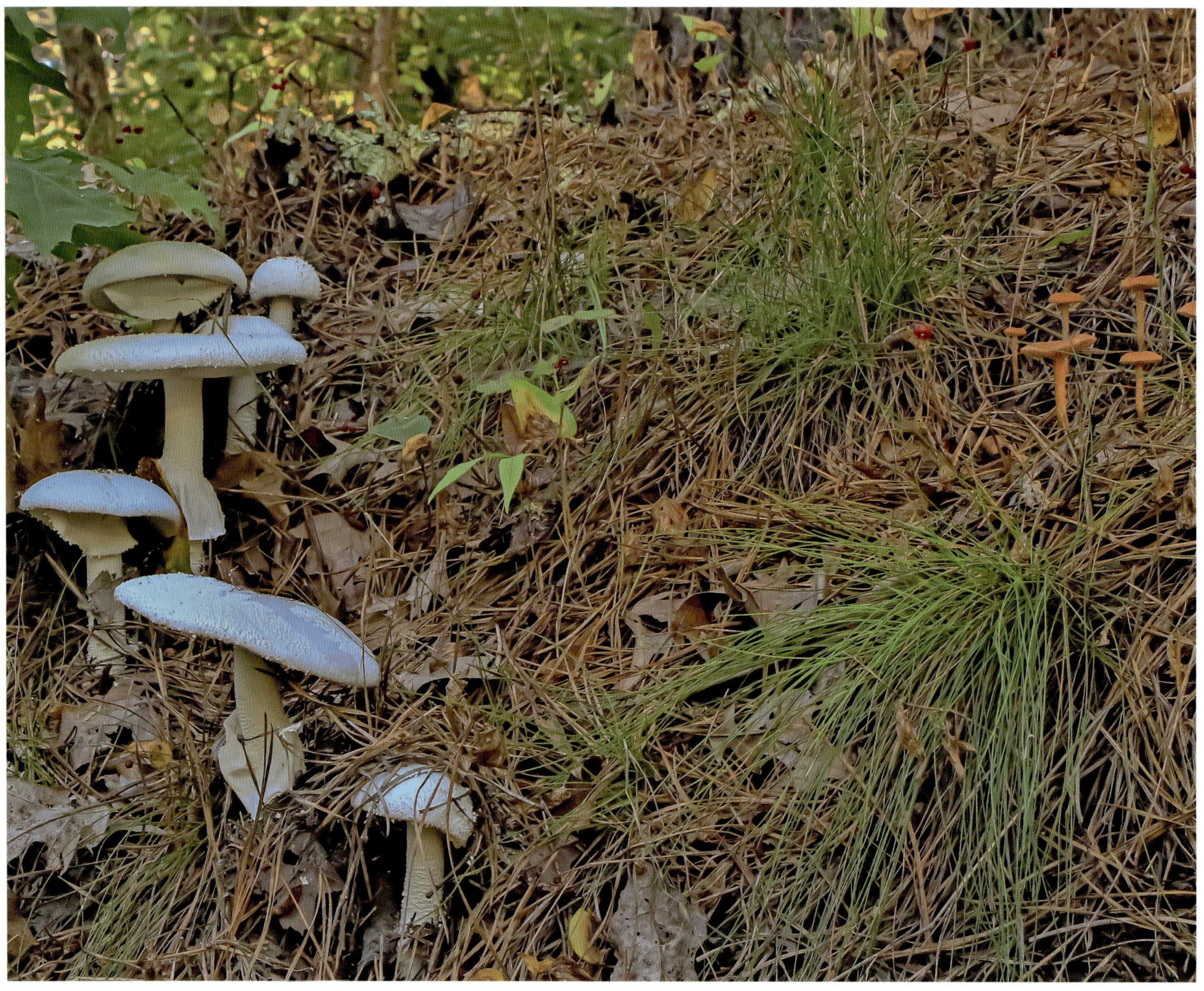

A walk through pine oak woodlands after a soaking autumn rain will offer a delightful diversity of colorful mushrooms. Growing on a wooded bank in Harwich below the oaks and tupelos, we find the white and rusty-orange varieties. The whites are amanita, many of them highly toxic. The mushrooms on the right are in the genus *Laccaria*, some of which are edible. One should never eat wild mushrooms without checking with an experienced mycologist.

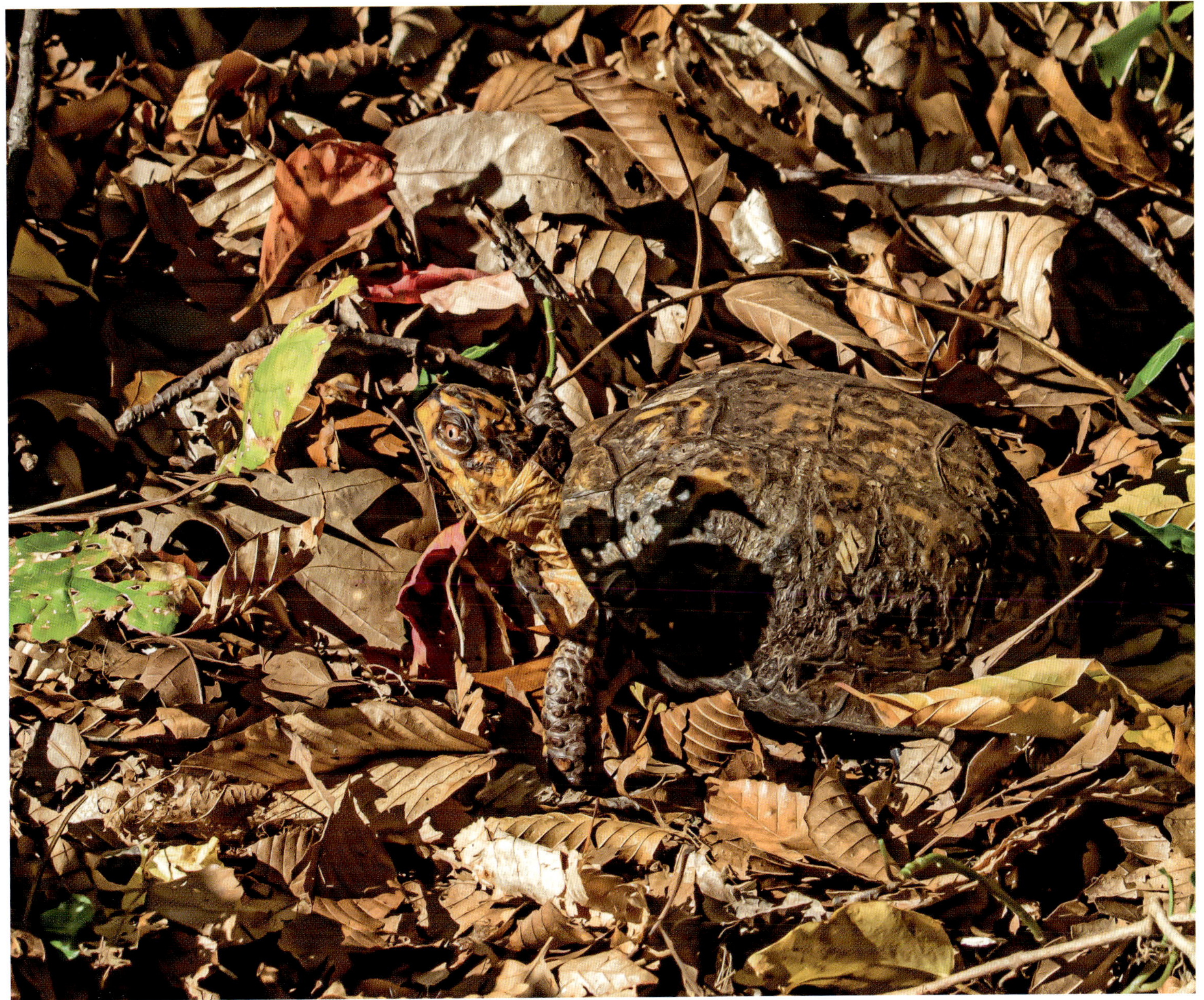

Beautifully camouflaged in the leaf litter, this box turtle will eat just about anything, including wild mushrooms of any sort. These hard-to-find turtles are listed as a species of special concern in Massachusetts.

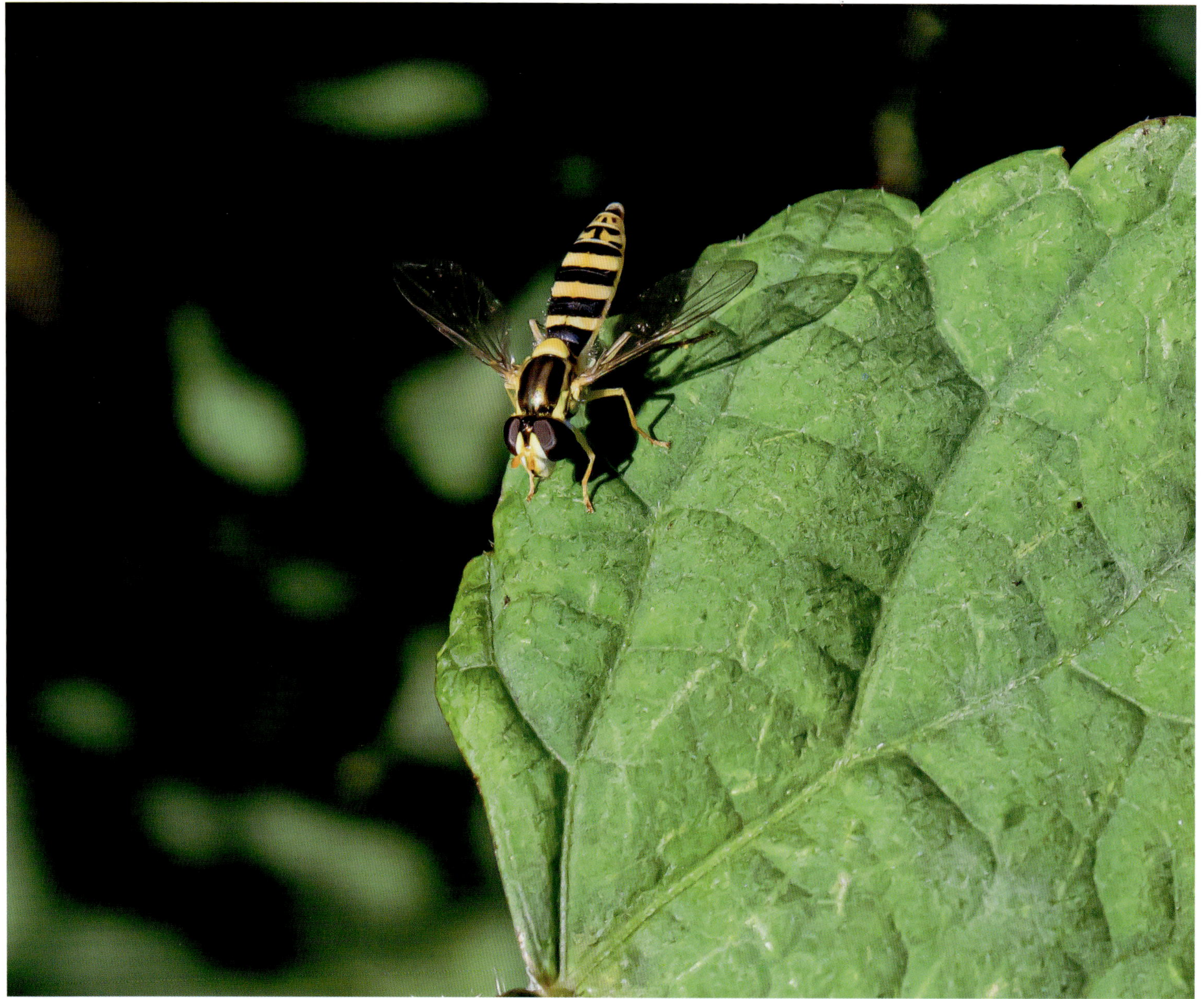

This tiny hoverfly, mimicking a wasp, is about a quarter inch long. There are over 6,000 species of hoverflies worldwide, with 870 species in North America zipping around in our gardens and meadows virtually unnoticed. These and many other flying insects are a food source for migratory birds in the fall.

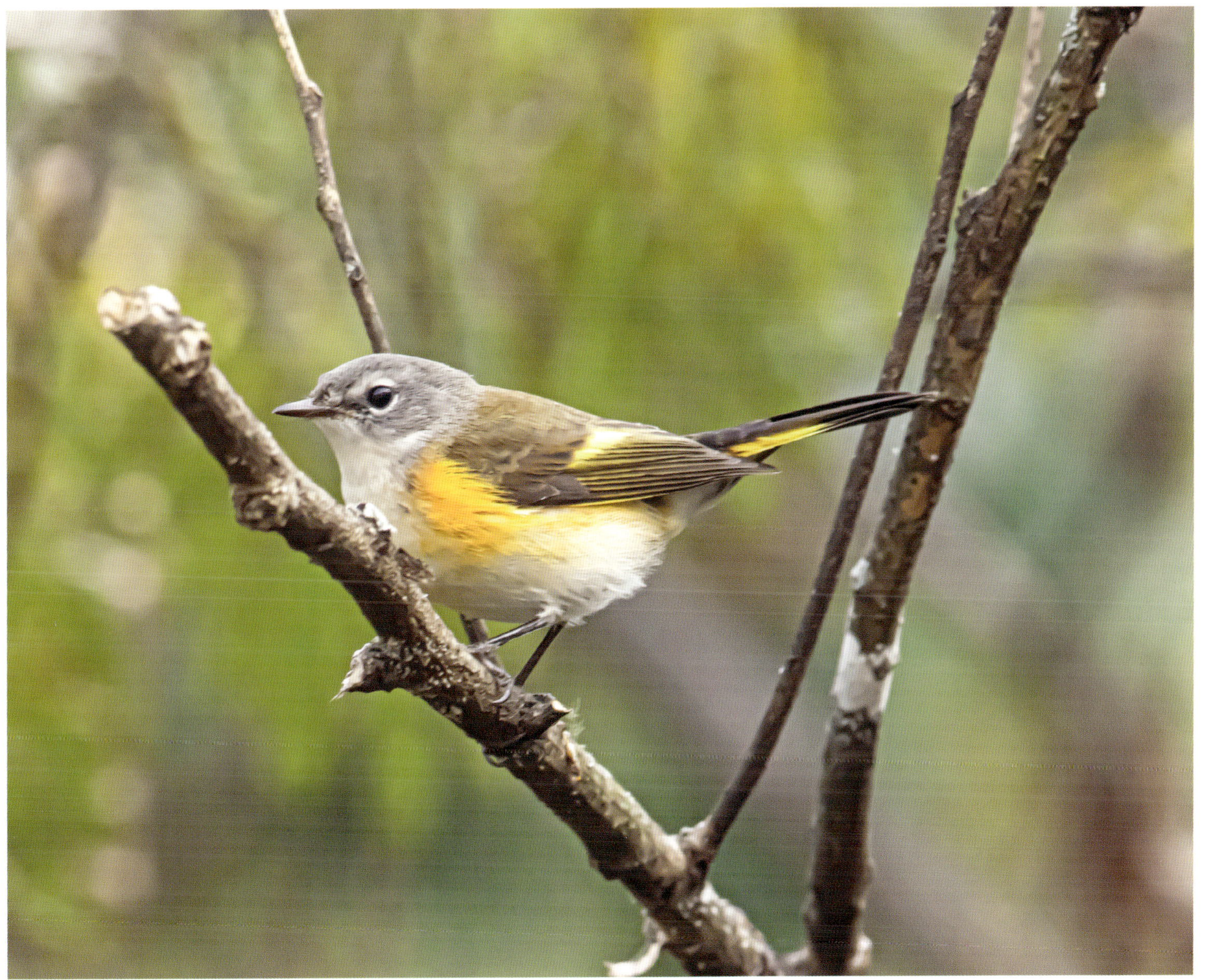

This tiny woodland sprite, American redstart, breeds widely across eastern North America and into Canada. Redstarts migrate each fall to Central and South America, plucking flies, caterpillars, midges, and any small insect from the foliage and twigs. This young male redstart hatched out in May or June and has not yet molted into its adult plumage.

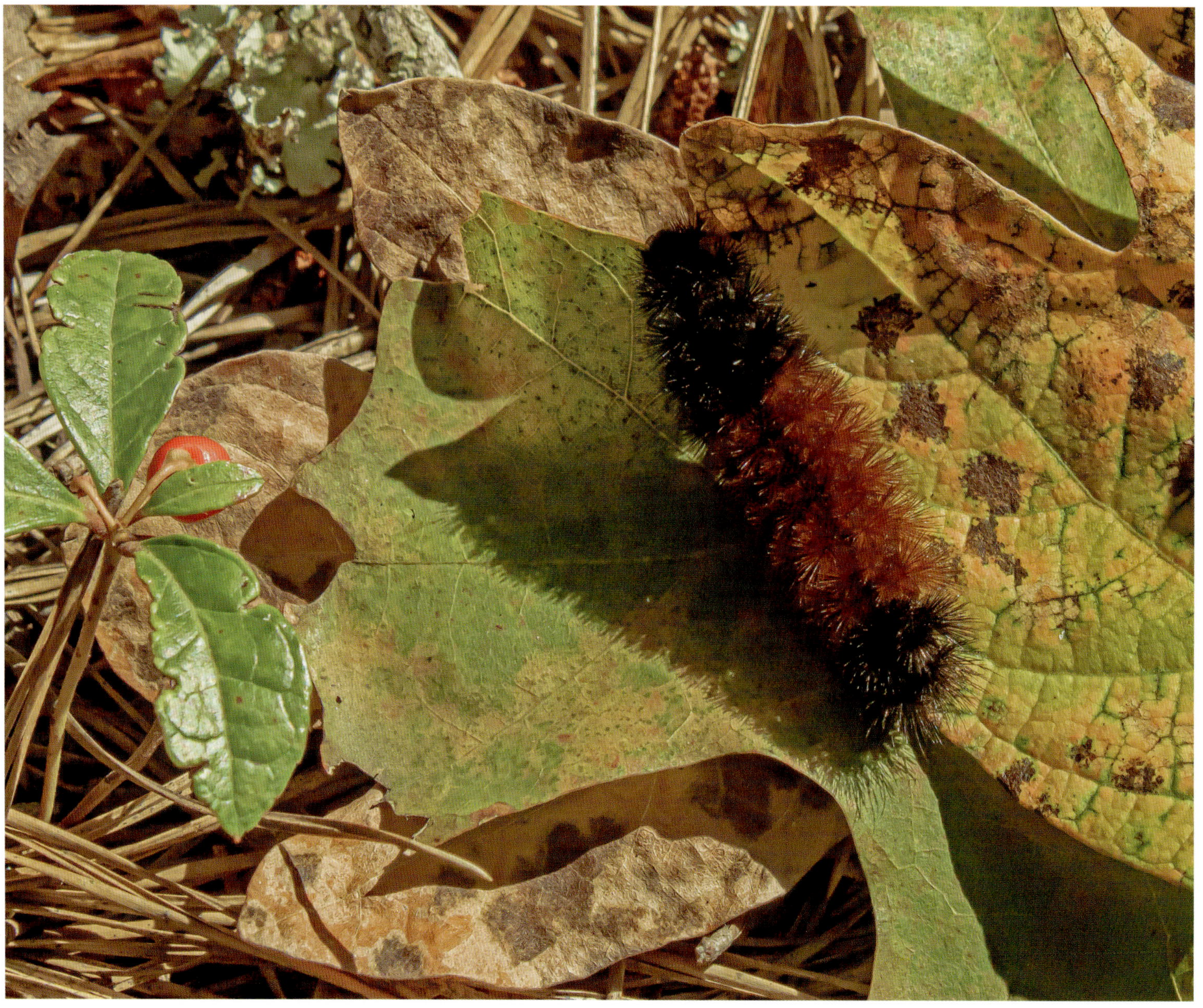

According to folklore, this woolly bear caterpillar is predicting a mild winter, with more reddish brown on its body than black. Prominent black coloration would suggest a cold, hard winter. Sassafras leaves and wintergreen are nearby.

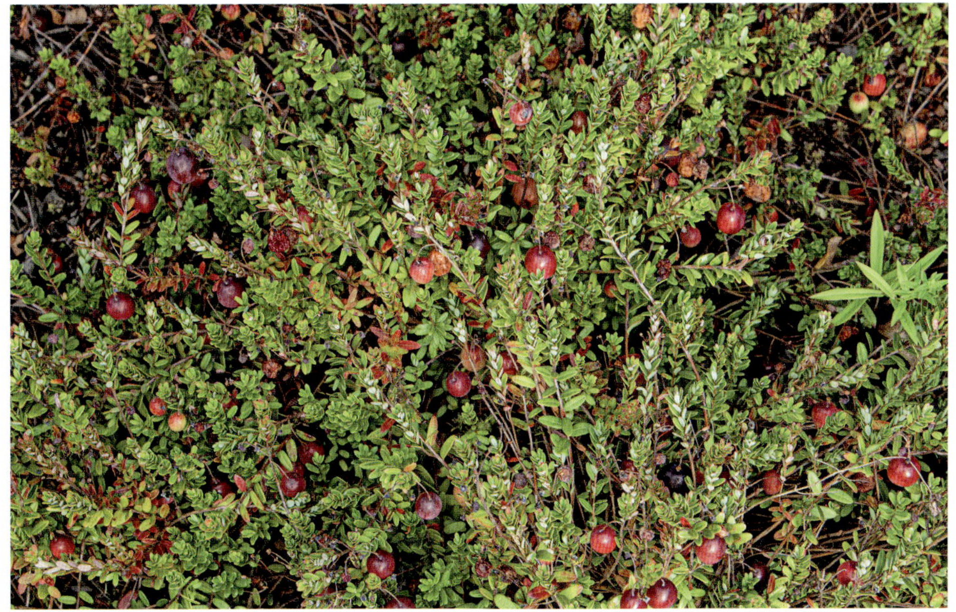

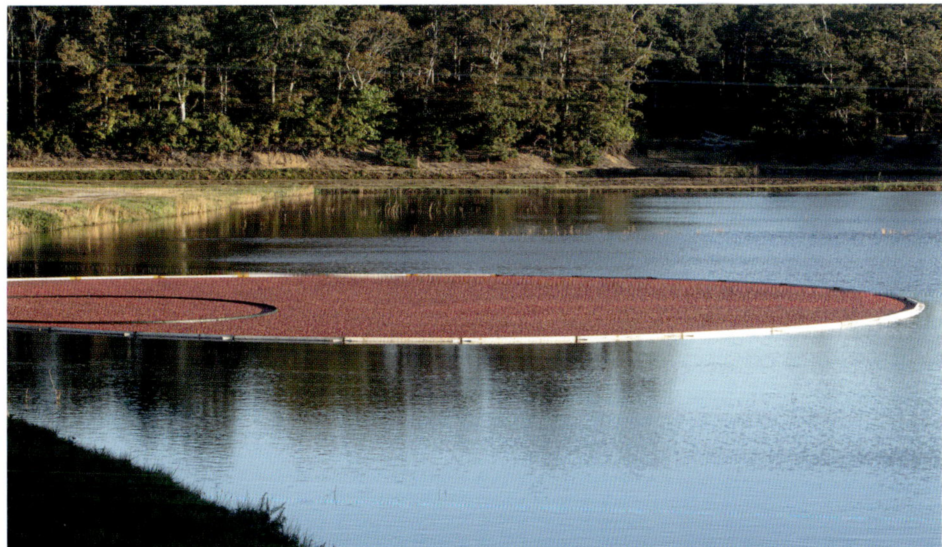

Cranberries grow wild from Mashpee to Provincetown. Truckloads are also harvested in commercial bogs, floated and contained in a boom, and "vacuumed" into trucks to be transported away for juice or other products.

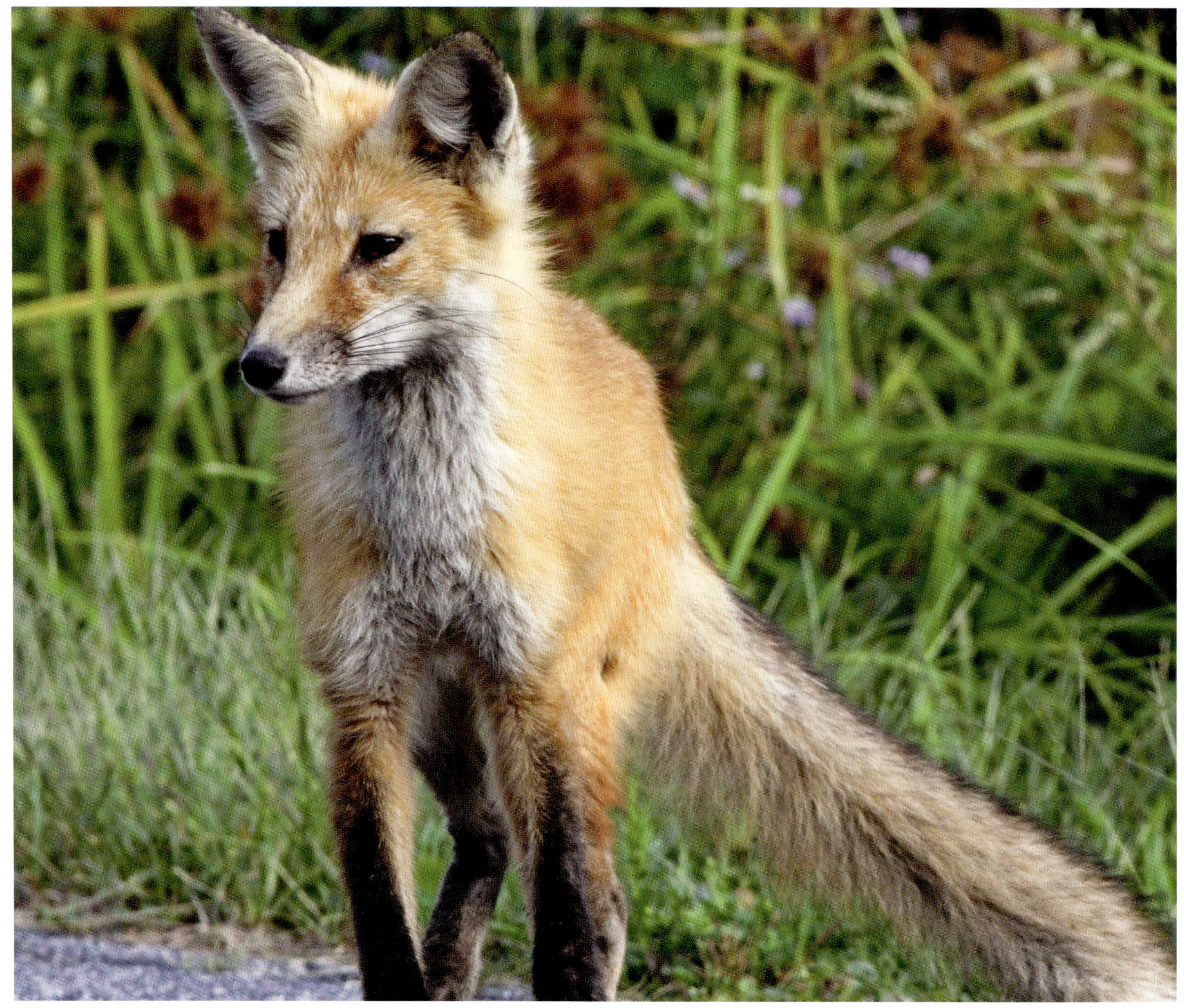

A red fox trots along the roadway.

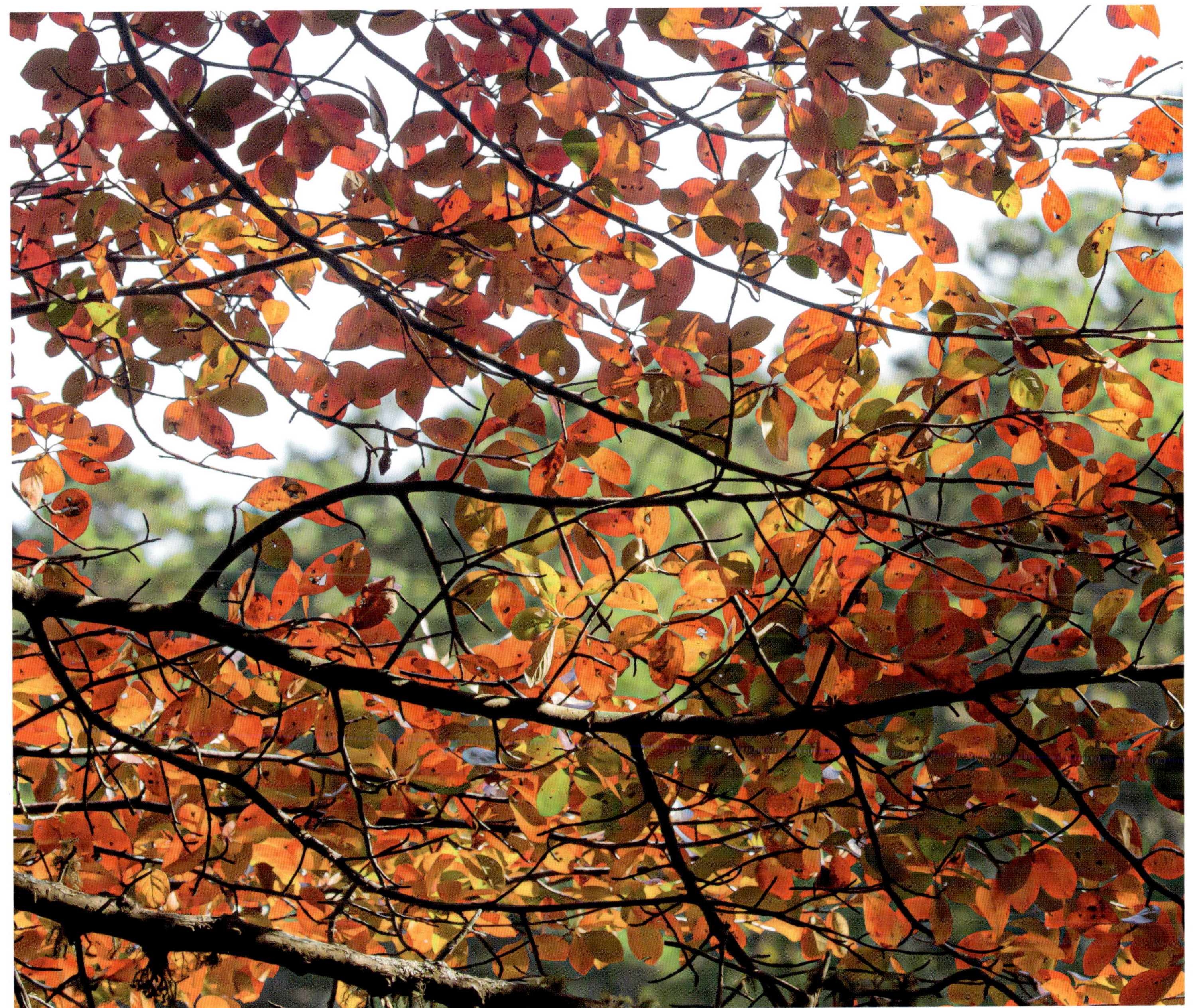

Tupelo leaves are flaming red in October.

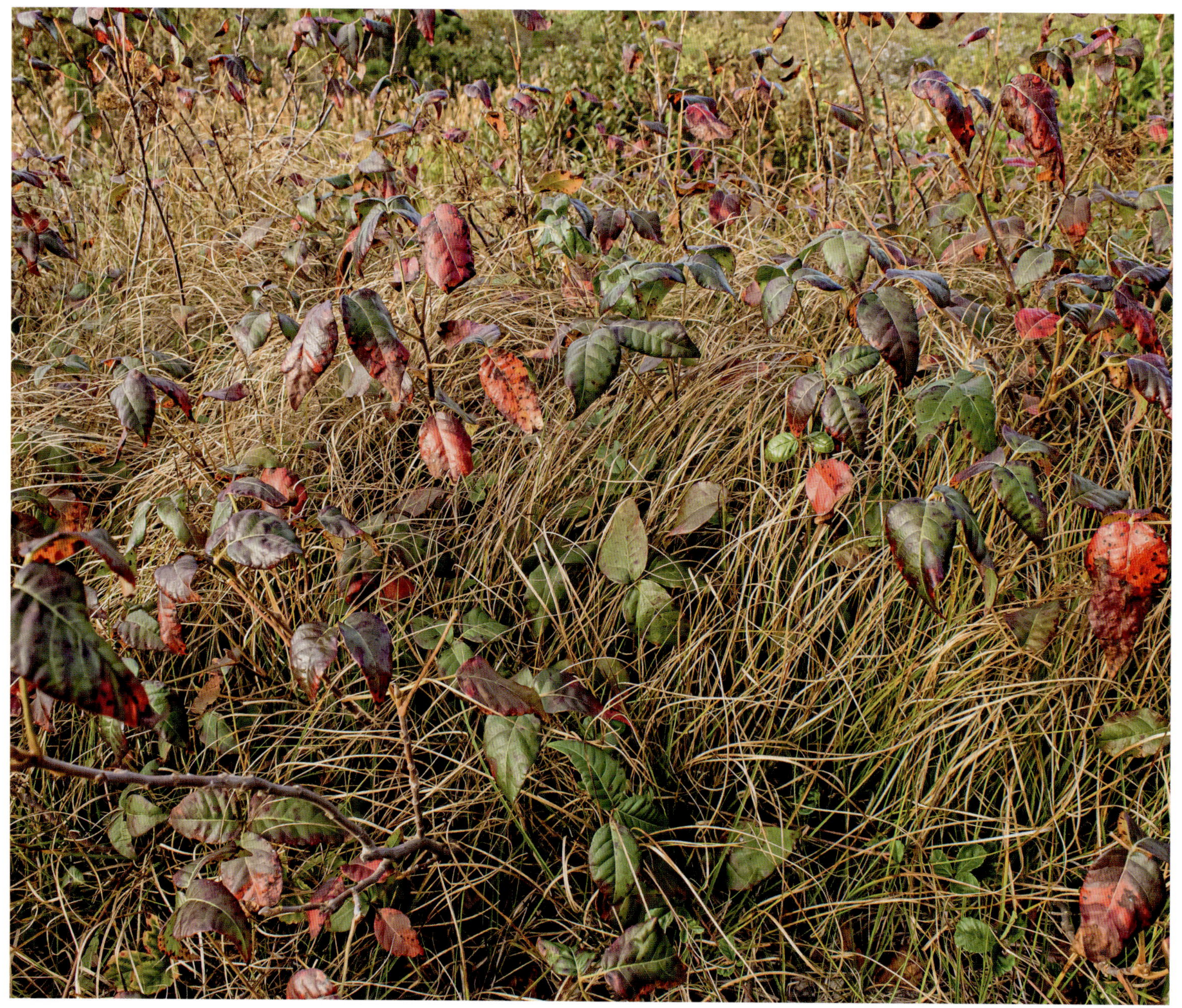

Red leaves to stay away from—poison ivy.

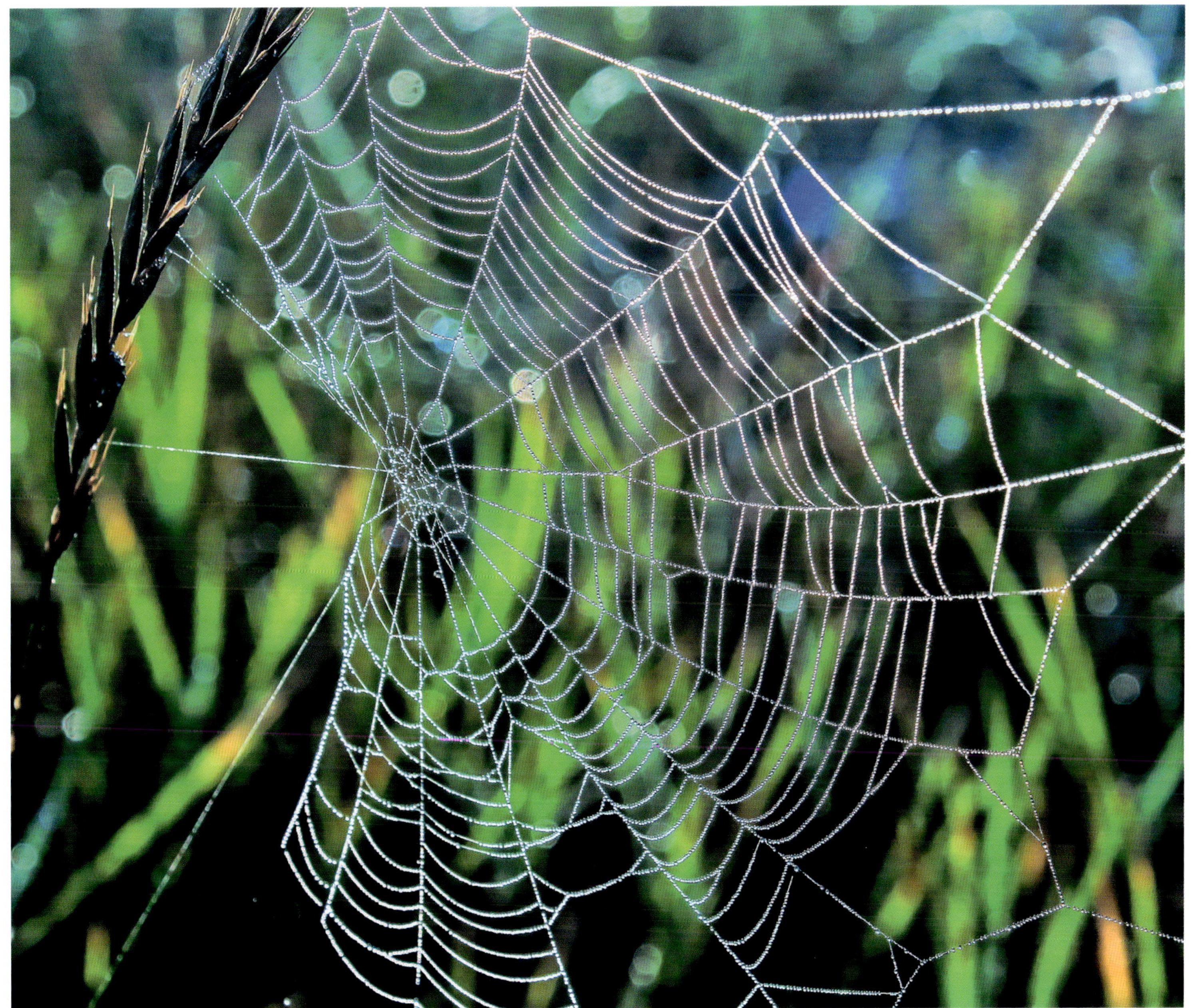

Illuminated by the sunrise, dew clings to the web of an orb weaver spider. A marsh or meadow may have hundreds of these dew-covered webs on an October morning.

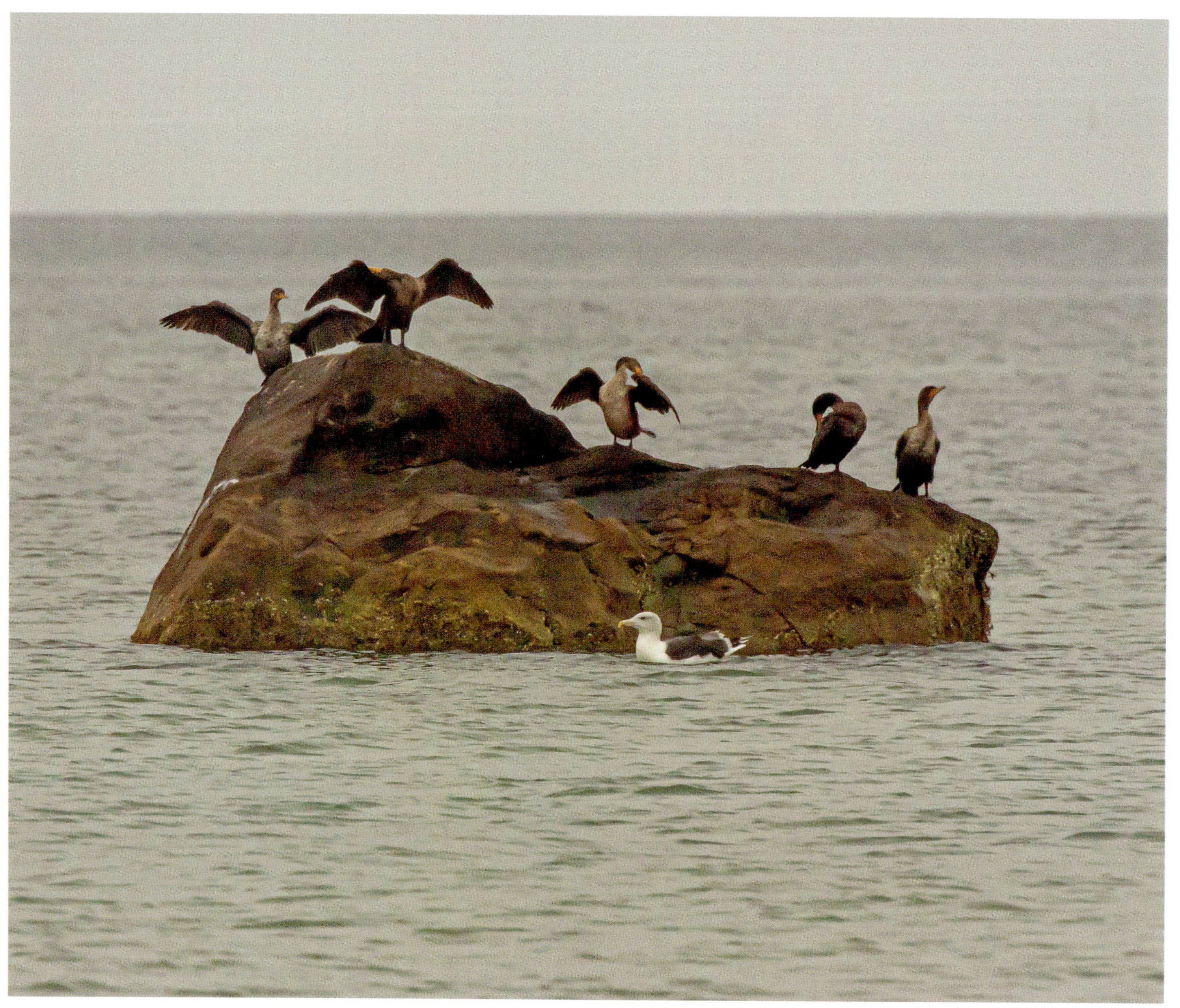

Double-crested cormorants will soon migrate south to the Gulf coast, returning to these Cape Cod Bay rocks in April.

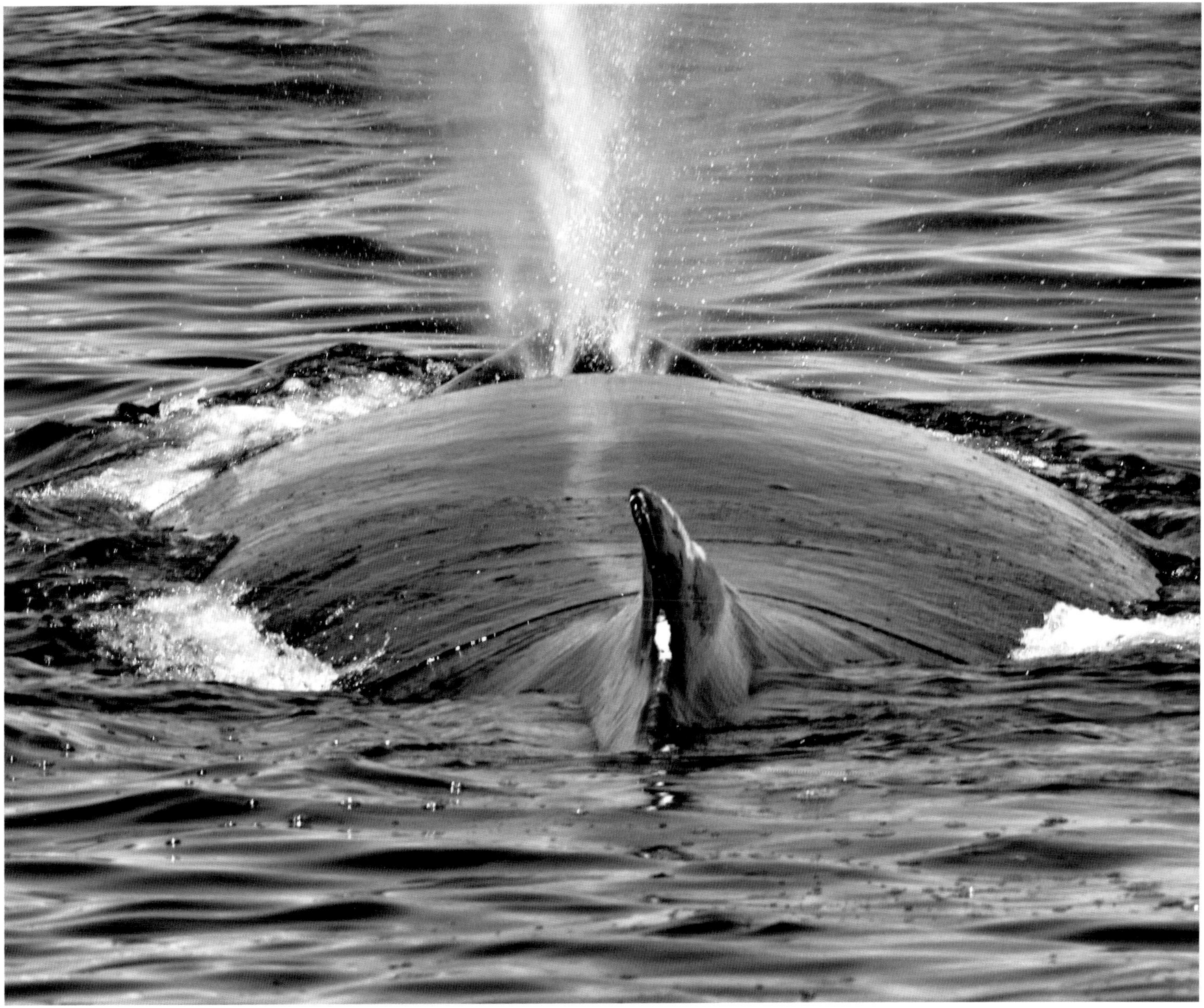

Humpback whales that have frequented the waters of Stellwagen Bank since April migrate to waters off Puerto Rico and the Dominican Republic to breed and give birth during our winter months.

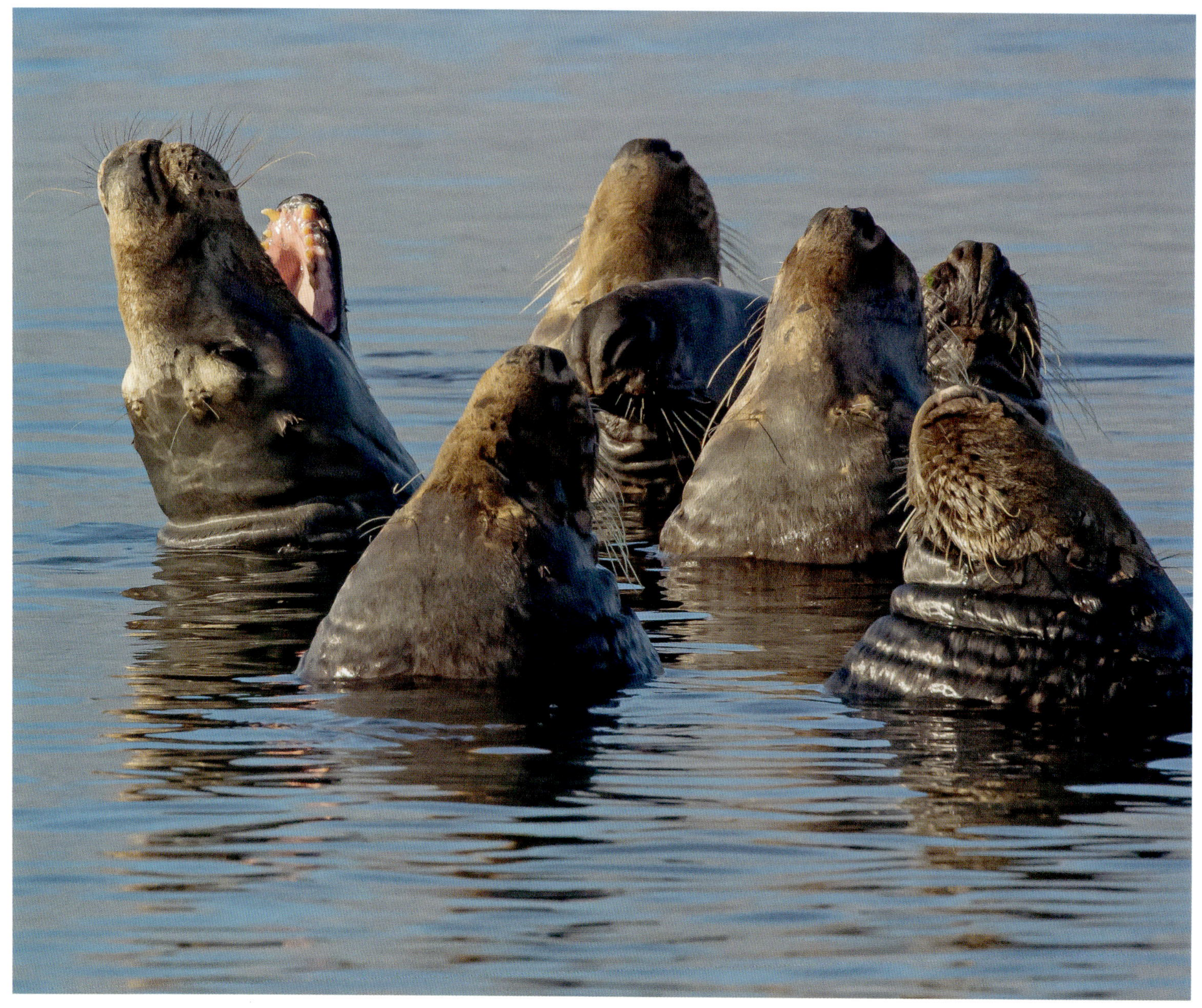

After lounging and feeding around the Chatham bars all summer, these gray seals will move to the shores of Monomoy Island and Nantucket to breed and give birth in January.

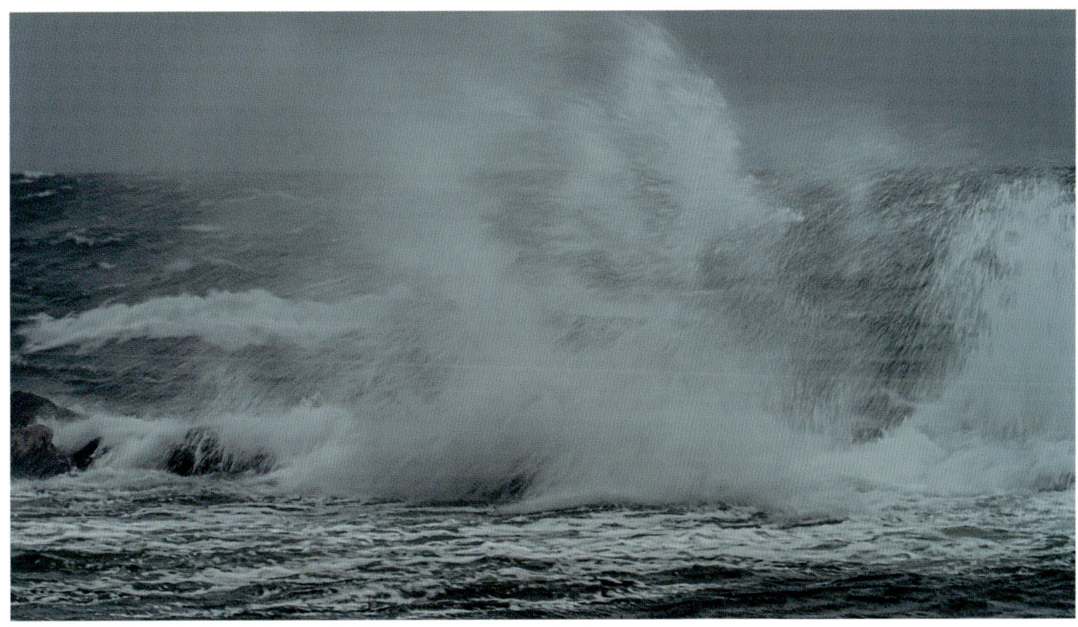

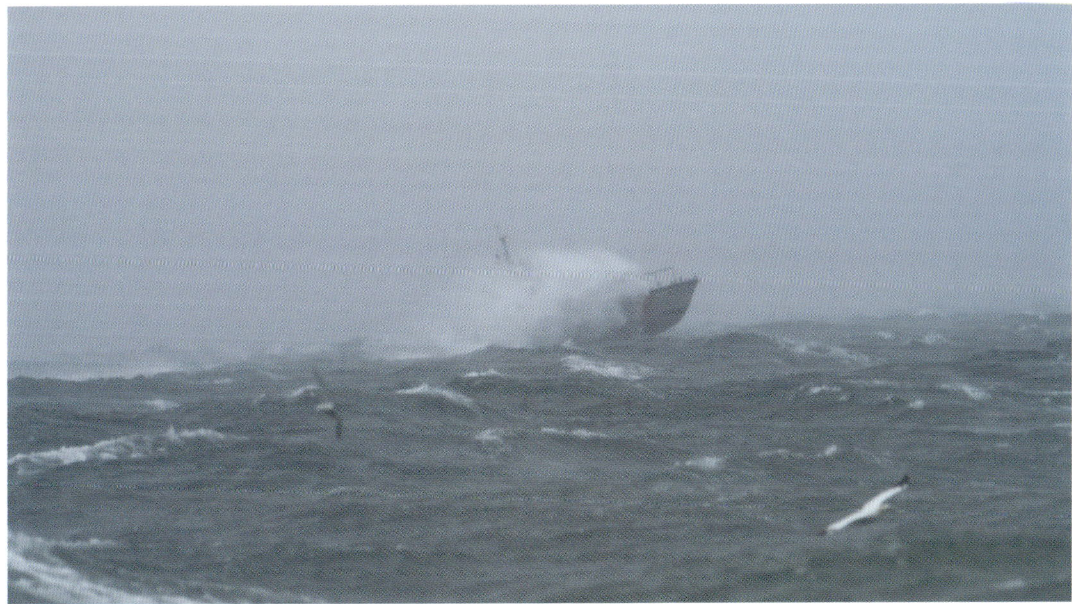

The wind really cranks up in October, crashing onshore and giving the US Coast Guard some exciting times at sea.

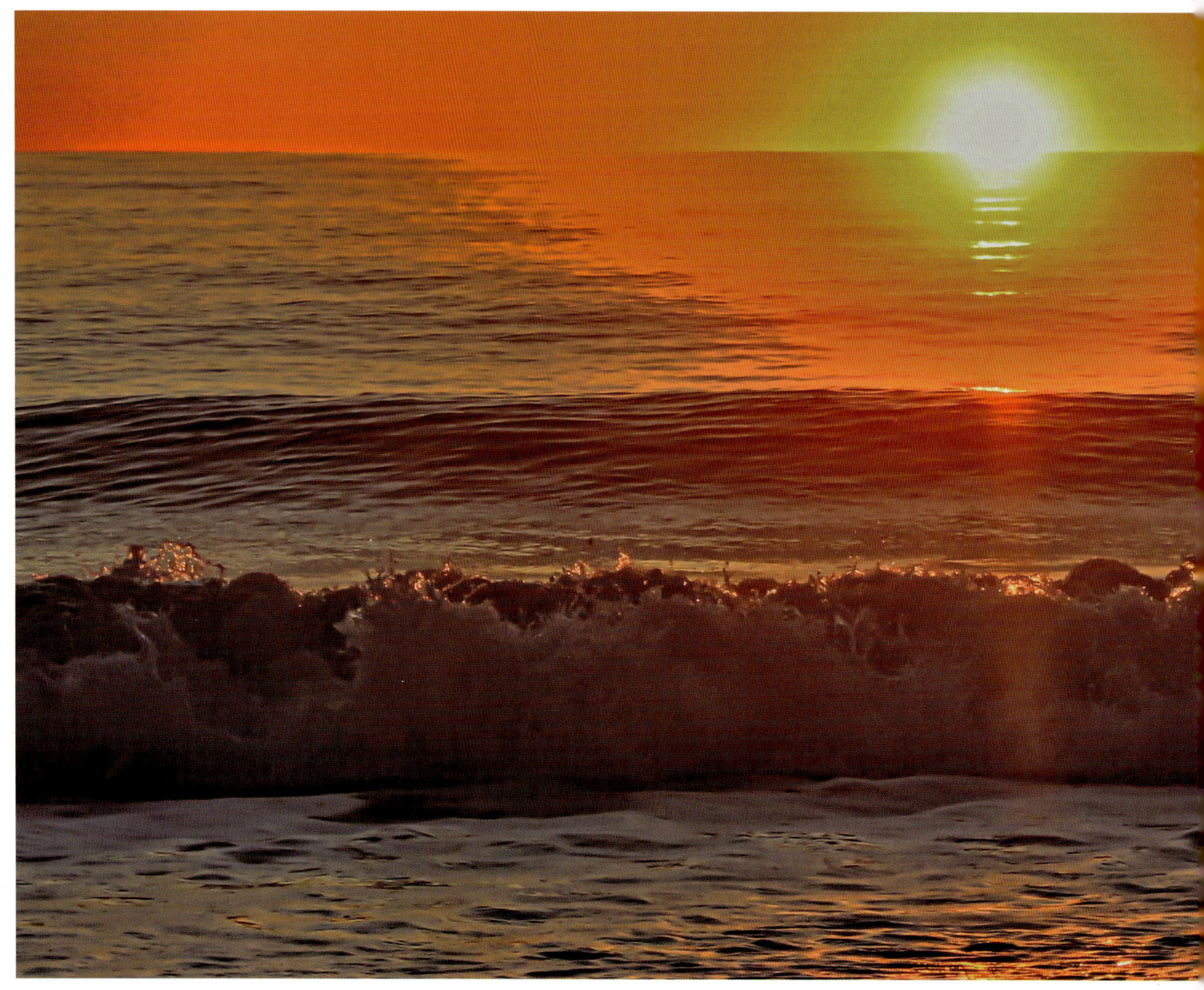

As the sun sets on October, and November winds blow from the north, we begin to see the first signs of shorter days and a cooling atmosphere.

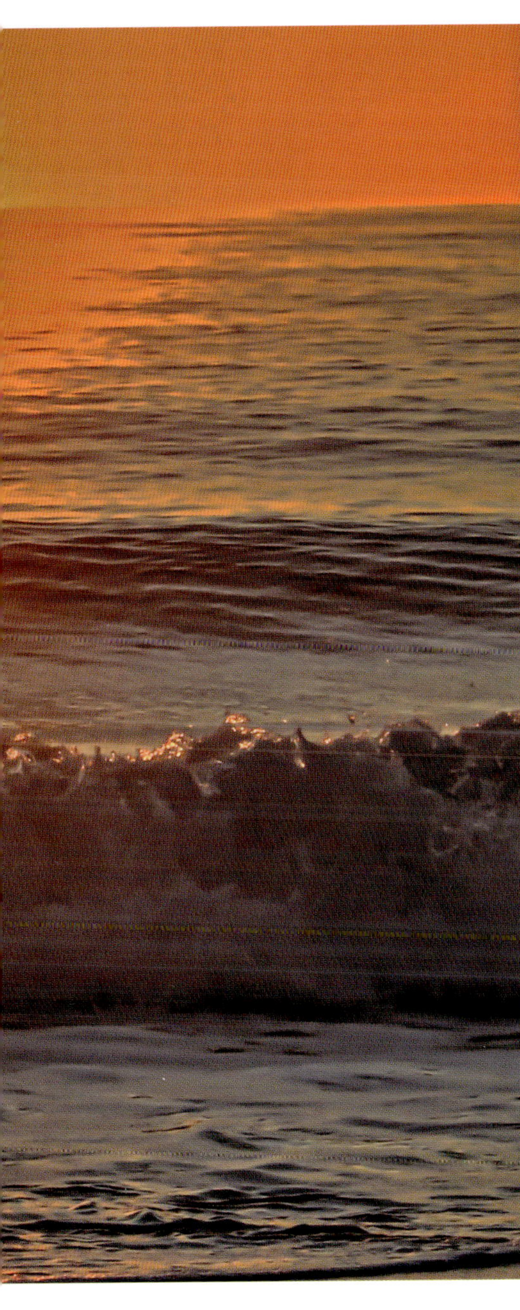

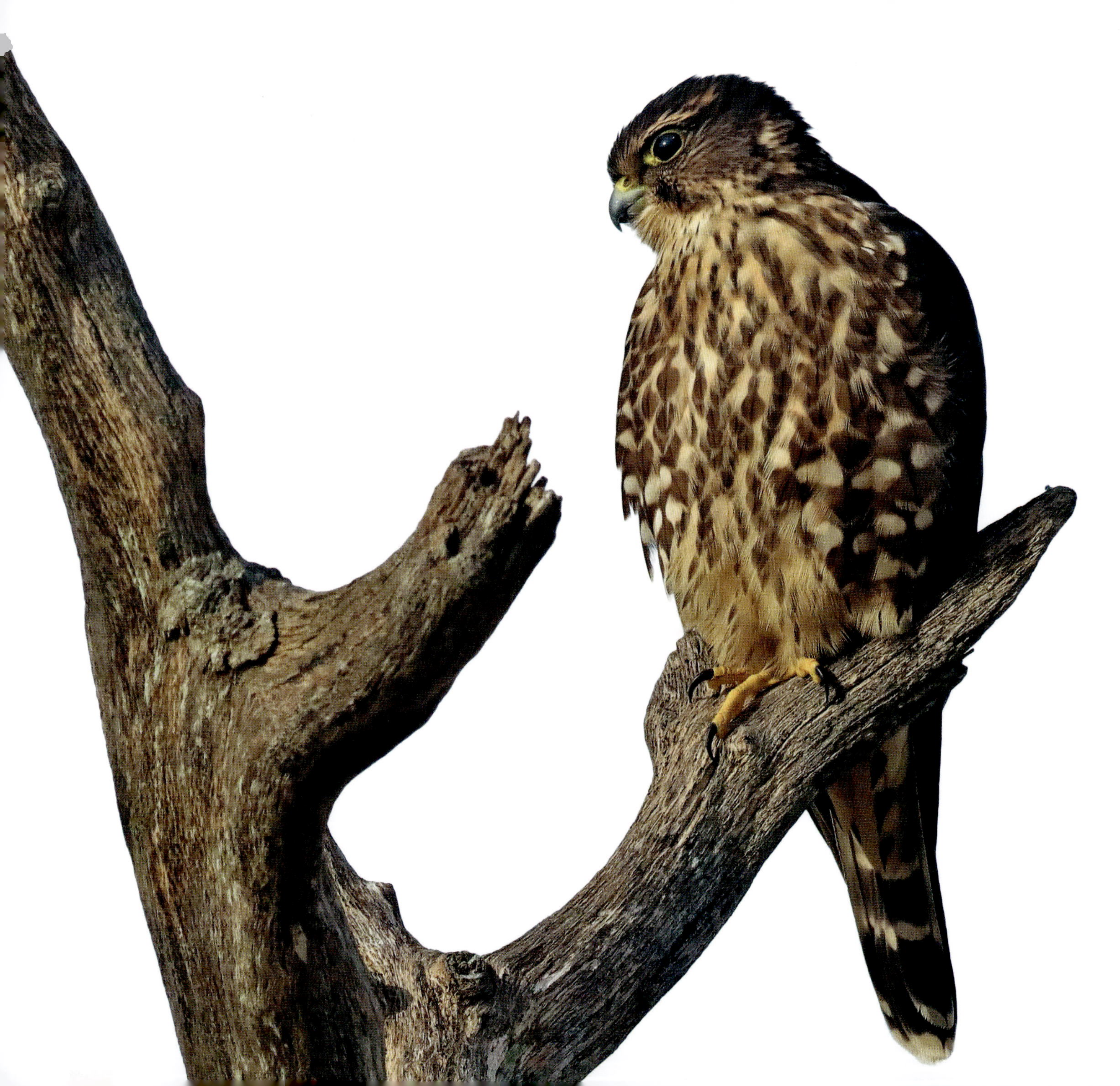

NOVEMBER AND DECEMBER

Life on the Tundra

As November and December roll around, we are introduced to the earliest signs of the oncoming winter. It may simply be a cold day, or a November snow flurry. However, we all recall occasional December surprises when temperatures climbed into the sixties and we were in shirtsleeves. Yes, the months of November and December can be perplexing, but winter is coming. The sky takes on an ethereal glow now that the days are rapidly shortening and the arc of the sun is low in the southern sky. Wind out of the northwest has a bite to it. Leaves have fallen from the trees, except for the predominant oaks, whose foliage simply turns a crispy copper brown and stays put until spring growth forces them to let go. Northern birds begin to arrive in November, adding life to the ponds and coastal waters. Most of these species will be with us until spring. But spring is a long way off. The snow and wind; the barren, empty beaches; and the winter scenes that lure us out of our homes to the coastline and back roads over the next few months are part of a continual cycle as we make another journey around the sun.

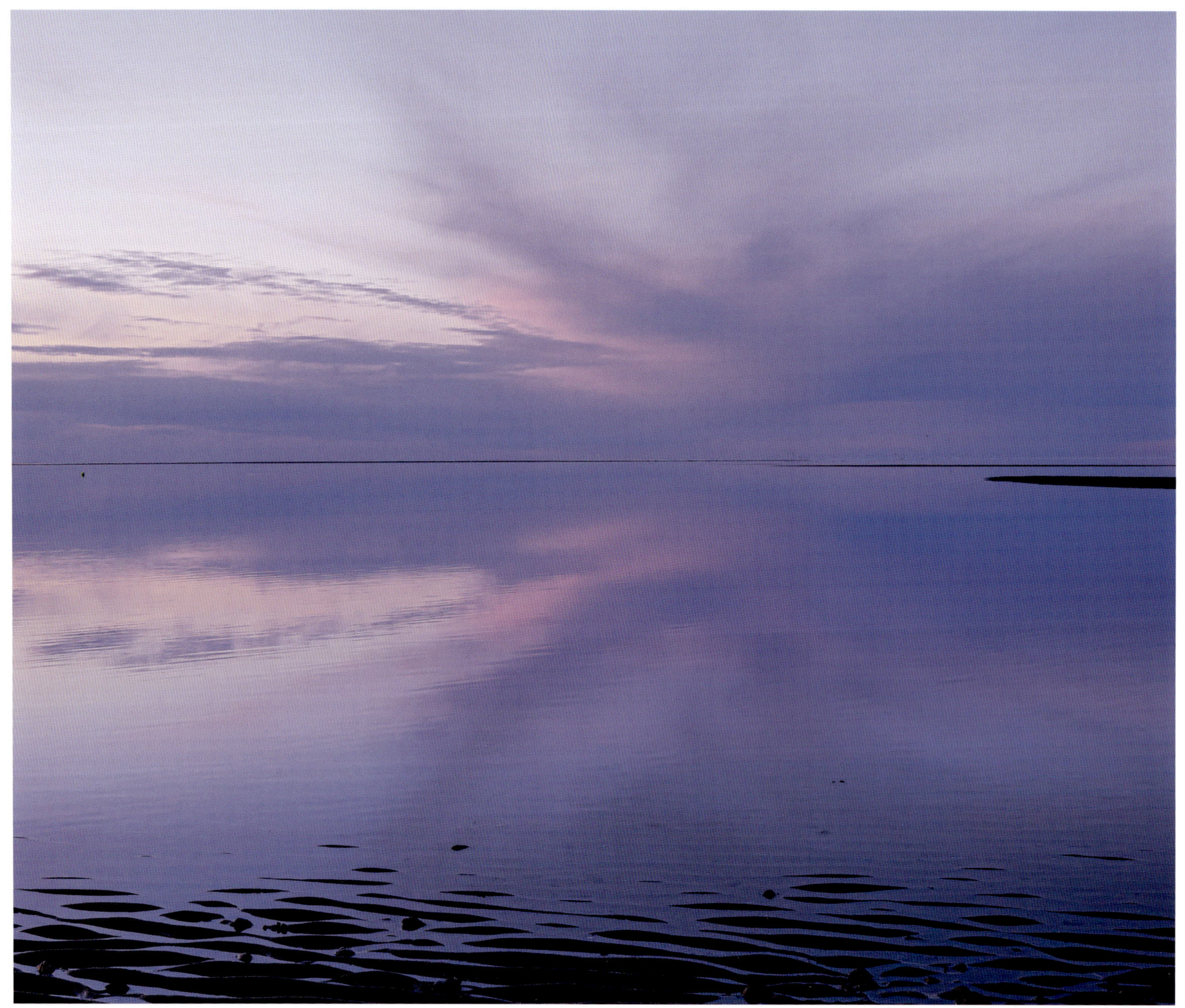

A mirror image of the late-day sky over Cape Cod Bay.

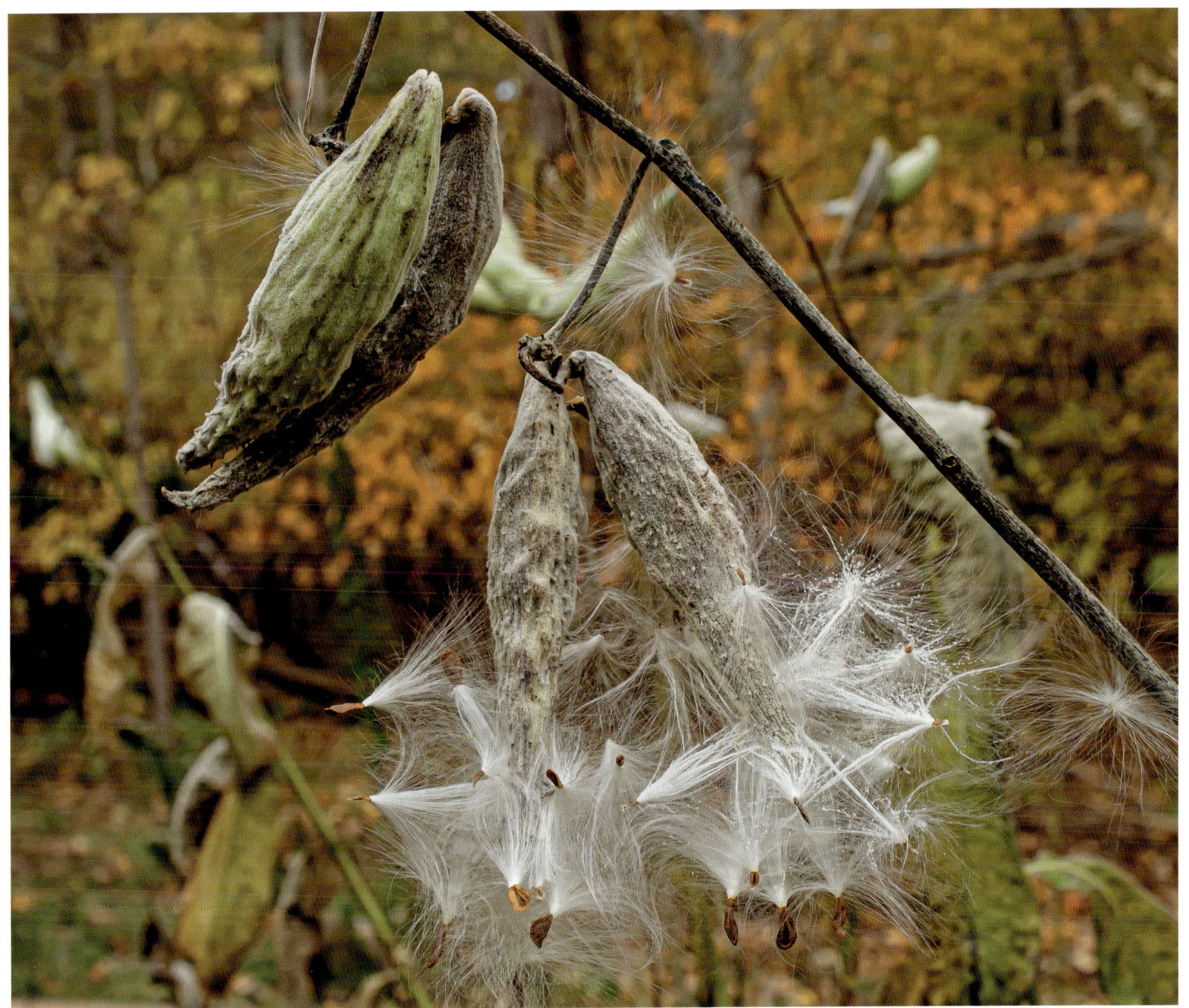

November brings the drying and opening of milkweed pods, allowing seeds to catch the wind on downy sails.

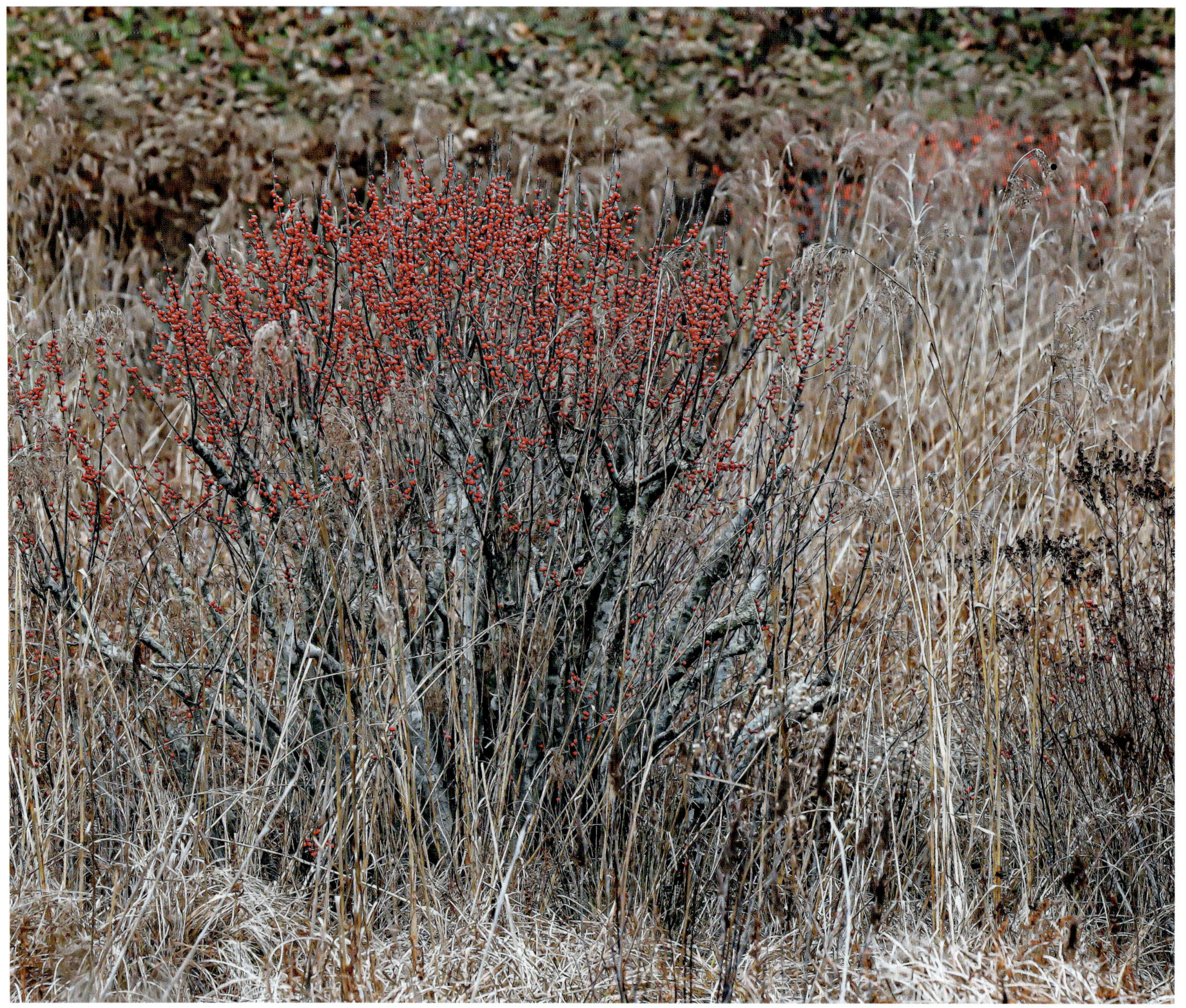

In abandoned bogs, in open meadows, and along roadsides, winterberry's scarlet fruit opposes the flat colors of November.

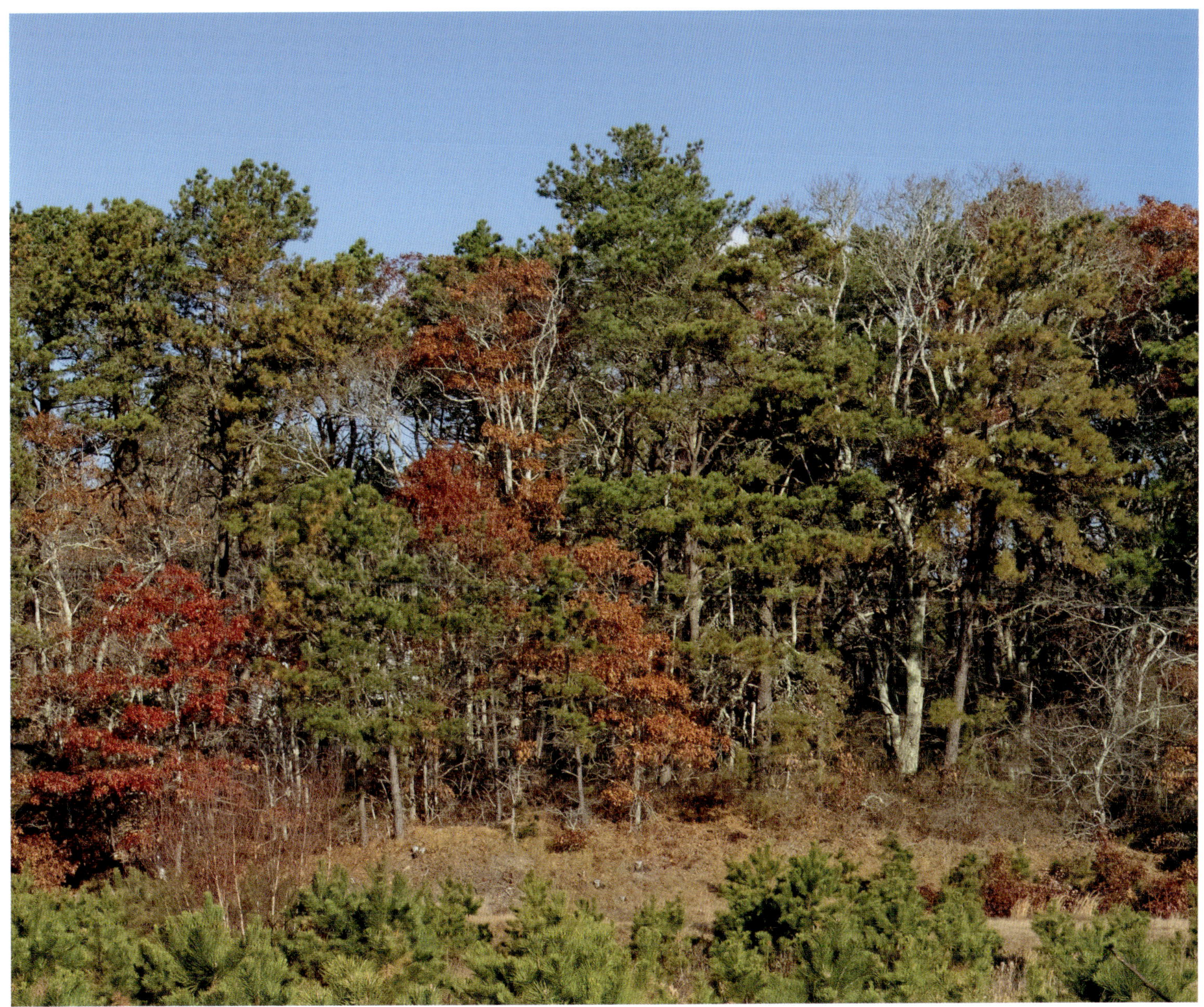

The woodland colors of November. A scarlet oak on the left lives up to its name, while black and white oaks exhibit the typical browns and coppers of winter, mixed with ubiquitous pitch pines.

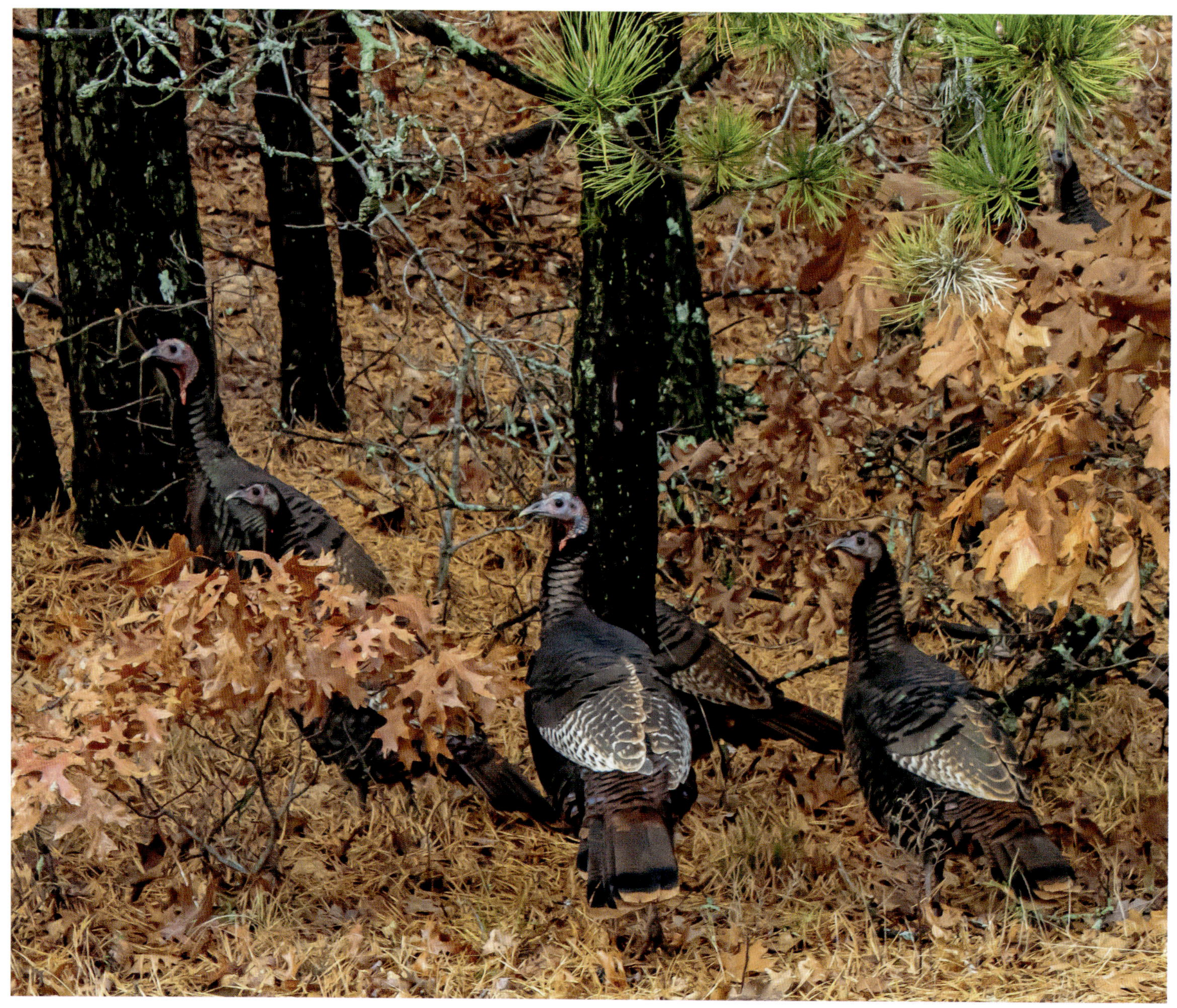

Turkeys forage among the pines and oaks. These woodland fowl consume acorns, berries, grubs, and especially ticks with vigor.

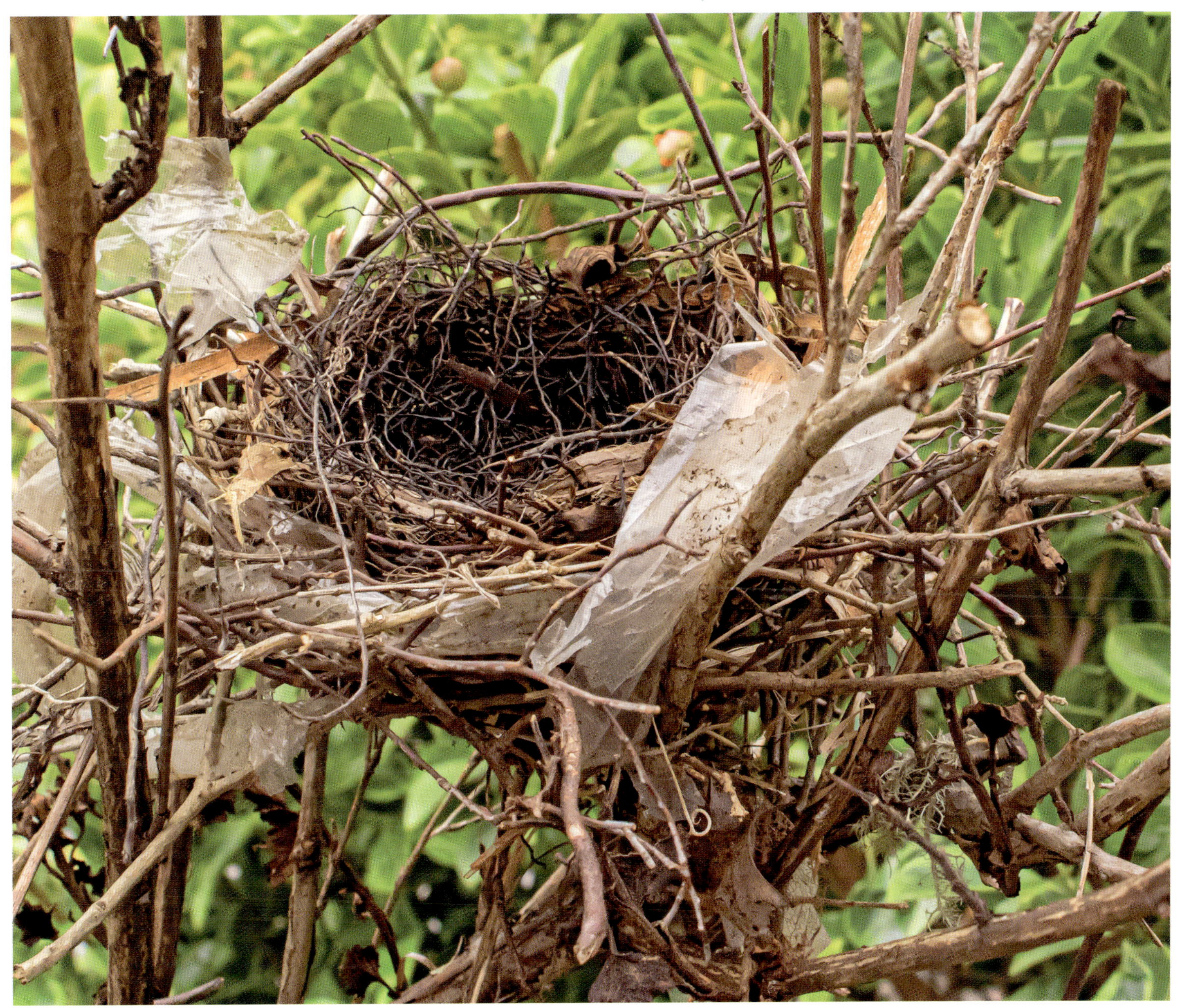

A catbird claims plastic trash for a well-woven nest, now abandoned after June nesting.

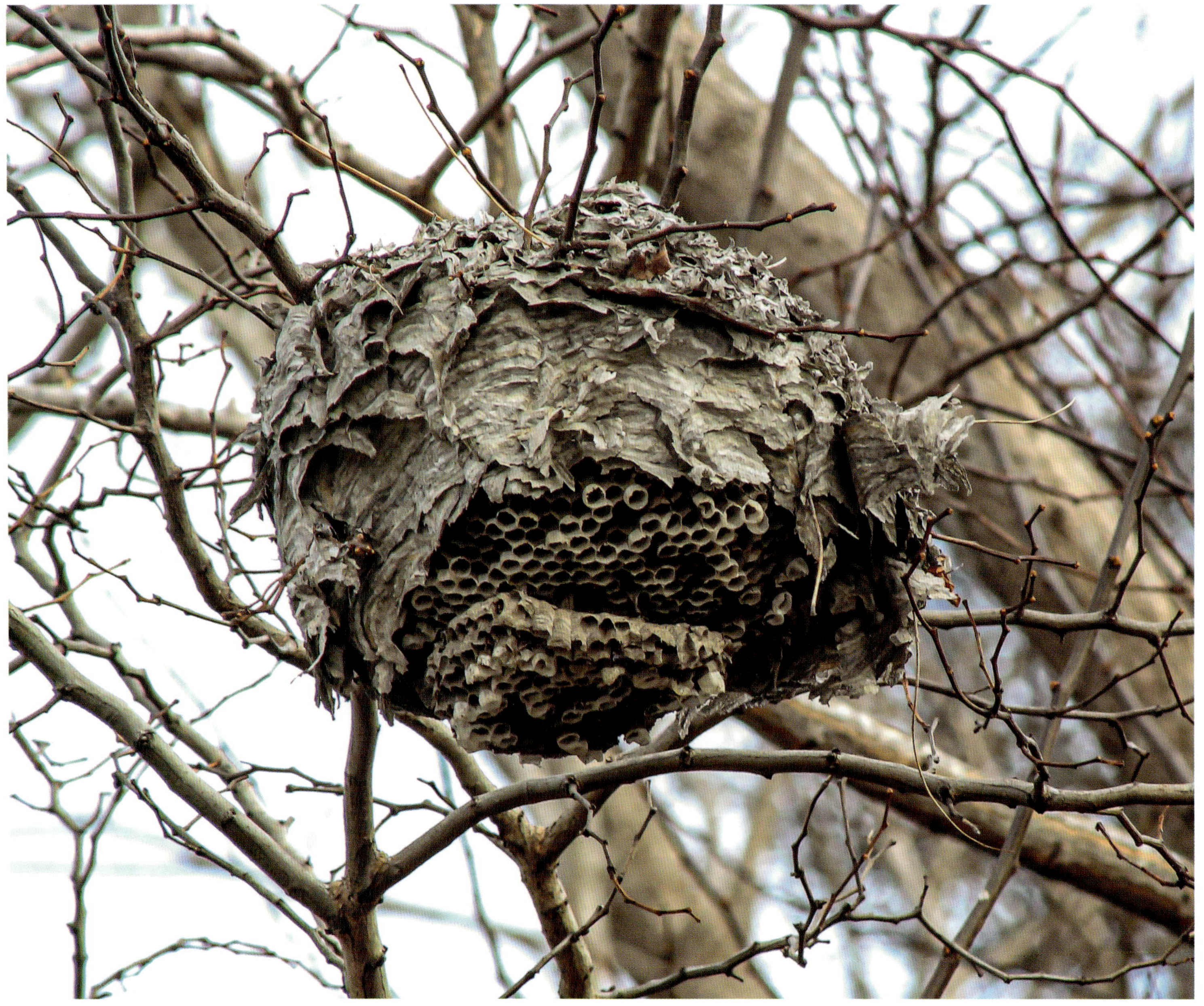

Now that the leaves have fallen from the branches of this tangle, a large wasp nest becomes evident. This is likely the nest of bald-faced hornets—not hornets at all, but true wasps, close relatives of yellowjackets.

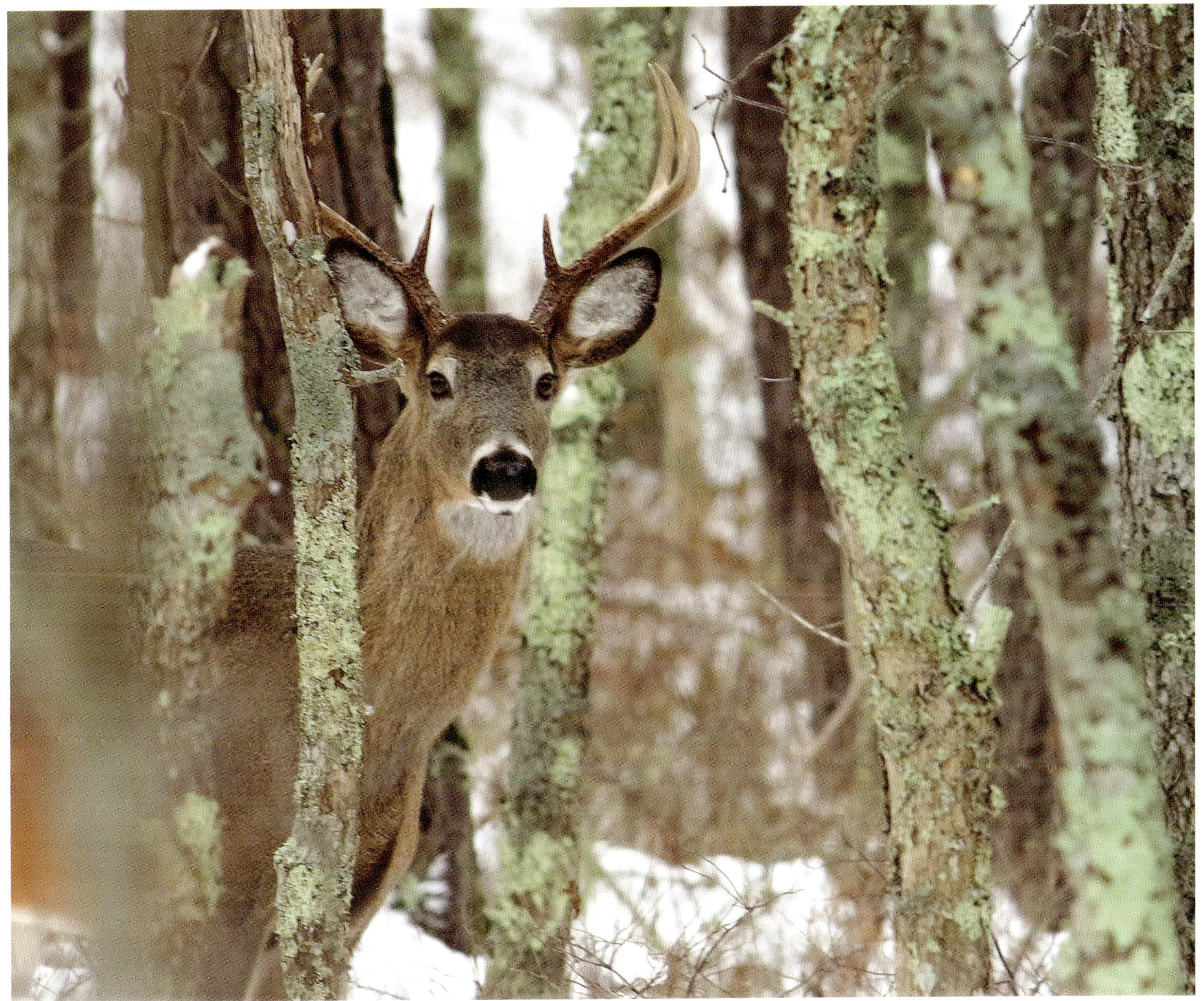

White-tailed deer are found in all habitats on the cape, often in proximity to people. After all, we provide them with grass, shrubs, and other edibles that bring them into our lives. Hunting season for this species extends from October to the end of December. This species thrives throughout the Northeast.

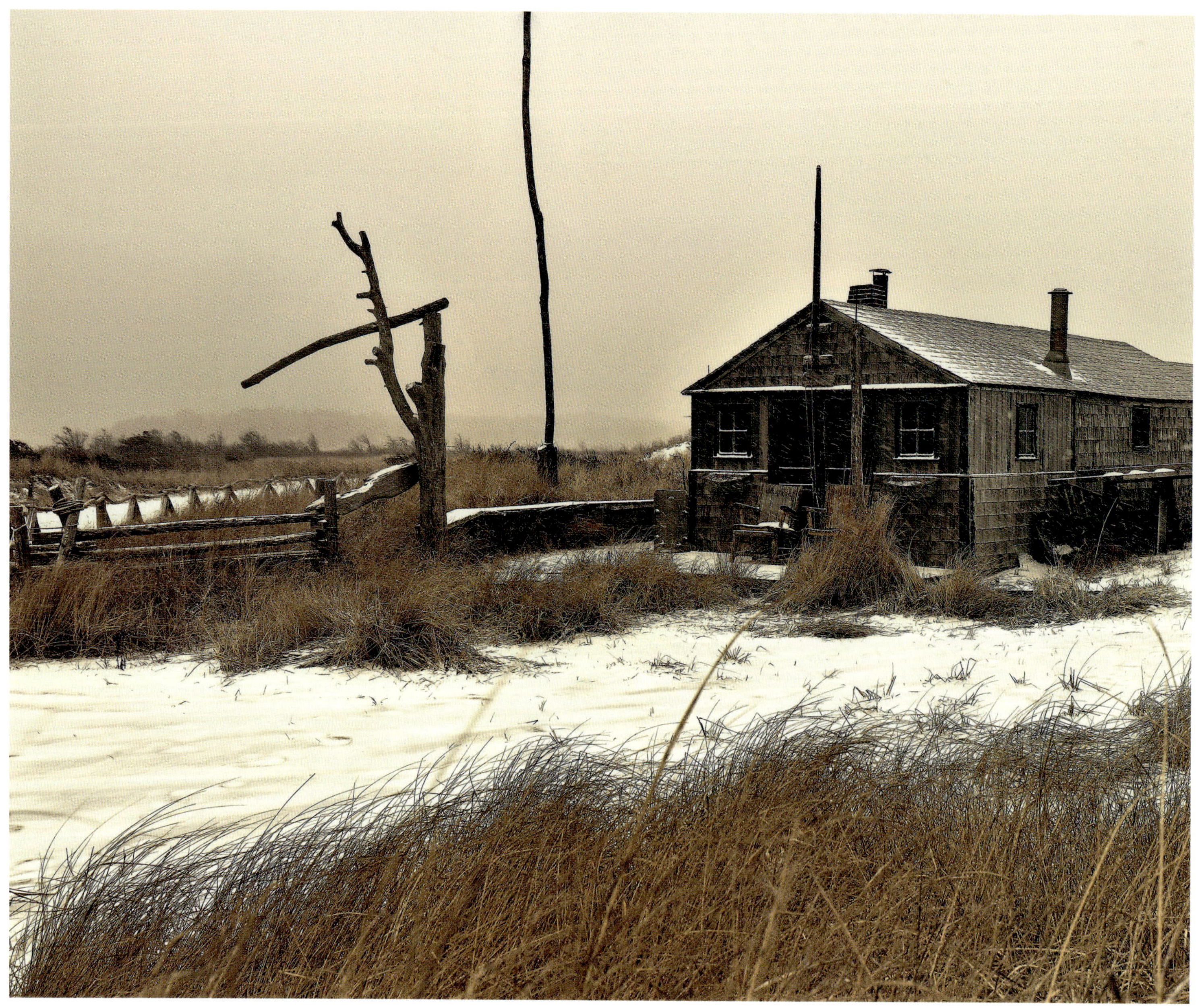

Who says it never snows on Cape Cod? From an abandoned cranberry bog to the outer beaches and quiet camps, November and December bring winter snows that lay a serene and quiet blanket of white over the entire cape.

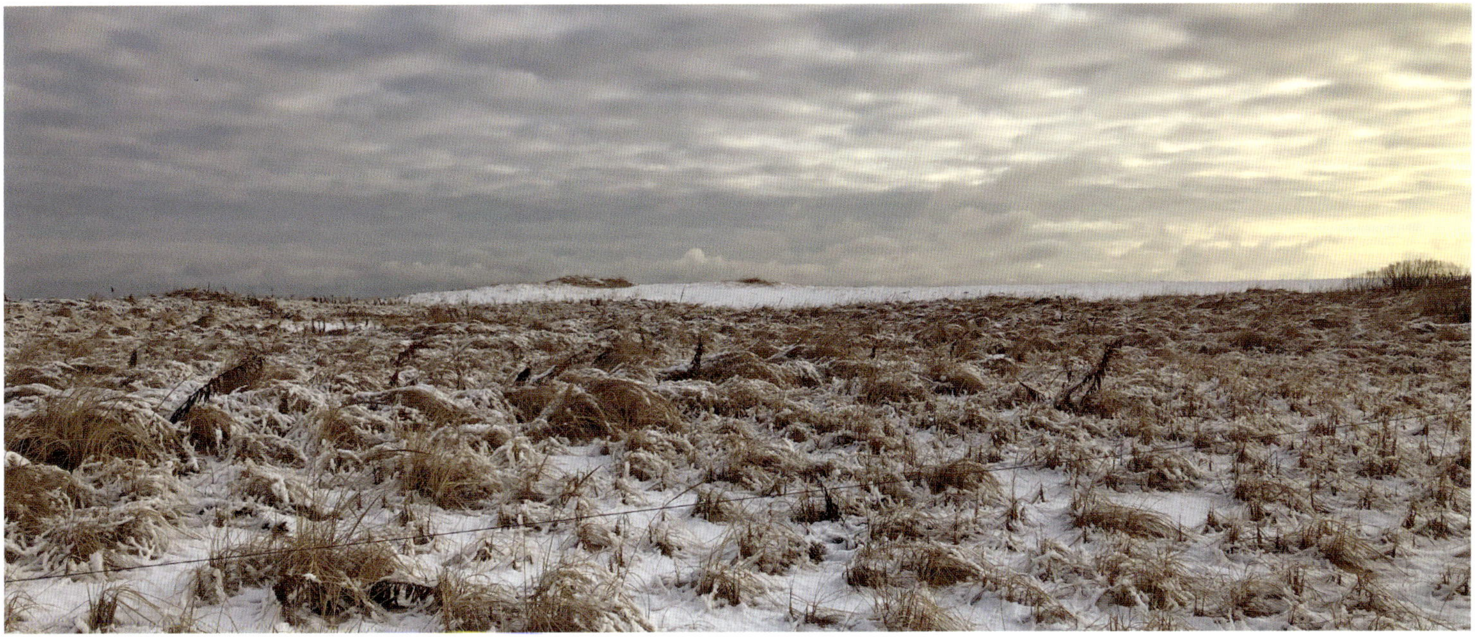

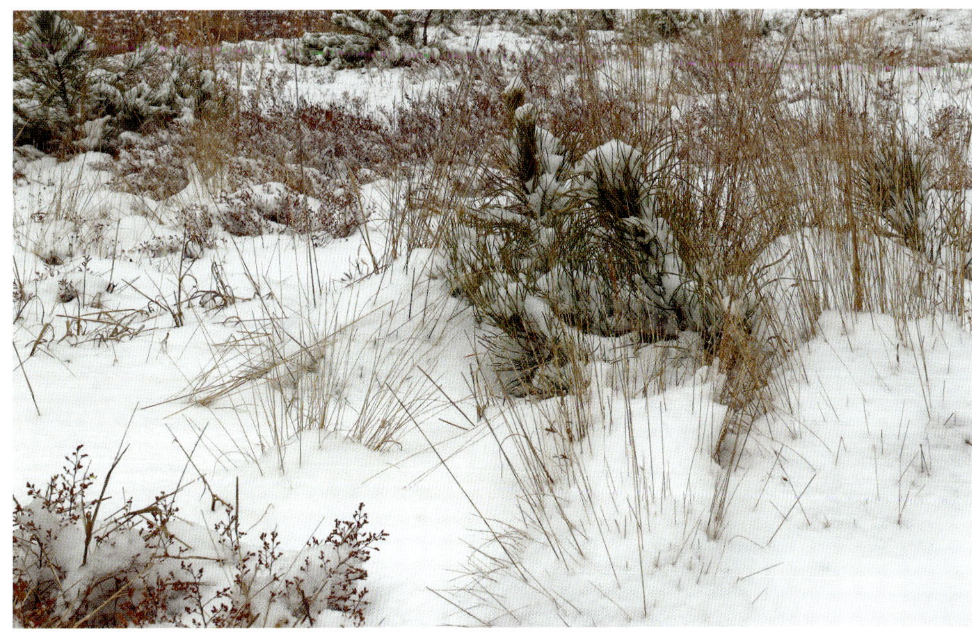

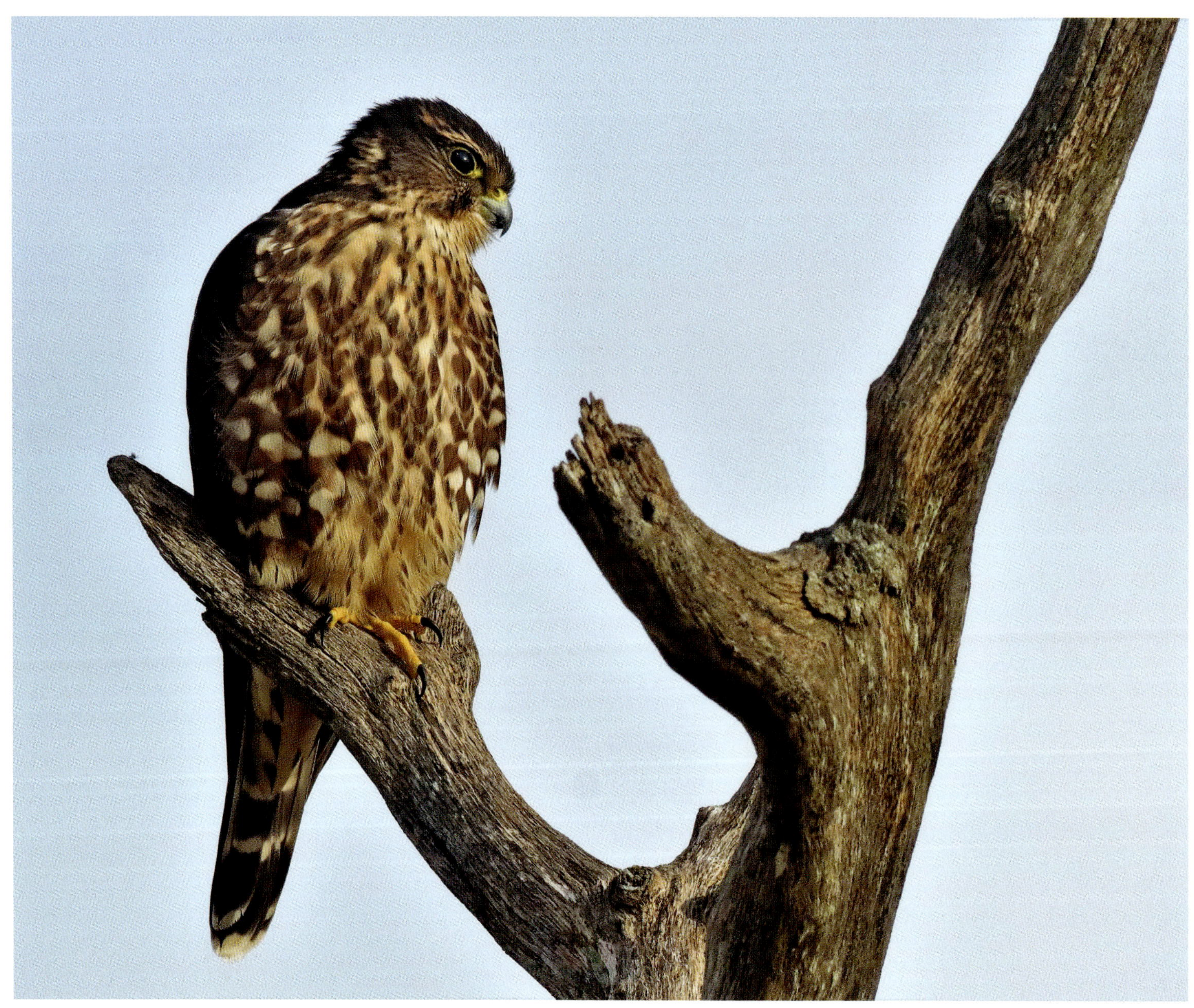

As colder temperatures move into the region, so does this medium-sized falcon, the merlin. Formerly called pigeon hawk, this powerful little falcon, larger than a kestrel, smaller than a peregrine, will feed on small birds throughout the winter.

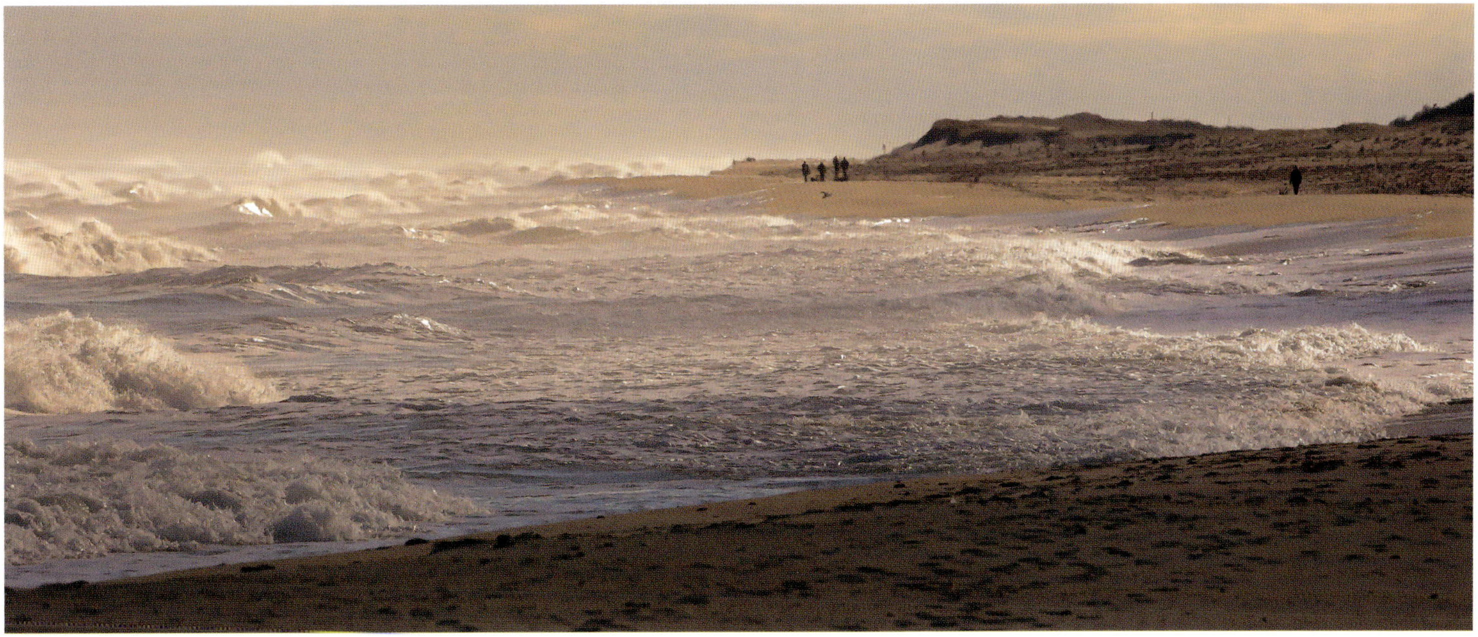

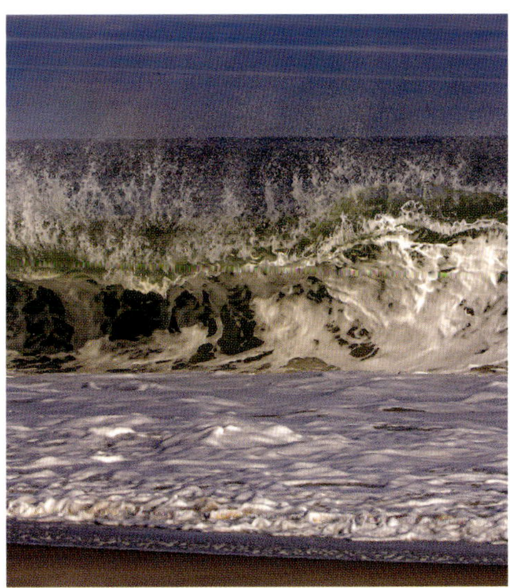

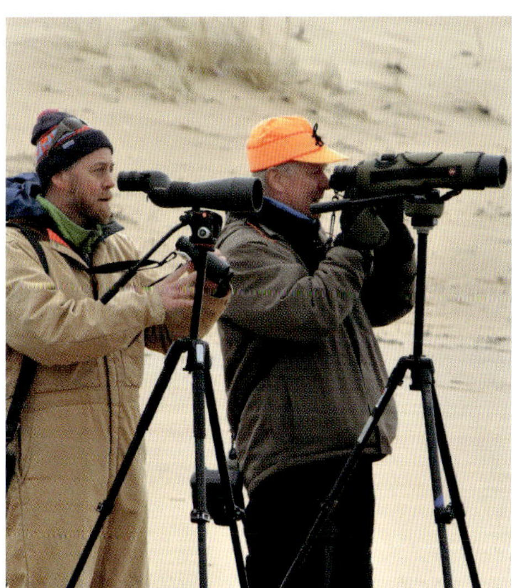

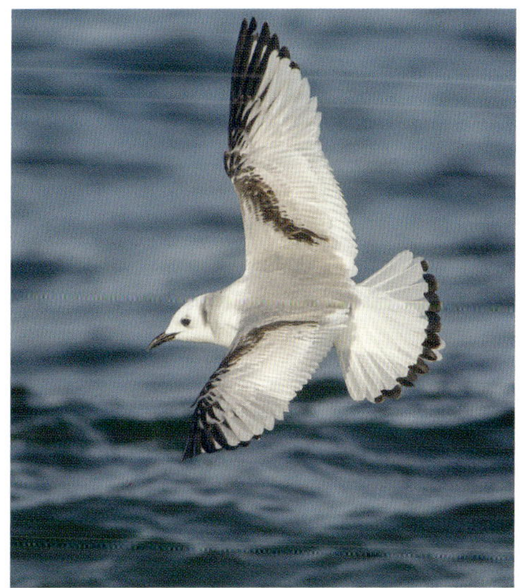

The sea roars as the wind blows frothy whitecaps along the outer beach. Some walk the great beach for quiet and solitude, while others stand firm, recording Arctic bird species that have flown south to Cape Cod's maritime climate. The father-and-son team of Jeremiah and Peter Trimble scopes the open ocean for birds. This Bonaparte's gull (*bottom right*) has migrated from the forests of Canada, where it nests in conifers as far west as Alaska.

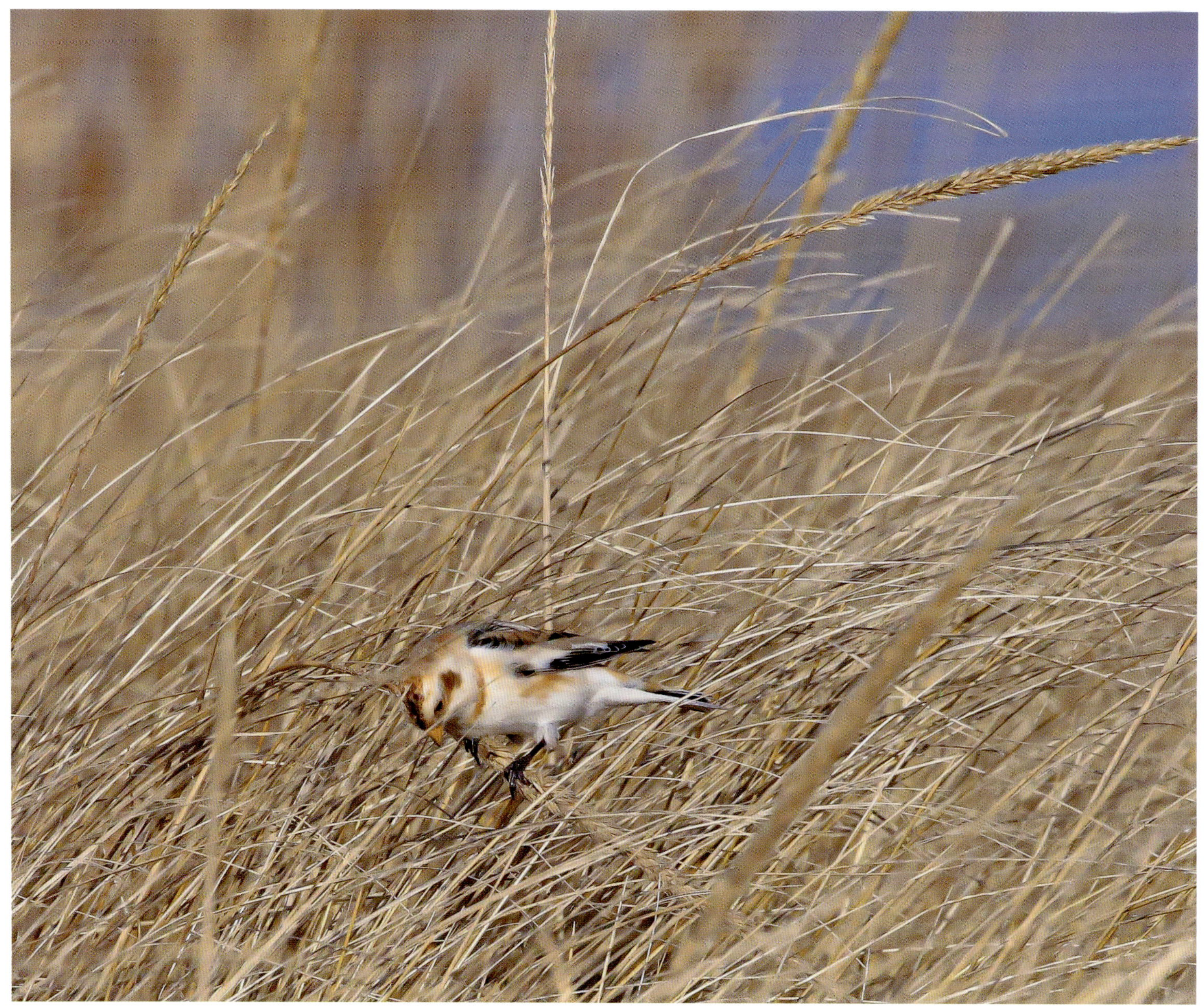

This Arctic finch, the snow bunting, is gorging on the flourishing seed heads of beach grass. Having nested in Earth's most northerly environment, the high tundra, it finds Cape Cod winters mild by comparison.

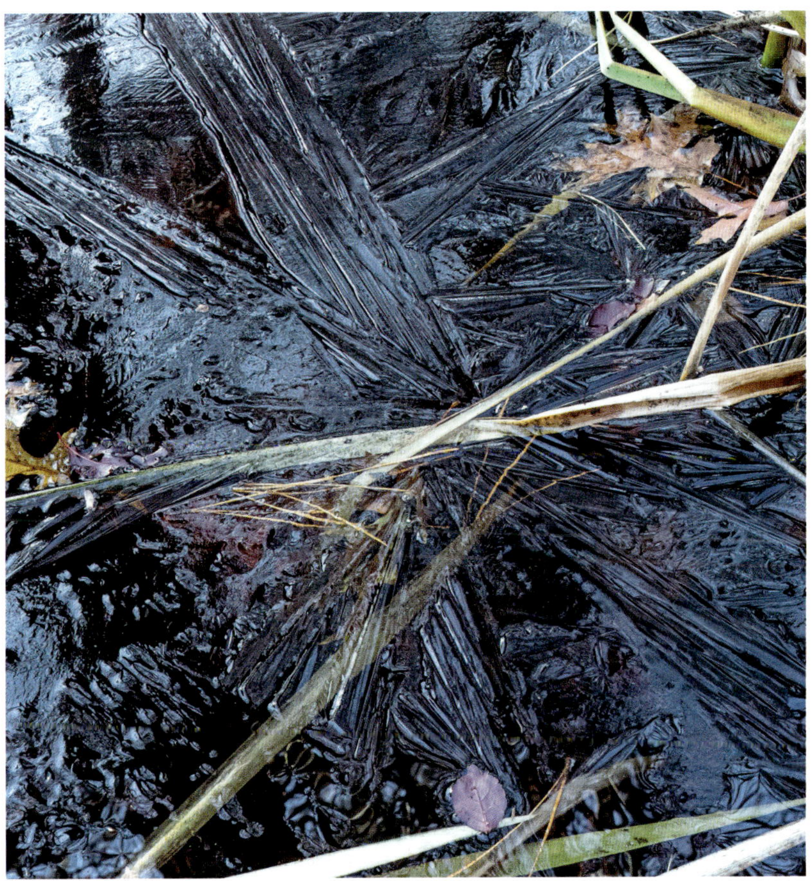

With a warming climate and a maritime biome, temperatures on the cape in November and December range from 30 to 50 degrees. A pond edge on a December morning may show glass-thin ice that quickly melts.

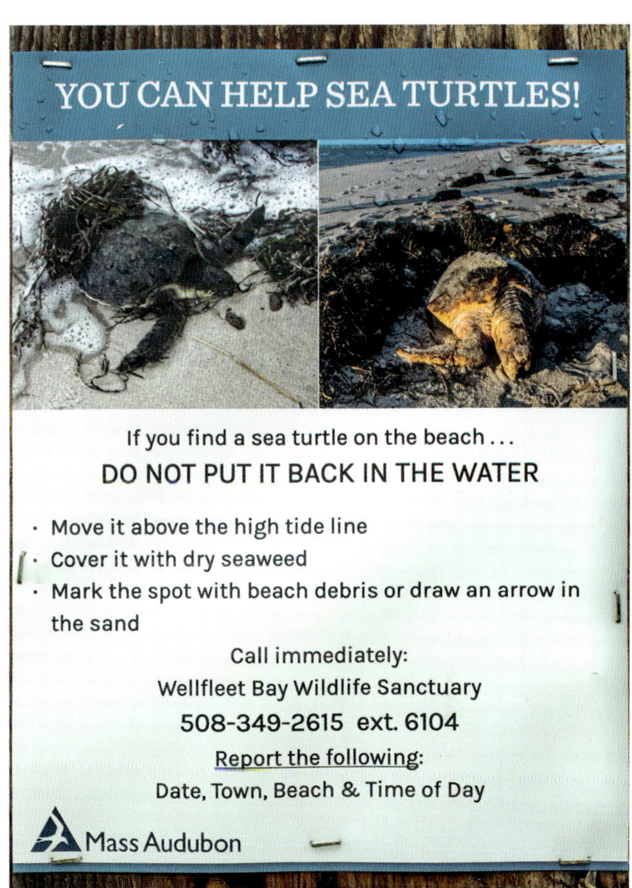

Volunteers walk for hours along the shores of Cape Cod Bay searching for the endangered Kemp's ridley turtles. The reptiles, on a southern migration, become cold-stunned in the waters of Cape Cod Bay, unaware of the Outer Cape's curling coastline.

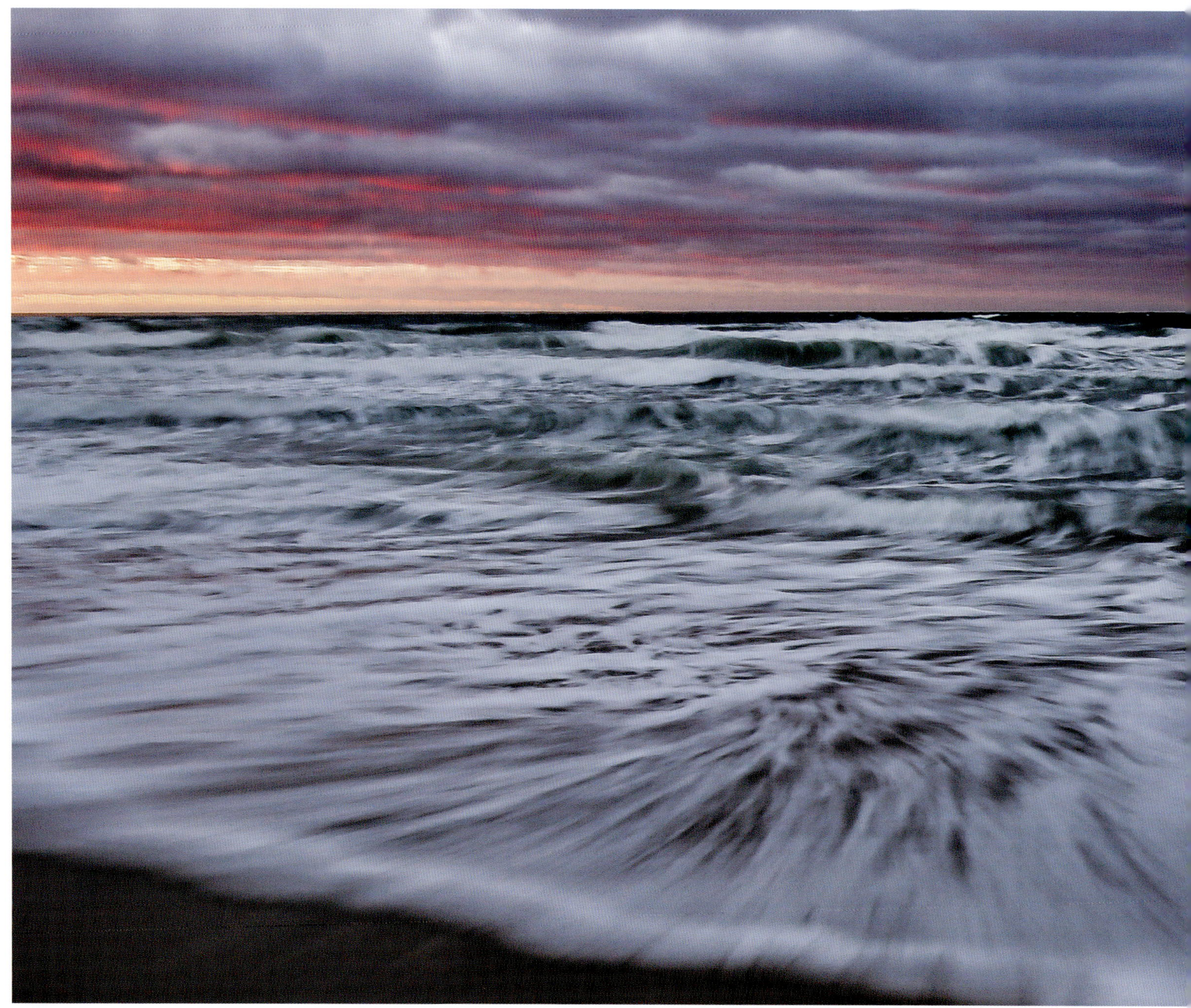

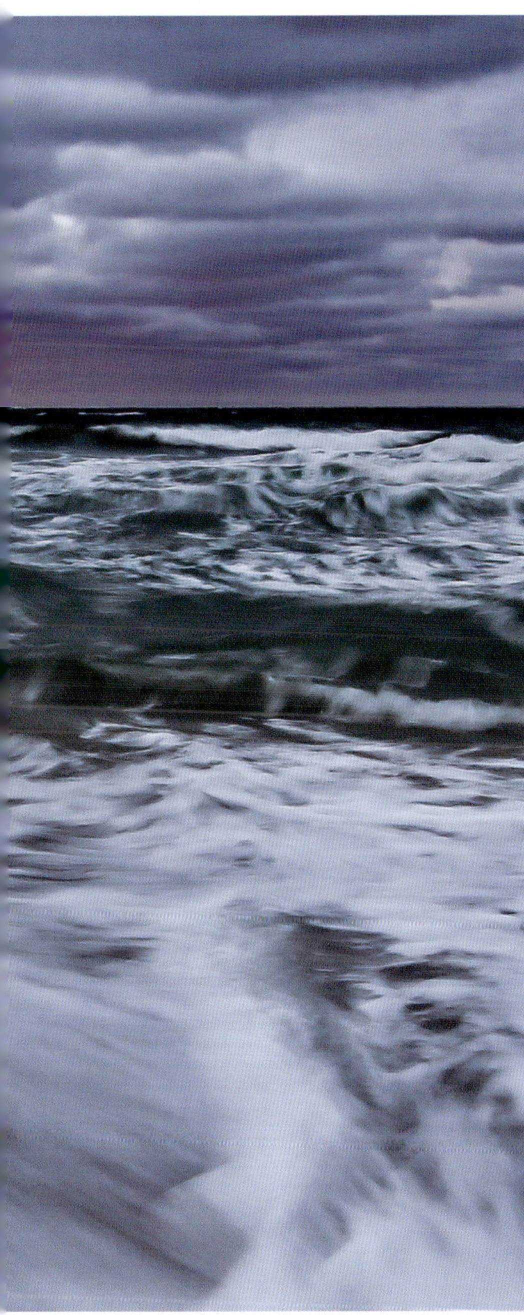

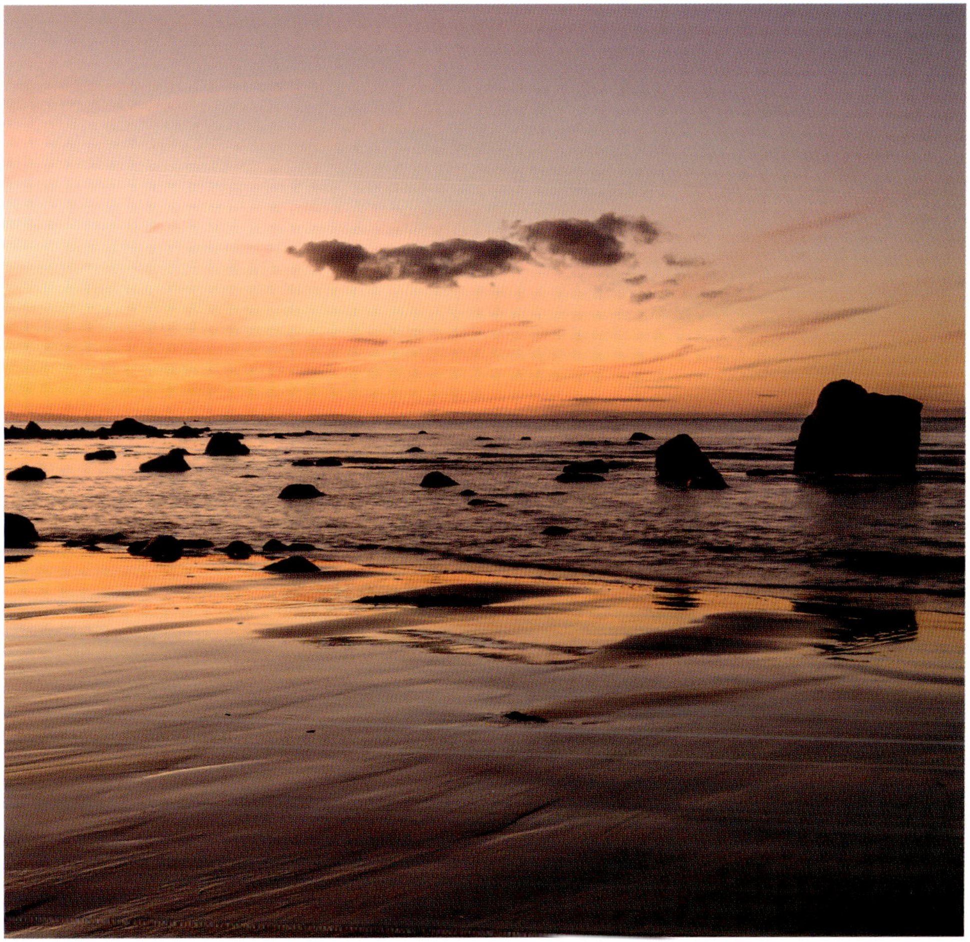

The sun sets on two December evenings as the calendar year comes to an end. Yet winter is only beginning to show her true colors. As the sun moves across the low southern sky, longer days beckon as the cold of January and February sets in.

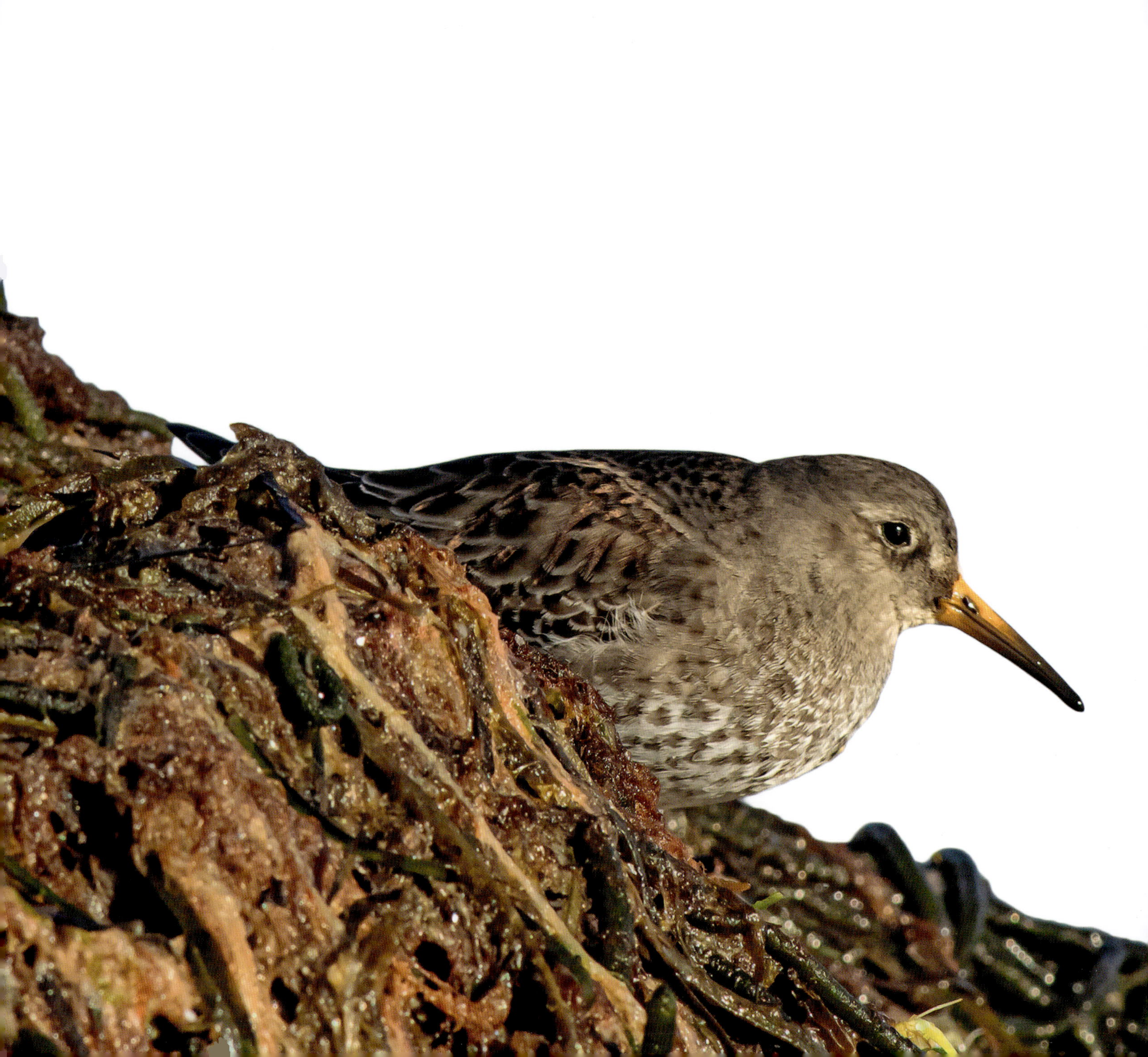

JANUARY AND FEBRUARY
Dead of Winter, but Not Deserted

There is a quiet about these two months. January is the center of the winter season, the beginning of a new year, and a time when the days begin to lengthen and a hint of the new beginning emerges. January brings tourists over the bridges to experience "the quiet" of Cape Cod. For thousands of years, the cape has evolved to support a specialized diversity of life, with each species of plant and animal adapted to survive in a sandy, saline, windswept environment.

January is the coldest month of the year on Cape Cod, with February seeming to give way to the higher arc of the sun in the sky. The woodlands are dormant, the beaches windblown and barren, and the ponds rarely frozen. Some years, the kettle ponds may freeze for a few weeks, inviting skating and ice fishing, but most years the frigid pond water supports a variety of waterfowl.

January has an average high temperature of 37 degrees and an average low temperature of 21 degrees. Many describe winters here as mild, and in fact, for many Arctic bird species, from sandpipers to ducks to gulls, the winter range of temperatures is just right. Winter season on Cape Cod lasts about three and a half months, from early December to late March. During that time, the average daily high temperature is about 44 degrees. Let's begin by looking at some winter scenes and the animals that thrive here in January and February.

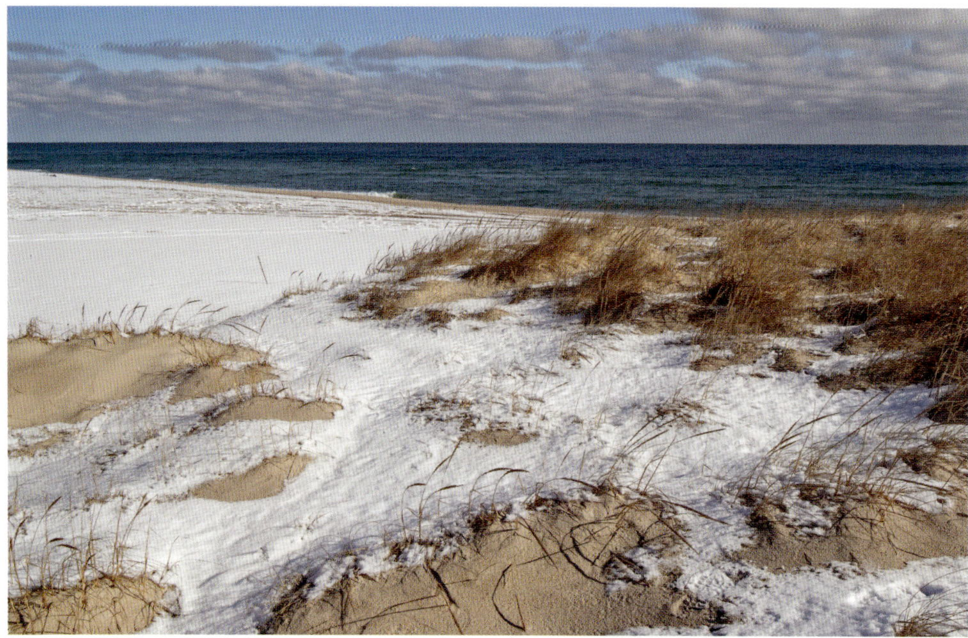

Weather on the outer beach area from Provincetown to Chatham is crisp, calm, and clear on any given January day. Ominous clouds coming in on a north wind turn Race Point, Provincetown, into a churning sea with birds gliding and swirling through the air.

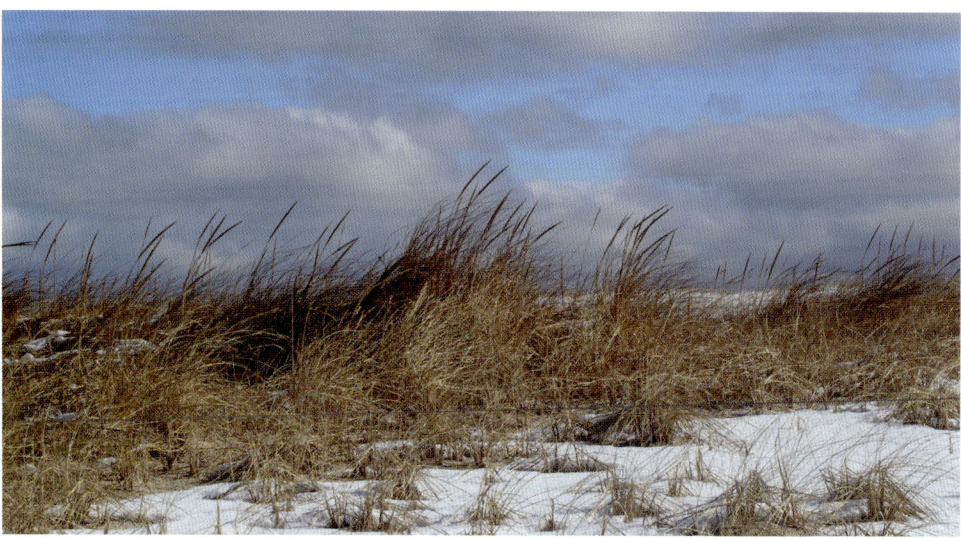

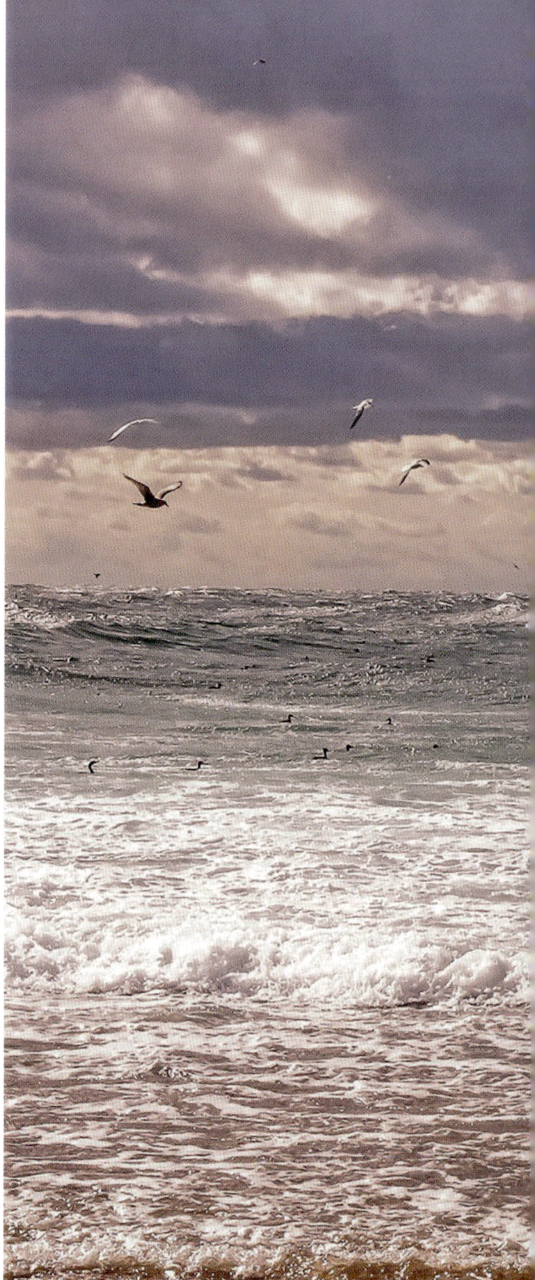

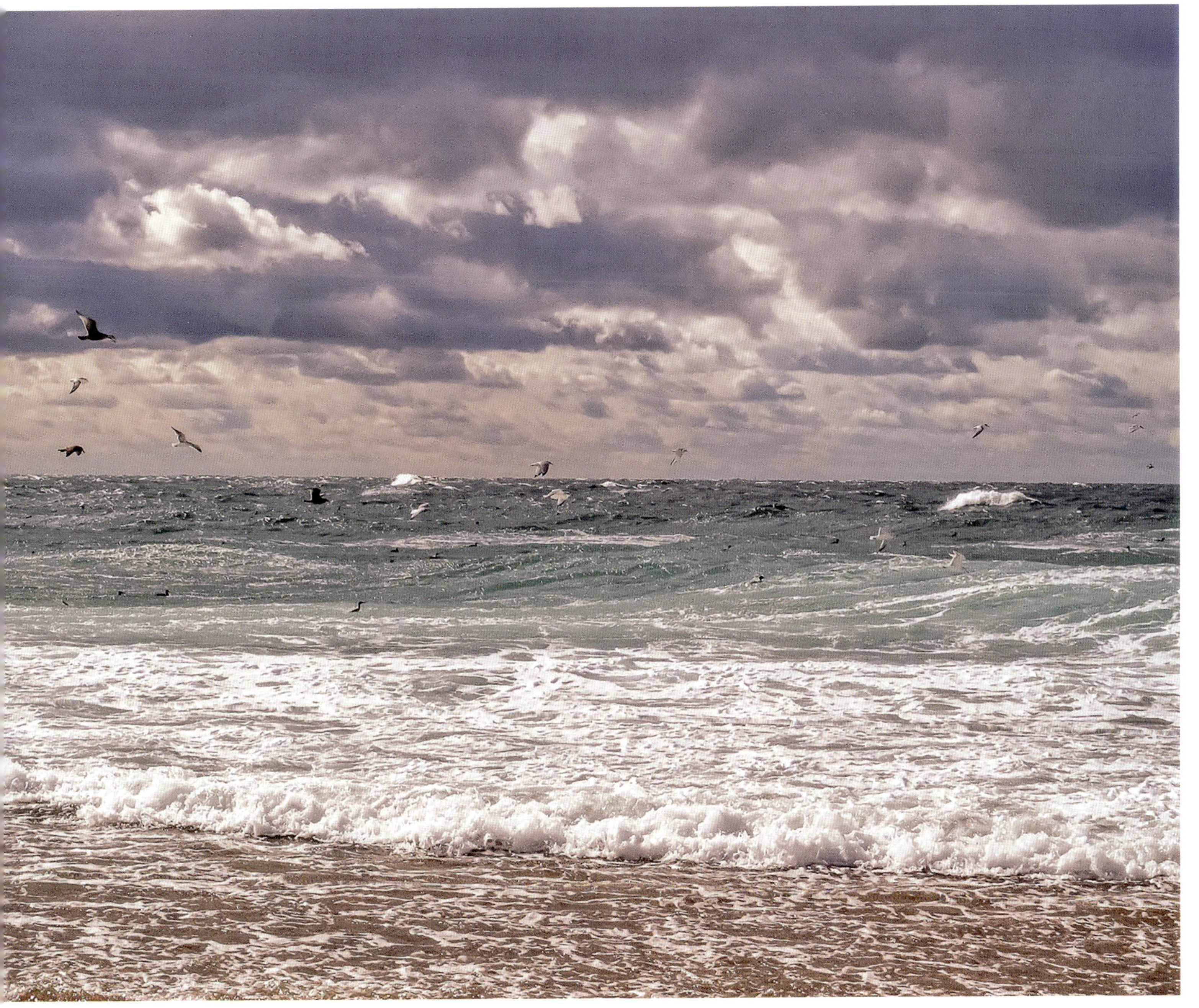

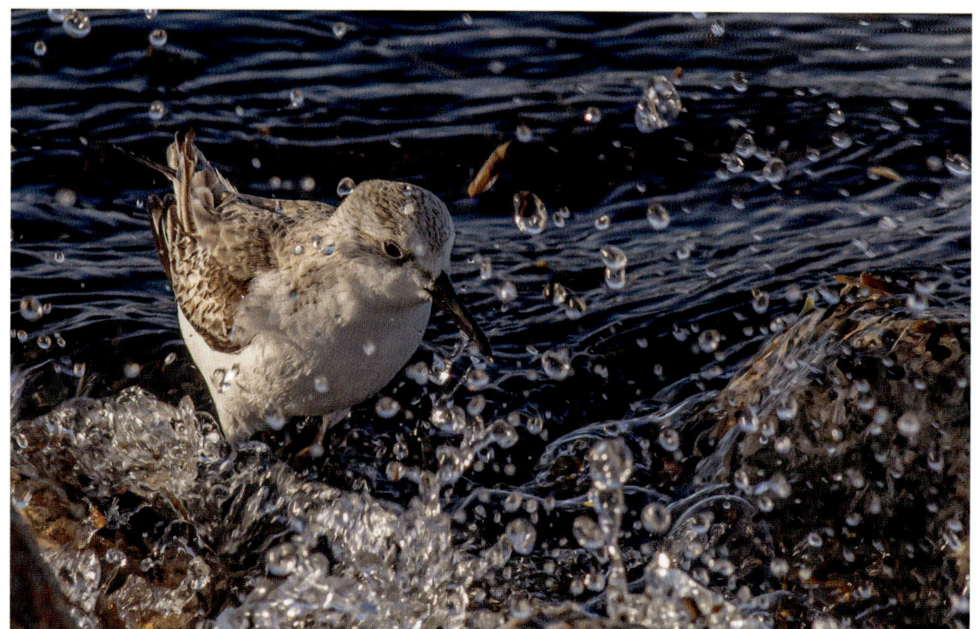

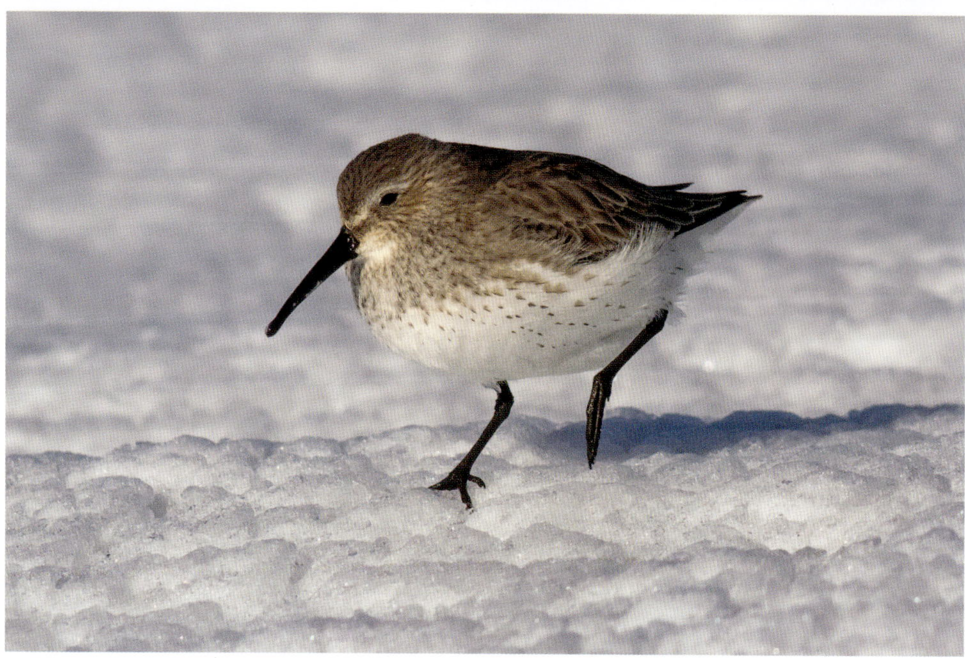

Along the beach, one may observe wintering shorebirds. Both the sanderling, in a splash of icy wave, and the dunlin, walking across snow, are comfortable on cold winter days. Both of these birds are high-Arctic nesters, often incubating eggs in snow and ice. These two species need to migrate south only as far as Cape Cod, where they feed on invertebrates and plankton that abound along this rich shoreline.

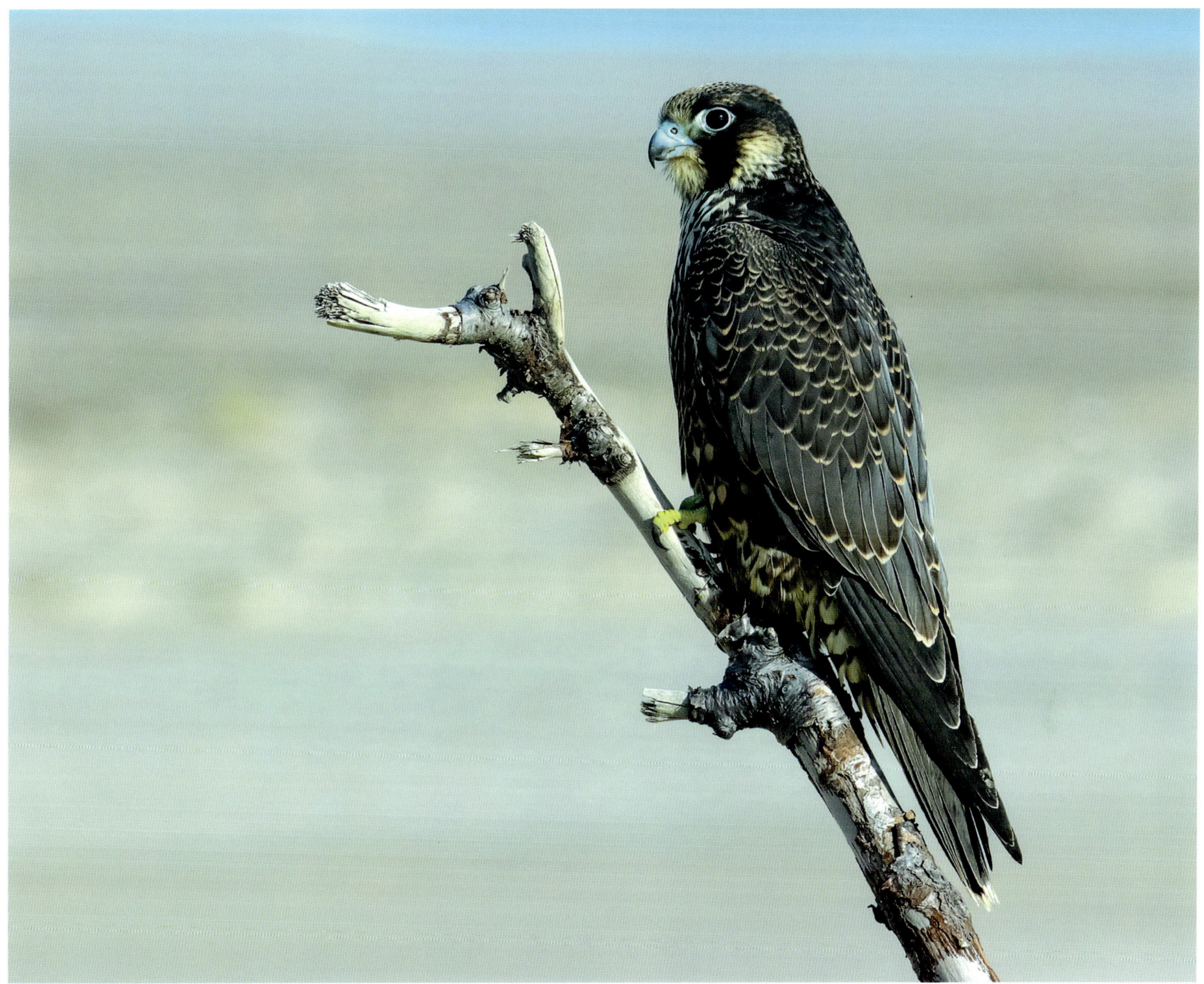

This sleek, elegant peregrine falcon, an immature bird, carries the distinction of being the fastest animal on Earth. During the cold days of January and February, on the expanses of outer beaches, we'll find this formidable falcon perched, statuesque, waiting for a sanderling or dunlin, snow bunting or small duck, to enter its field of view. Woe to the small bird that flies within a quarter mile of a hungry peregrine.

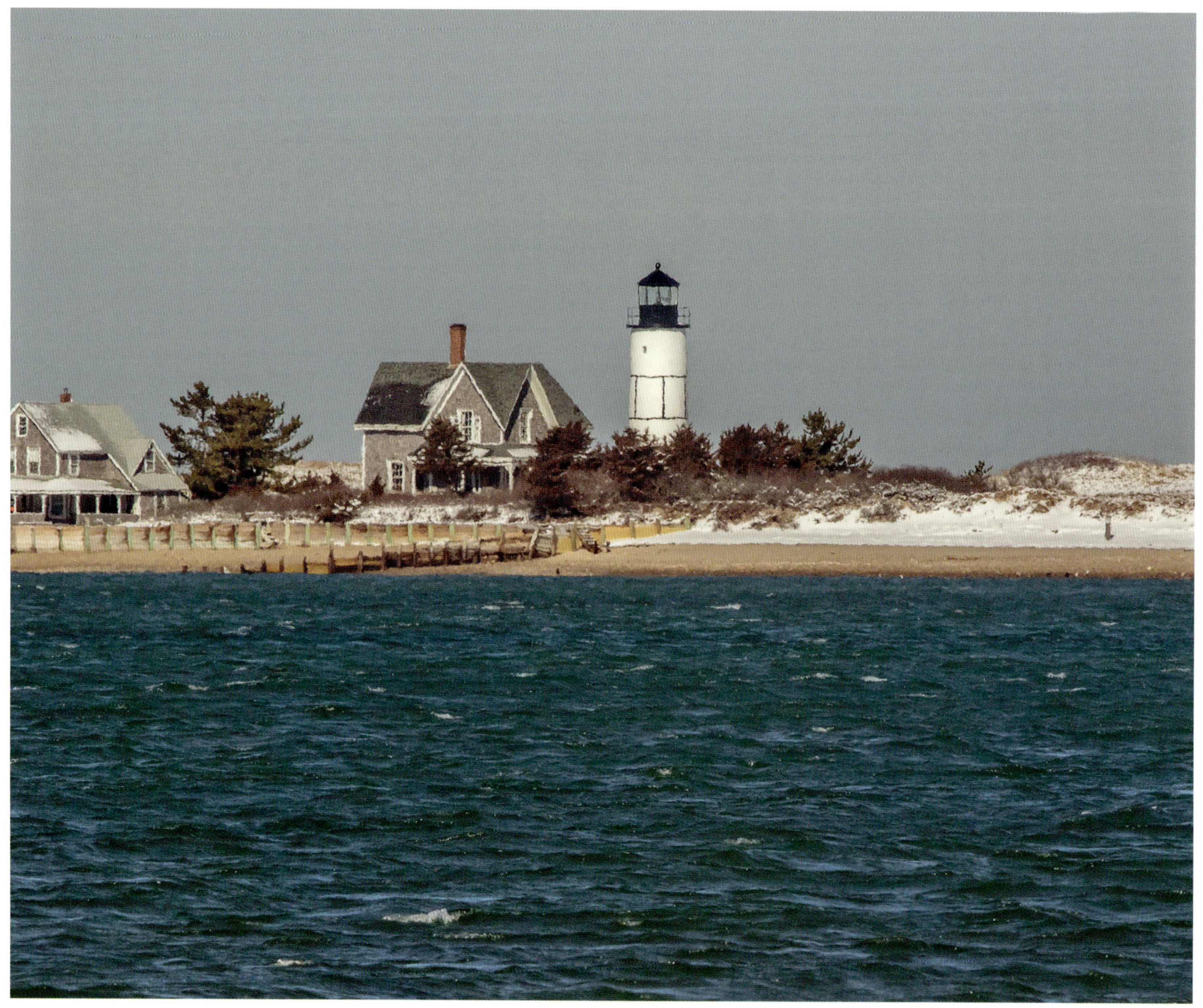

Over on the bayside, Sandy Neck Light stands at the entrance to Barnstable Harbor. Established in 1826, deactivated in 1931, and relighted in 2007, the lighthouse and keeper's house are a Cape Cod Bay landmark.

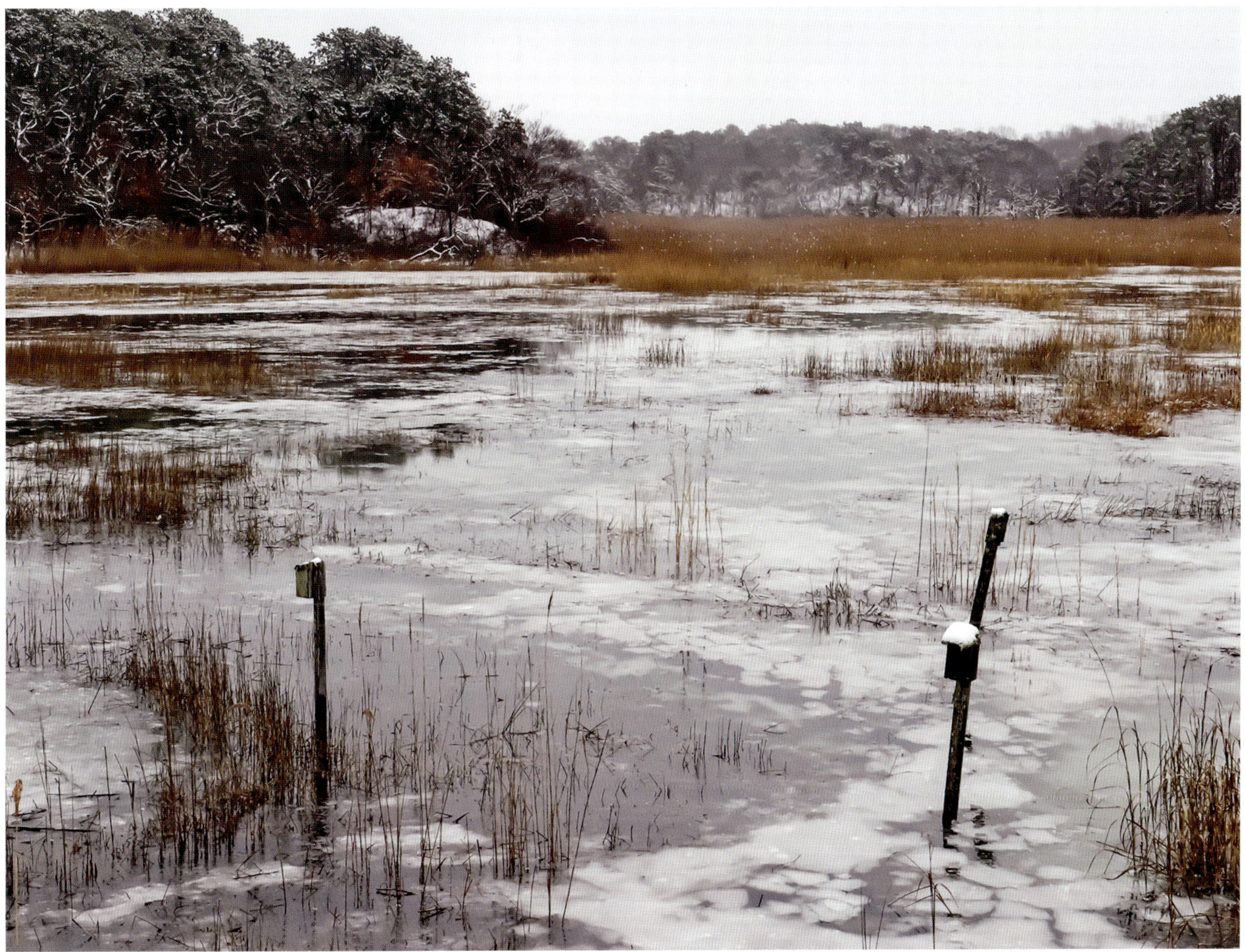

Each month during full moon and new moon, the tides are higher than normal. This is because of the gravitational force of the sun and moon. During the full moon, the earth is aligned with, and between, the sun and moon. The full moon rises as the sun sets, so the sun illuminates the moon on the opposite side of Earth. Gravitational pull from these celestial bodies causes the ocean waters to "bulge," causing tides to rise higher than normal. The same spring tides occur during a new moon, when the moon is between the earth and sun, with both bodies pulling in the same direction, causing very high tides. "Spring" does not refer to the season, but rather to the tides that spring or swell to higher levels. Here we see a wind-driven spring tide covering the marsh during a storm at the Cape Cod Museum of Natural History in Brewster.

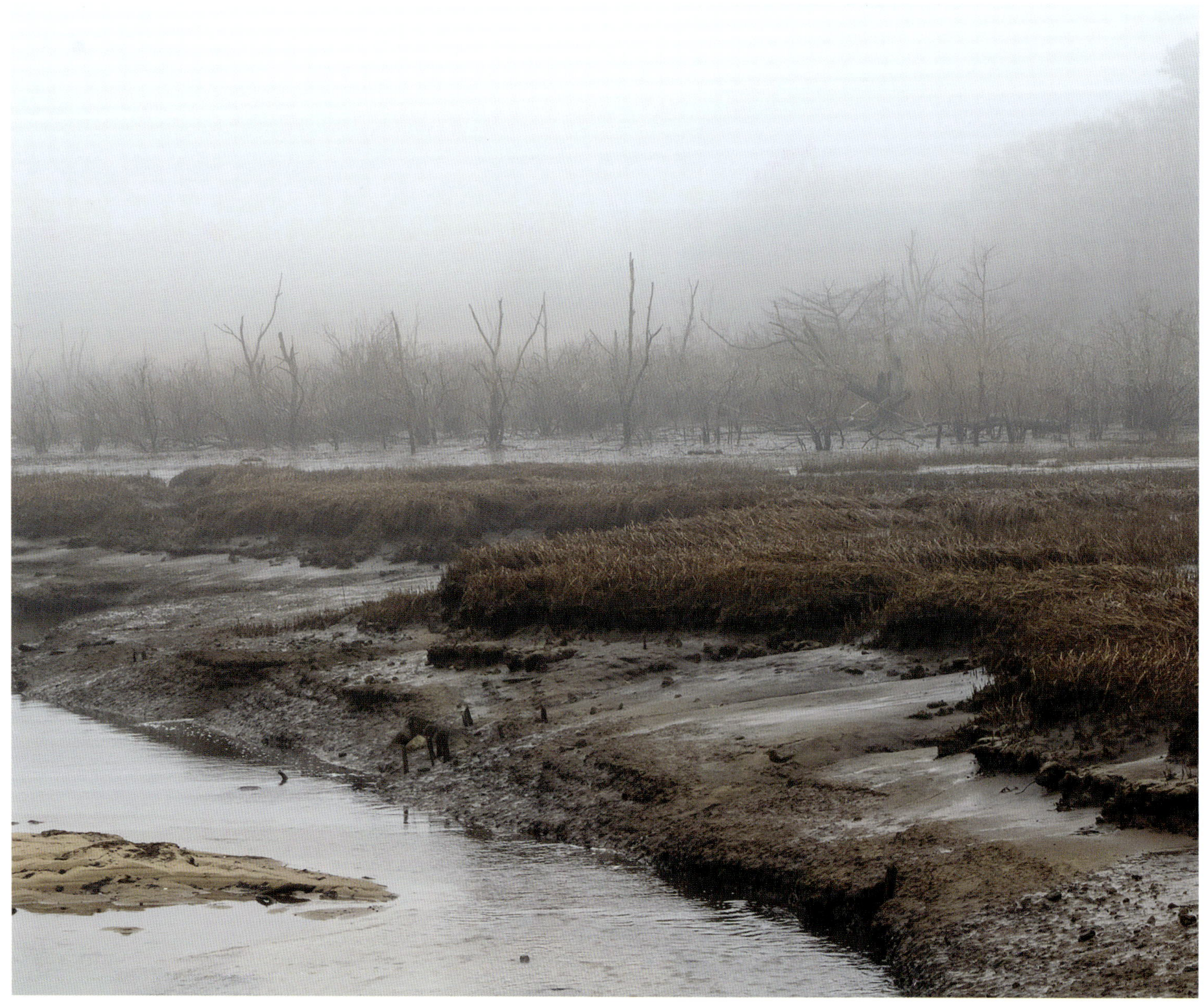

Fog occurs when water evaporates and condenses in cooler air. This mystifying scene, created by a rare winter fog, provides an unusual winter scene of muddy banks and dead trees killed by encroaching seawater.

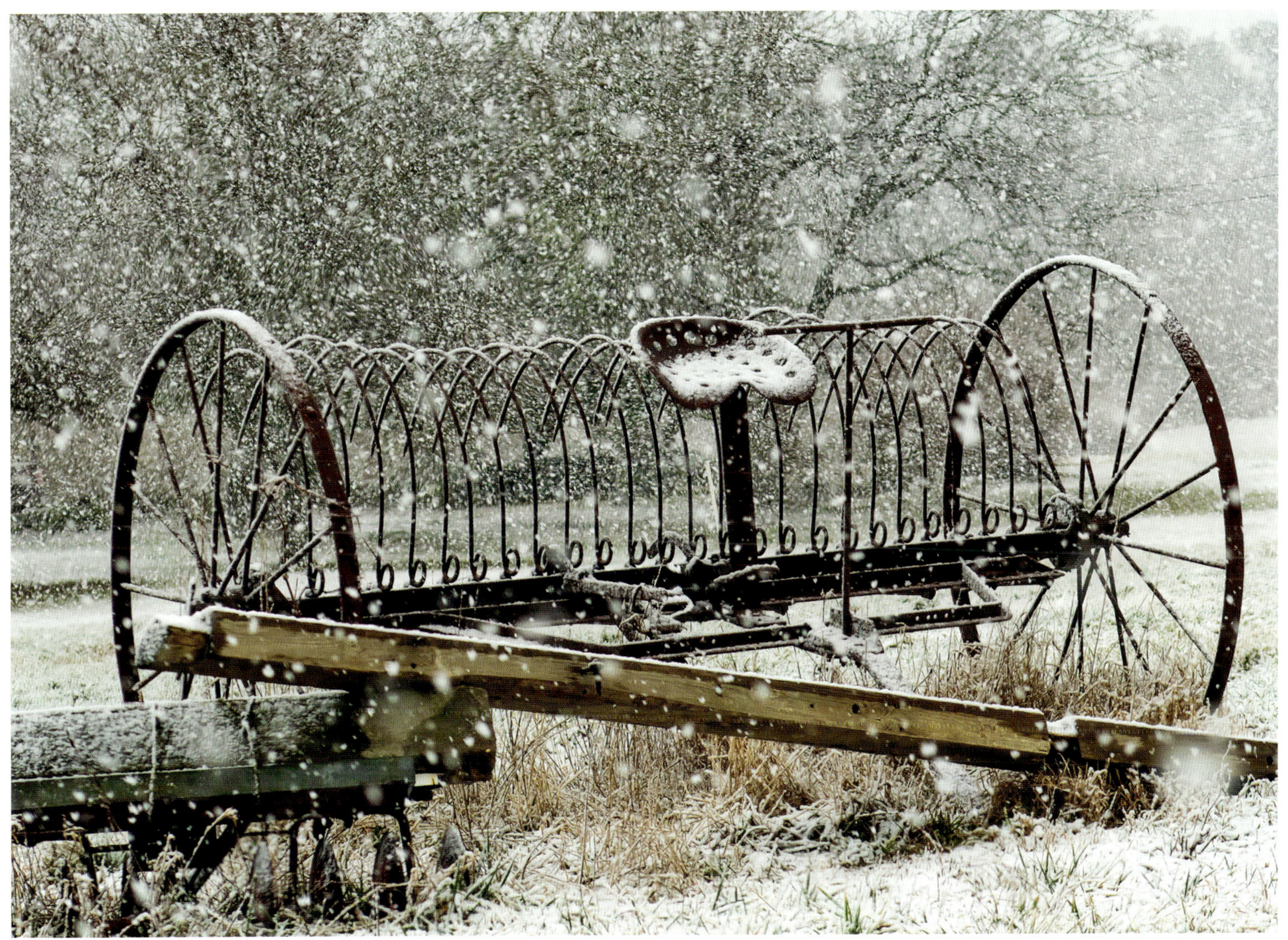

These photos prove the exception to the saying that "it never snows on Cape Cod." The woods after a snowfall provide tranquil scenes that may catch an artist's eye.

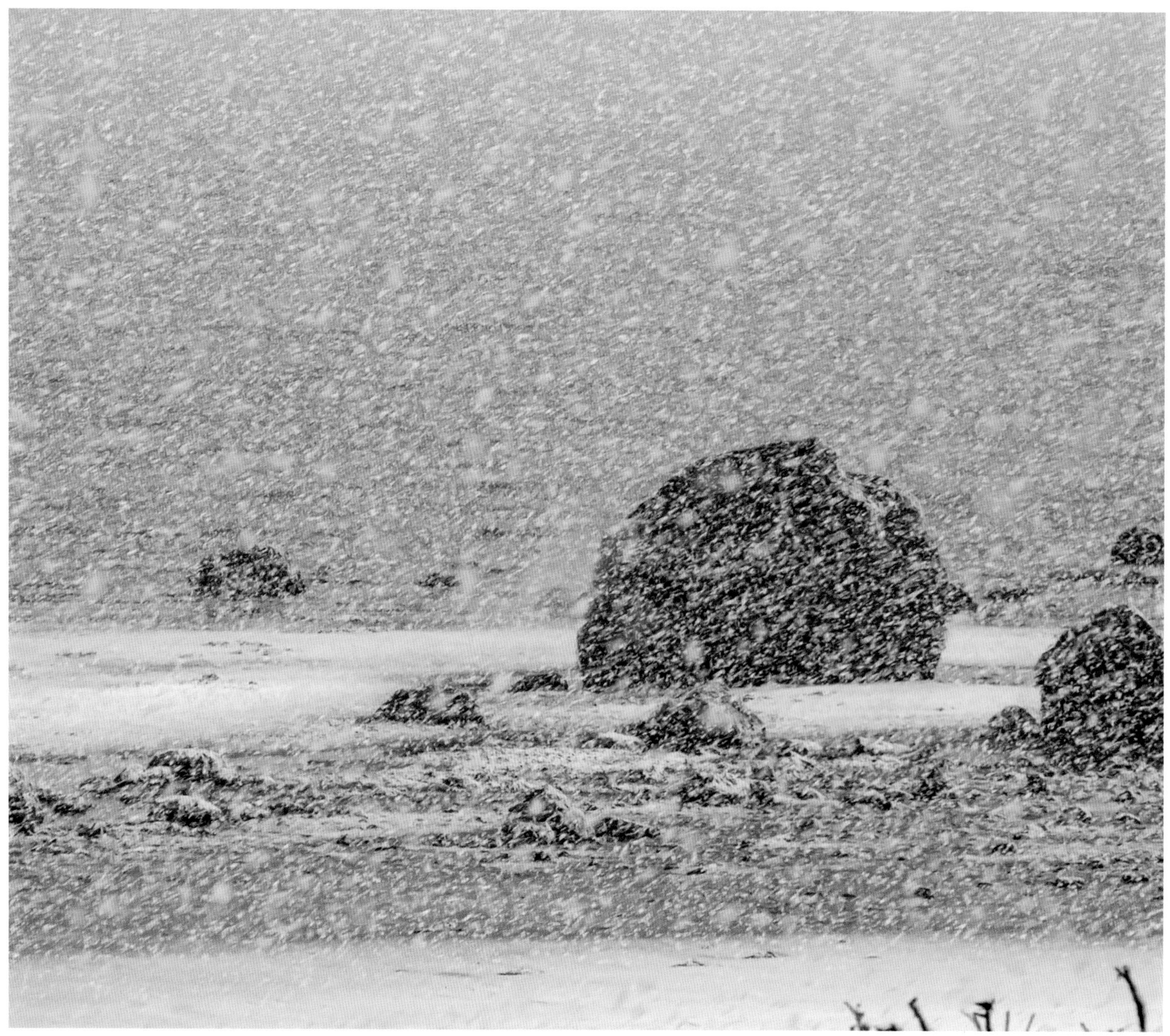

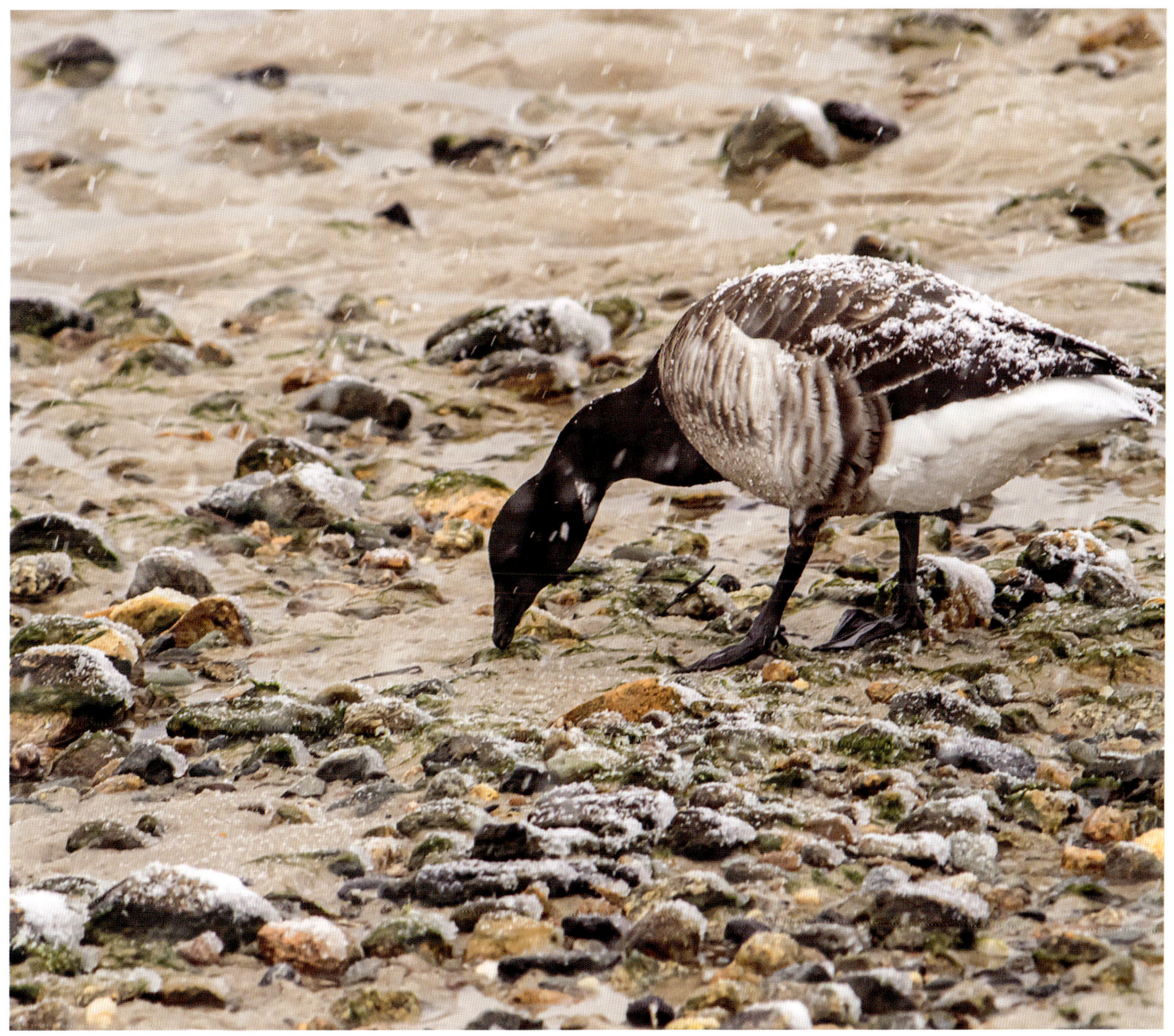

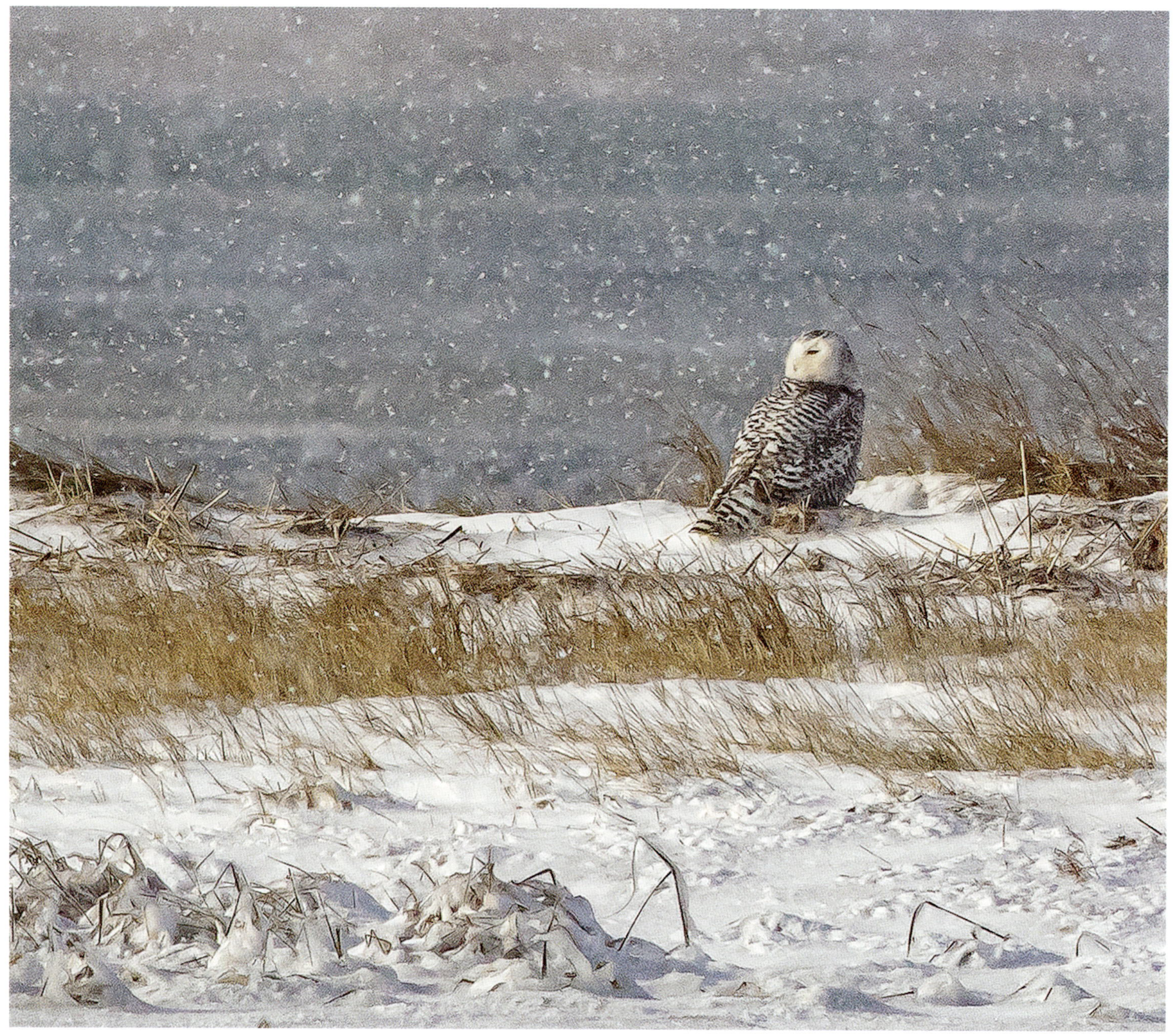

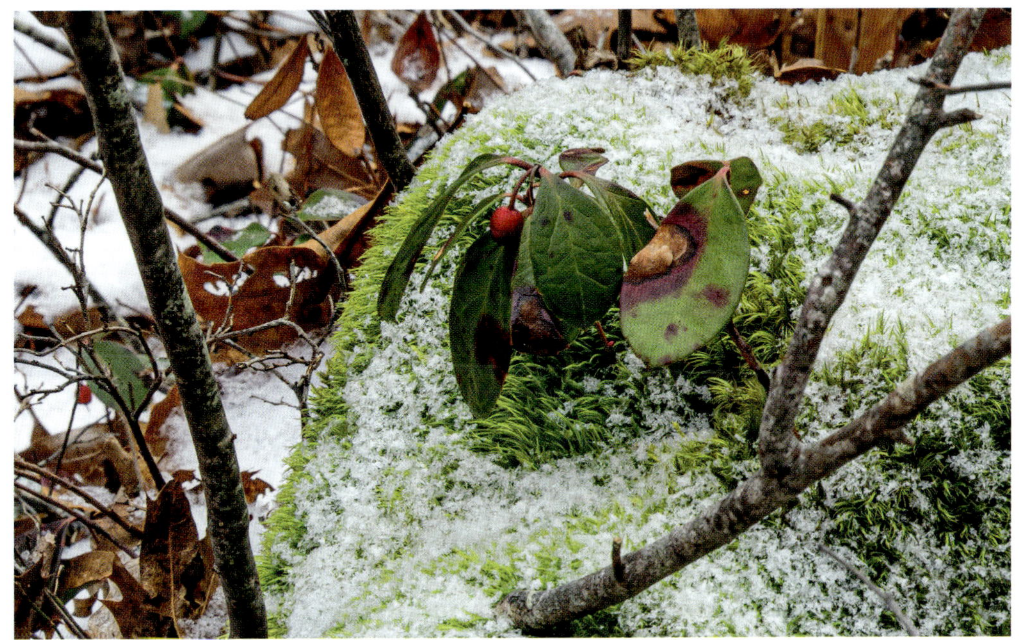

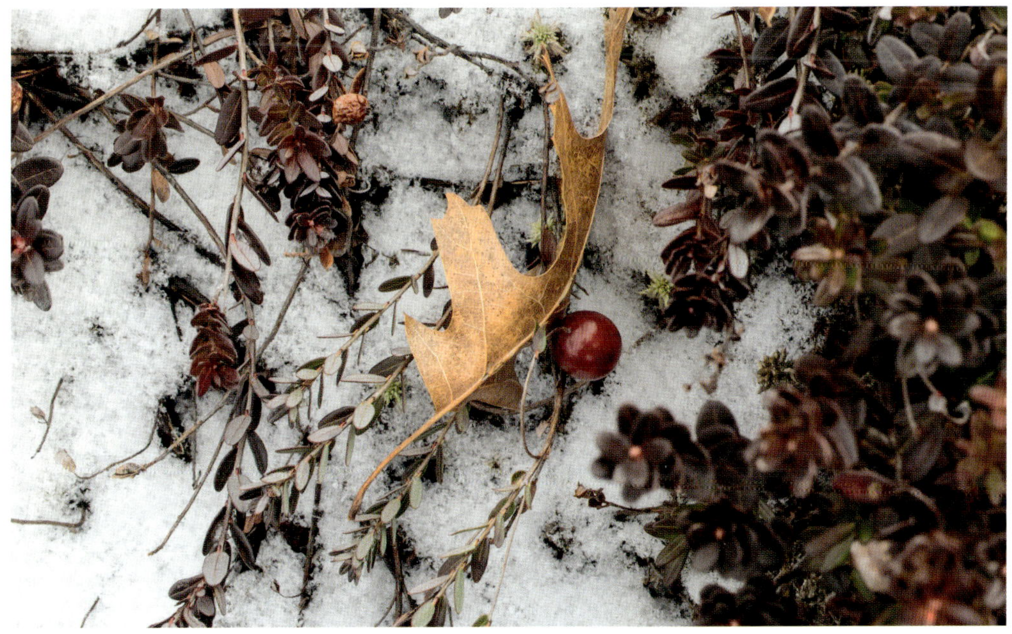

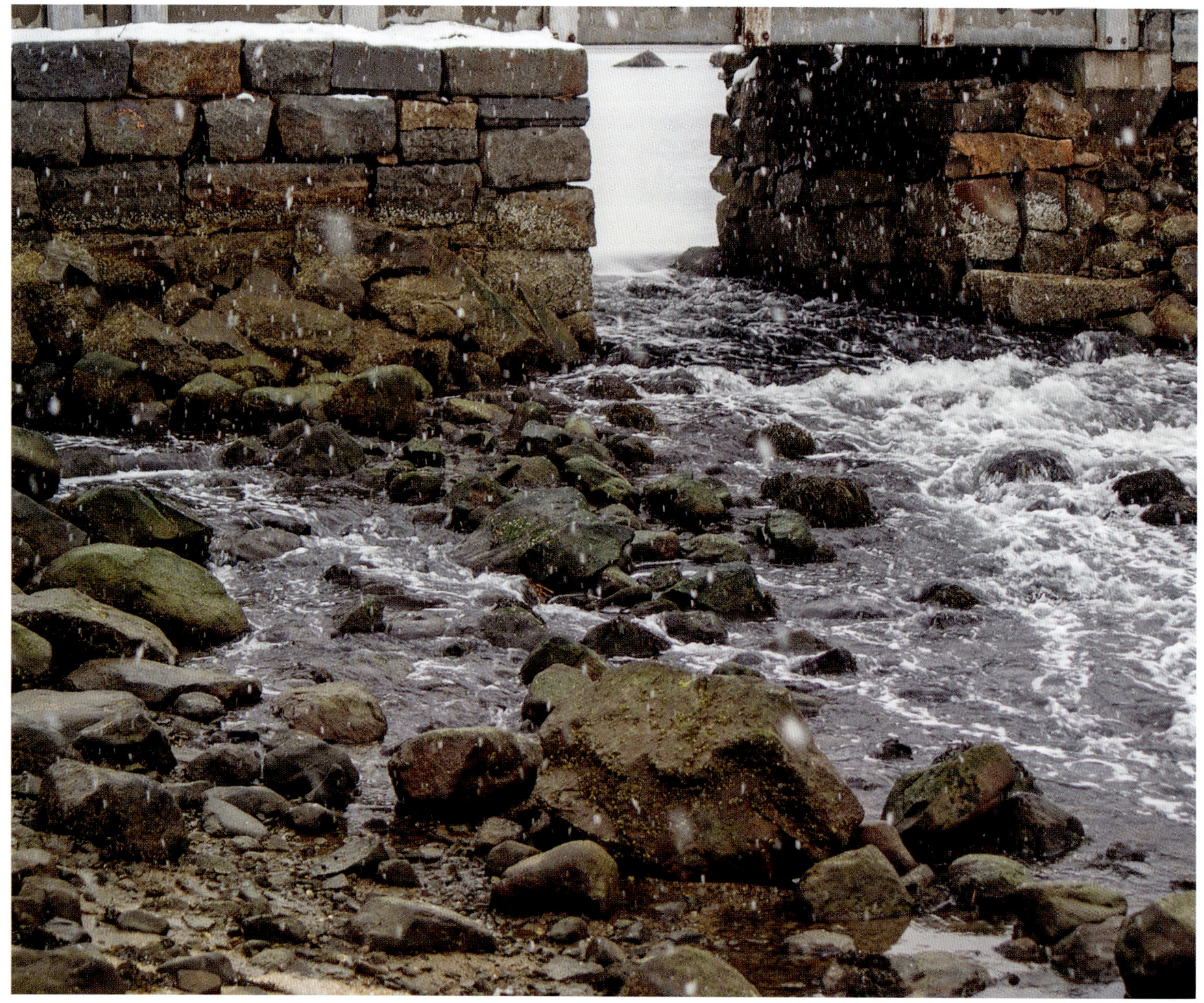

On the town boundary between Yarmouth and Barnstable, the Keveney Lane bridge is a favorite spot for many locals. The single-lane stone bridge marks the entrance to Hallet's Mill Pond. The falling tide is graced by a snow squall.

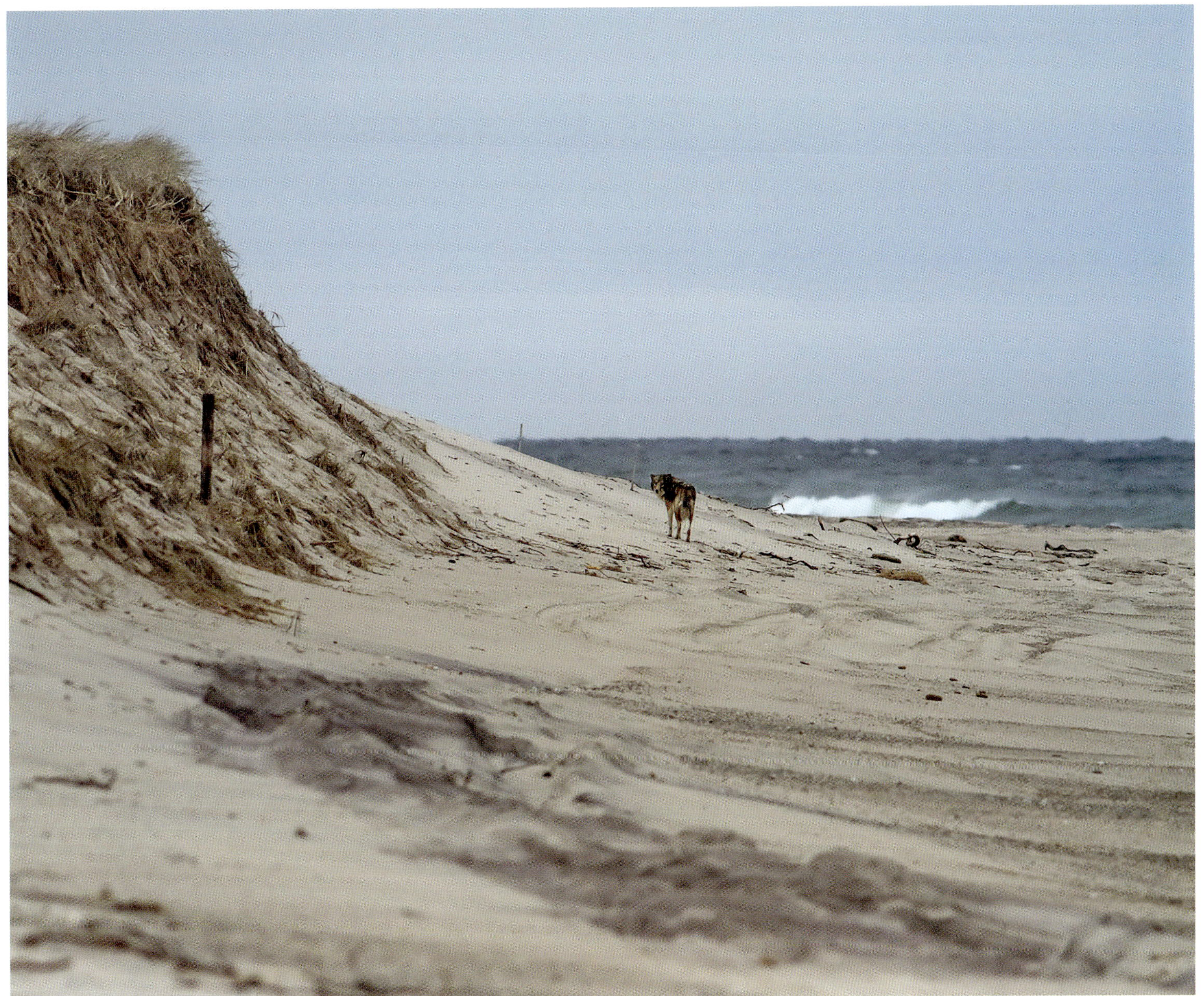

Oceanfront beaches are typically deserted in the dead of winter. As I walked from my truck to survey the winter seas for birds and seals, I felt I was being watched. To my left a few hundred feet down the beach, looking back over its shoulder, was an eastern coyote.

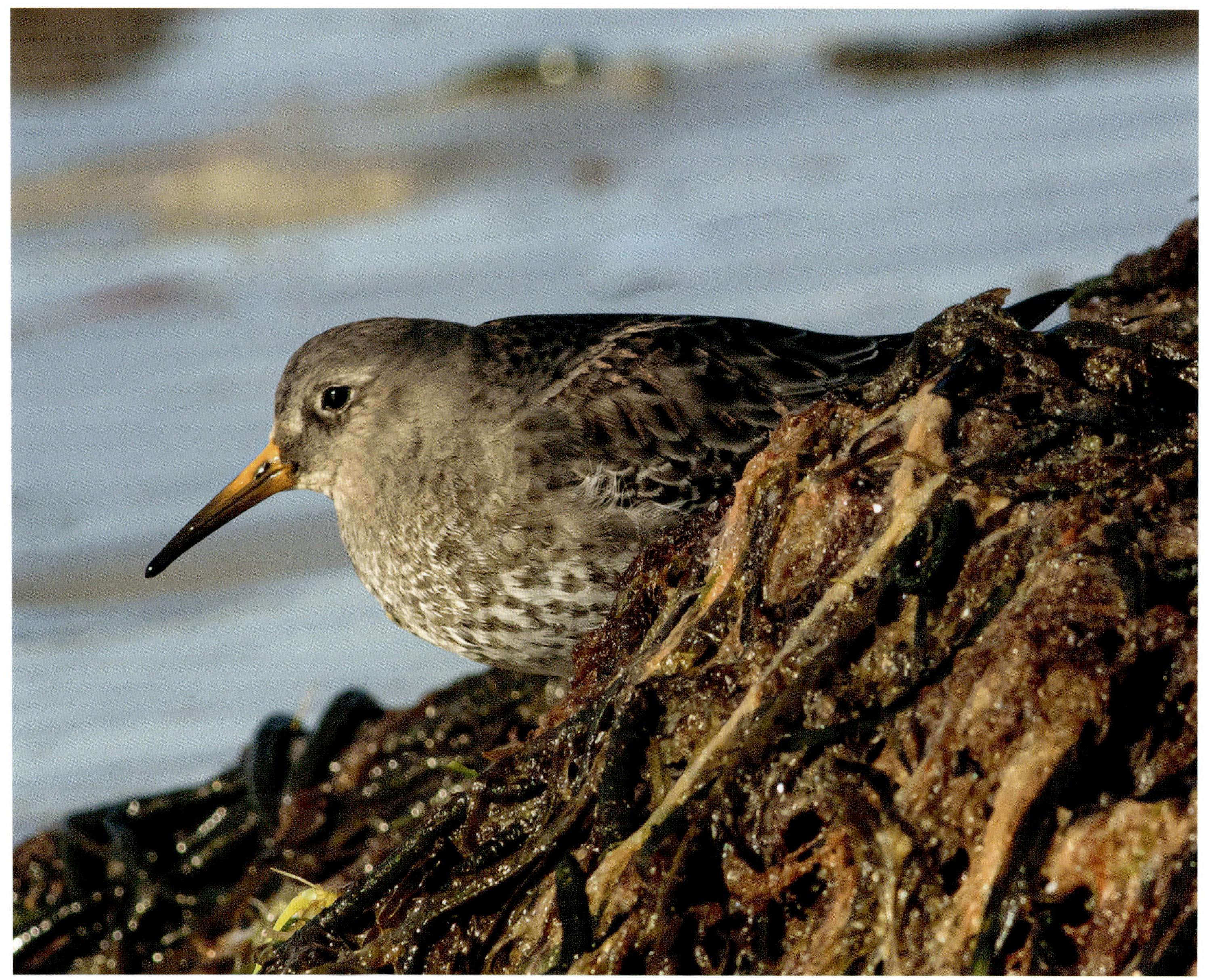

Strictly a winter resident, purple sandpipers are found mostly along rocky shores, feeding or resting along Nantucket Sound, where granite jetties are prevalent. This one is hunkered down out of the wind next to a pile of codium and other storm-washed algae (seaweed). Note the purplish tinge on the feathers that give this hardy sandpiper its name.

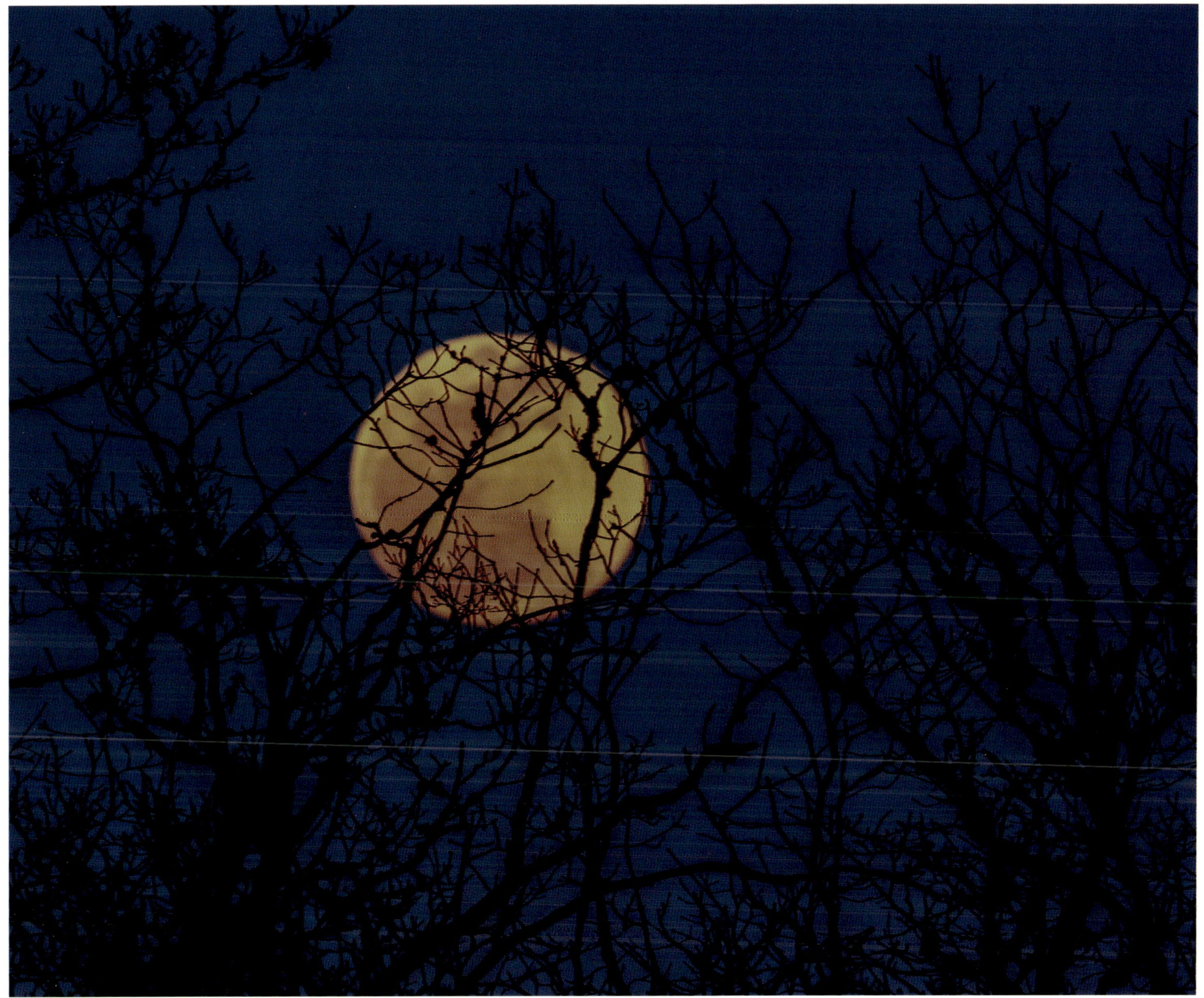

It looks cold, and it is. With dormant twigs and branches silhouetted against the "wolf moon" of January, one thinks of warmer days to come. The chill and wind of January and February will soon give way to the wet, warming days of March and April, when winter releases its grip on this wild cape.

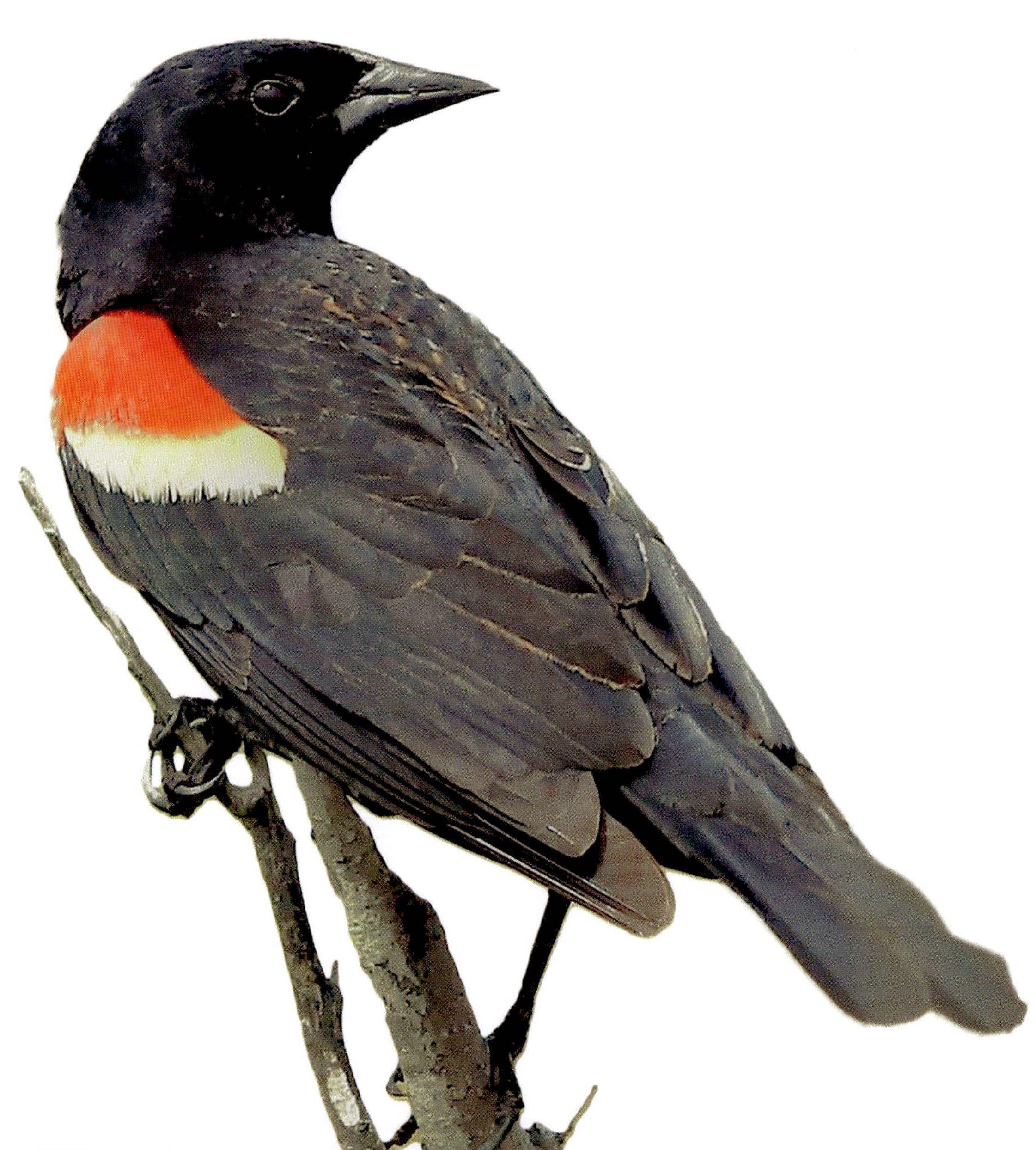

MARCH AND APRIL
Spring Peepers and Pops of Color

Spring shows herself along the wet and saturated edges of ponds in mid-March. We welcome the warmth from the heightened arc of the sun in the southern sky in late March and early April. Much has taken place over the weeks ending February and the lengthening days of early March. Now that the backbone of winter is broken, we find in our cold but thawing gardens crocus pushing up through the dead leaves, perhaps the first real color signifying the end of winter. Red-winged blackbirds, with brilliant, flaring wings and loud, somewhat unmusical calls, herald spring in the bordering foliage. They will soon nest in the emergent vegetation, safe from most terrestrial, egg-eating predators.

It is only a matter of days before the chorus of tiny frogs we know as spring peepers announces their percolation from last autumn's leaf litter. After the first rain on the backside of the March full moon, these frogs, in numbers too many to count, will emerge from hibernation, their bodies having been partially frozen under the leaf litter for most of the winter months, and immerse us in a deafening chorus. While many of us are aware of the spring peepers' chorus, let this be the spring that the hiker, dog walker, fisherman, or skateboarder finds a wetland and walks among them. It is a sound from another world. To be surrounded by this amphibious orgy in frenzied chorus is, in a way, overwhelming, because of its loudness, strangeness, and beauty, especially after dark. Spotted salamanders and wood frogs, both more secretive than the ubiquitous peepers, also emerge in great numbers. You just have to know where to find them.

The sweet but plaintive whistle of the piping plover has returned to the coastal beaches, and the herring are running, counted now by digital monitors. The ospreys, having spent the winter in South America, are back on Cape Cod to nest, tidying up last year's nest in between trips to the herring runs, where they catch and gorge themselves on these anadromous fish. Oaks swell their leaf buds, pushing off last year's remnant brown, dry leaves, while shadbush and forsythia show their colors. It's the end of the last winter's cold, so let's burn the last of the cordwood and step into the colors of spring.

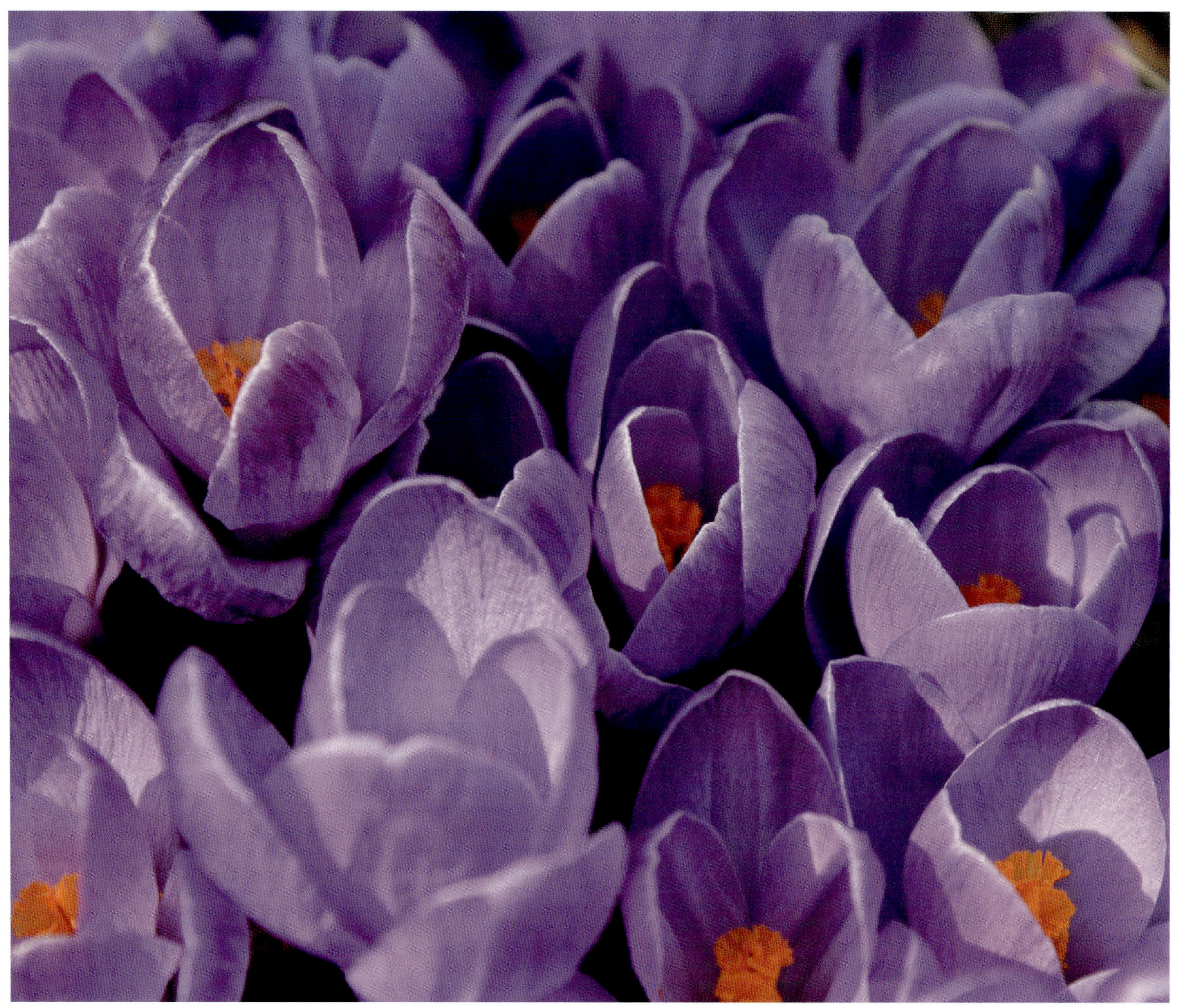

Crocus burst through leaf litter, signaling the end of winter.

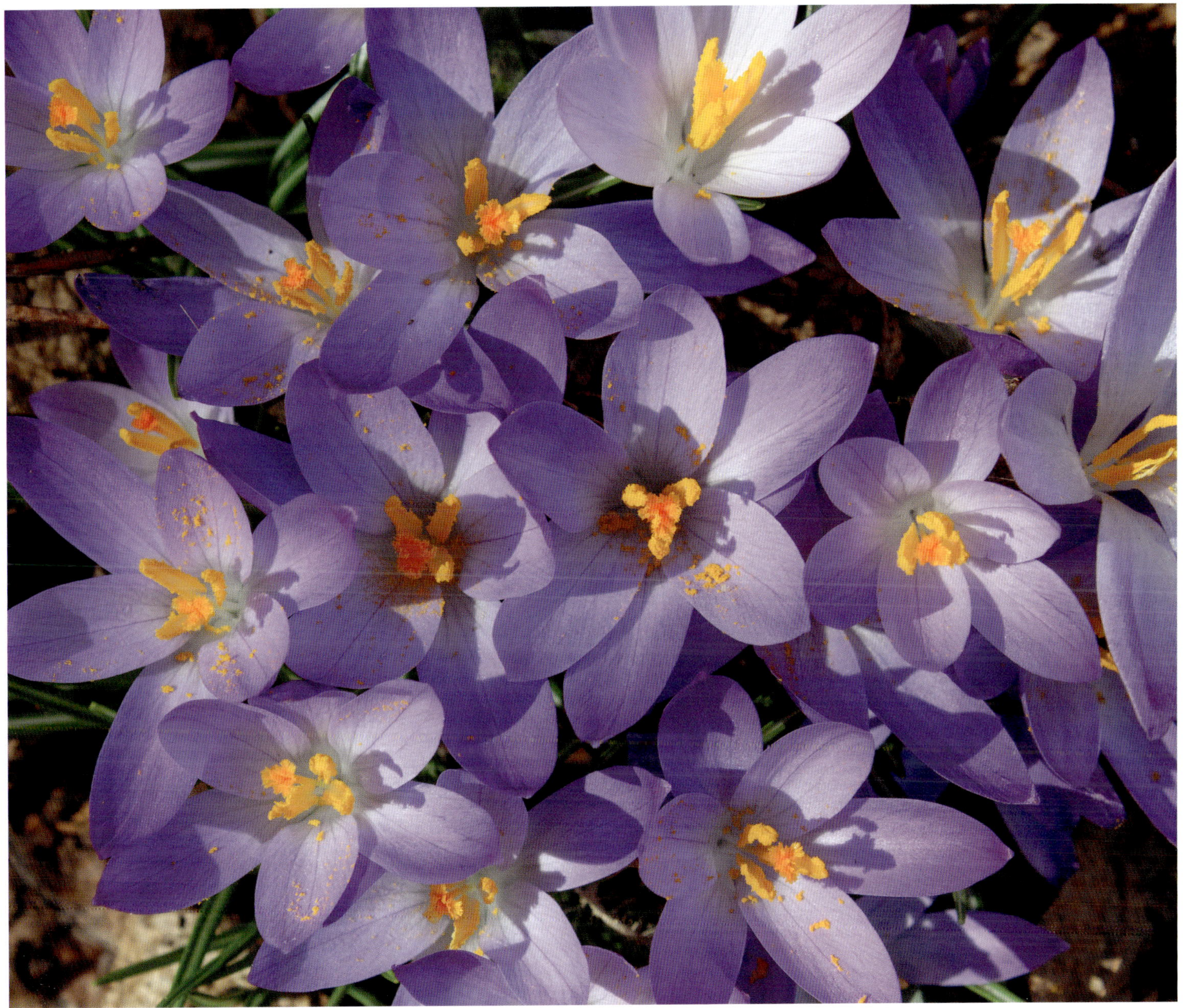

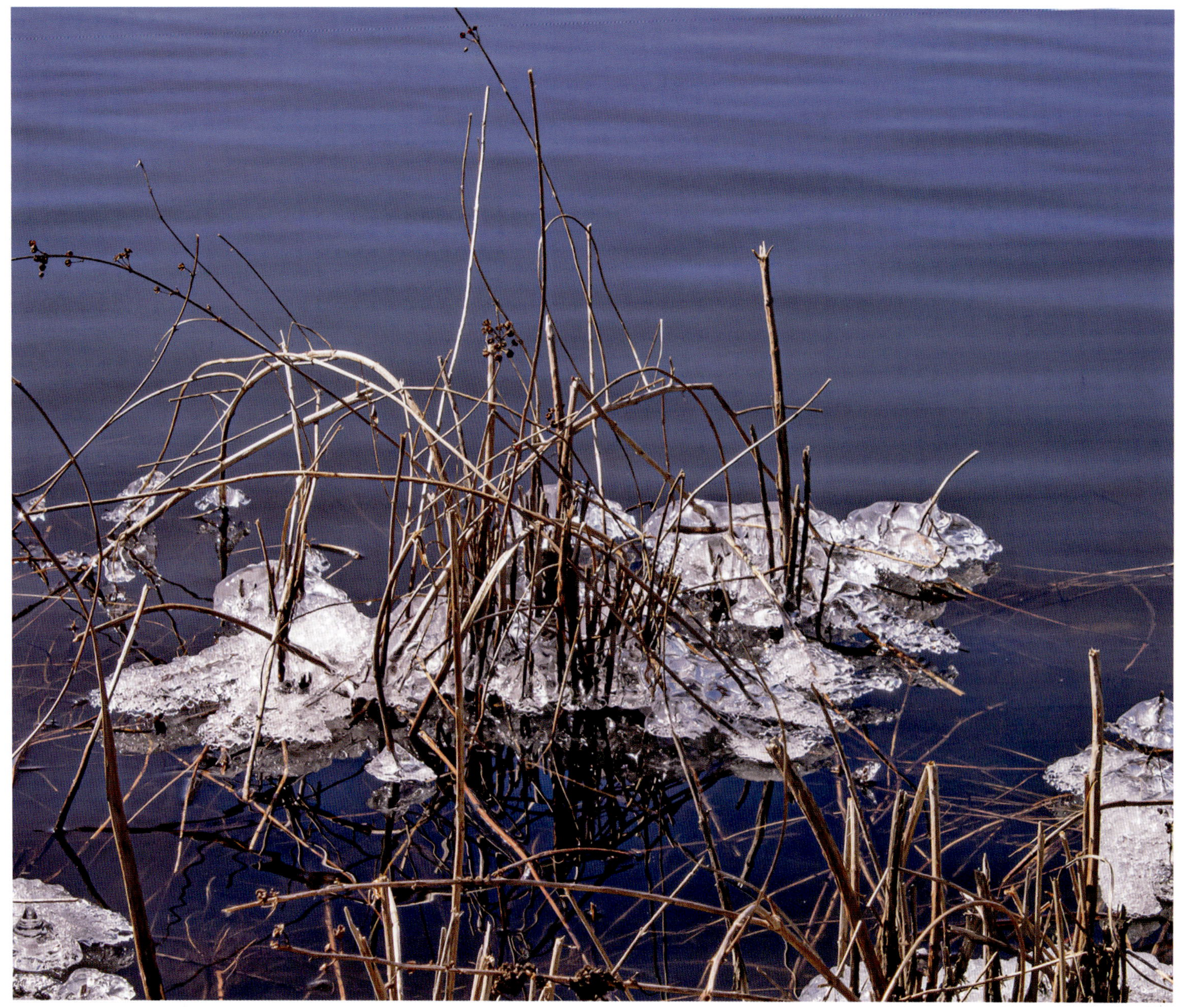

While warmer days bring on blossoms, nighttime temperatures still drop below freezing in March, leaving lingering, early-morning ice around emergent grasses and twigs.

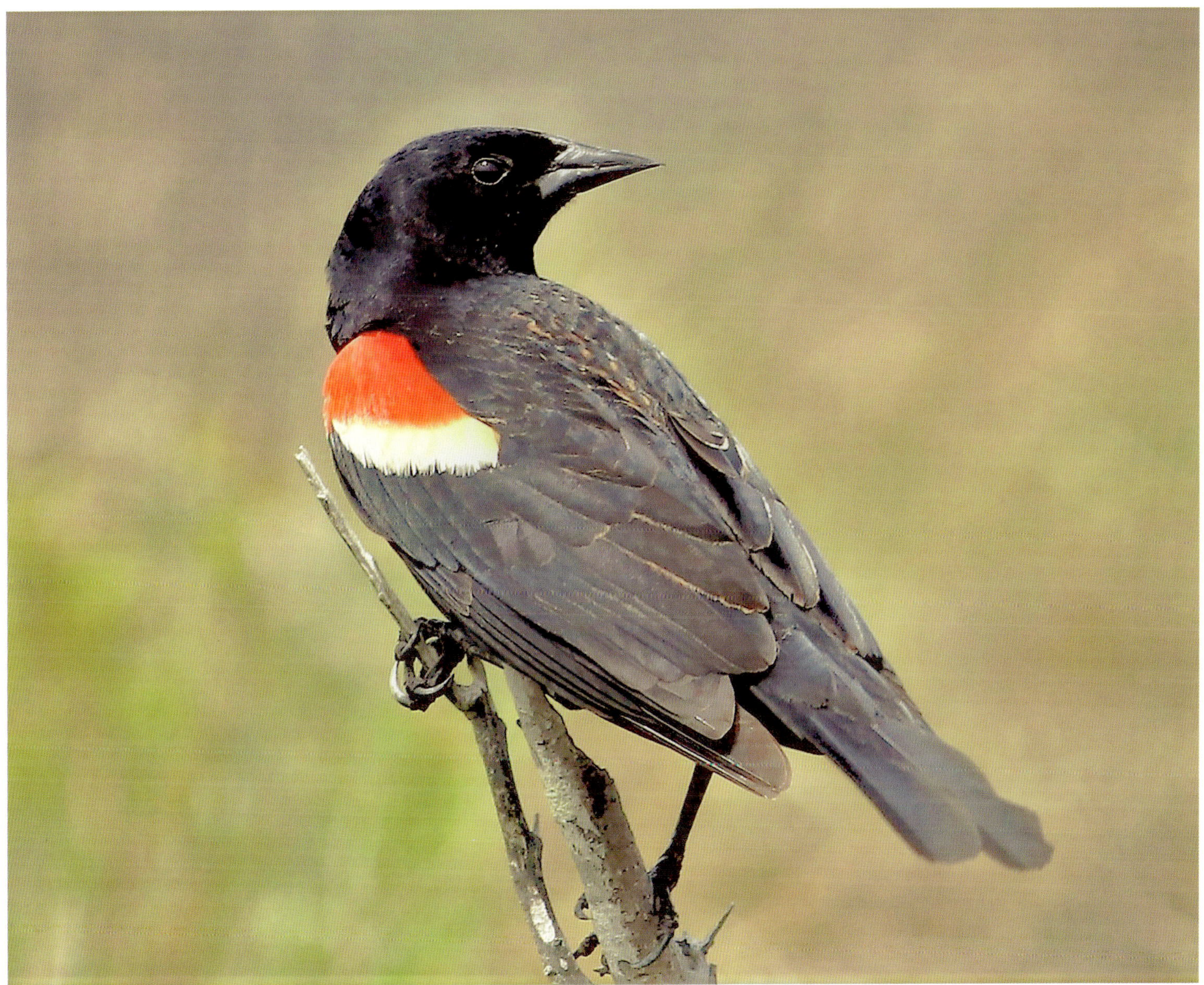

As we wait impatiently for spring's arrival, the red-winged blackbird's distinctive song reassures us that the new season is close at hand. This marsh-loving bird arrives from its wintering grounds, sometimes in late February, to call from the wetland edges. During the first week of March, they are often calling loudly to herald the end of winter.

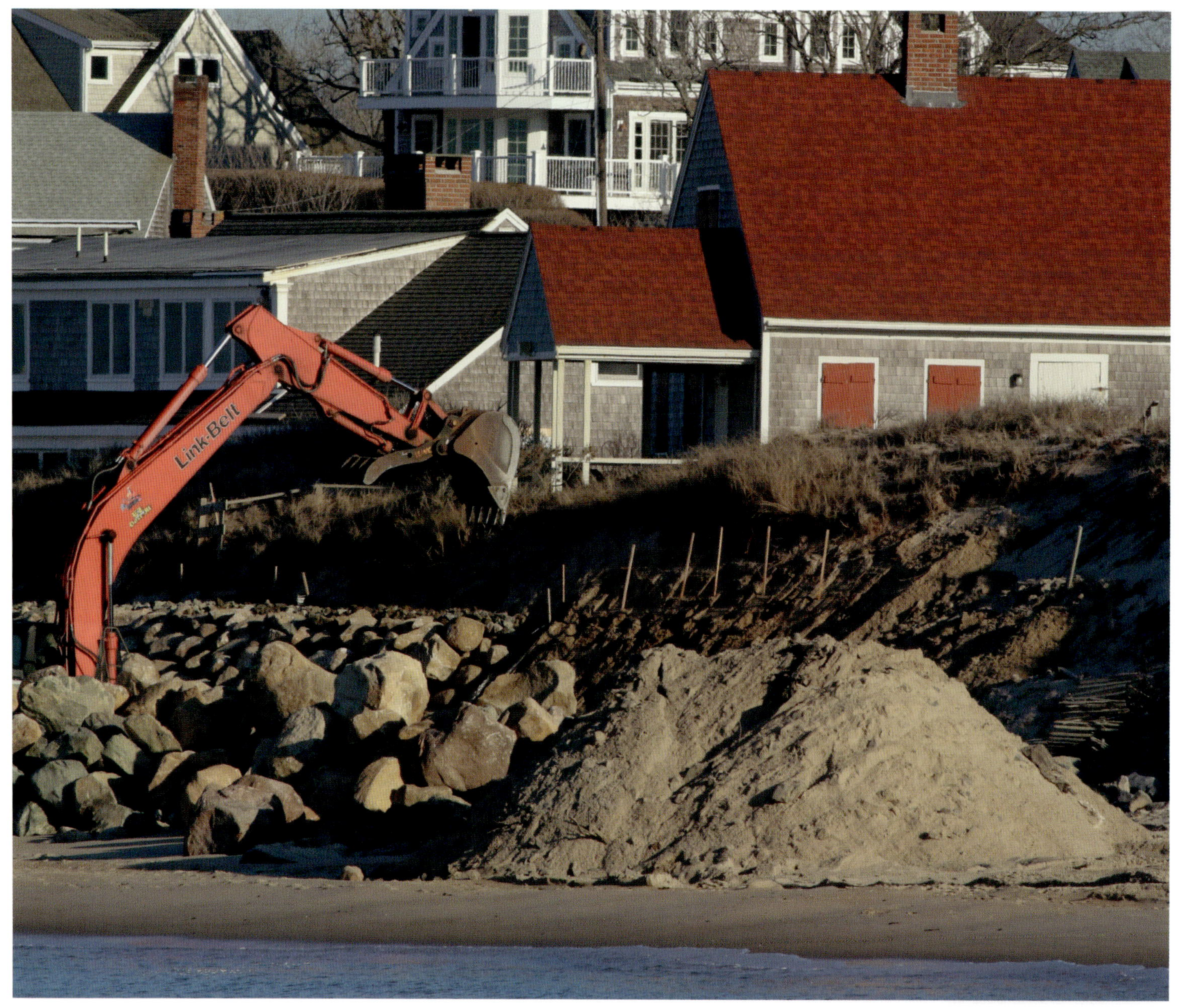

A common sight all along the beach this time of year: shoring up the dunes and rock jetties that protect cottages from the ever-threatening assault of the sea.

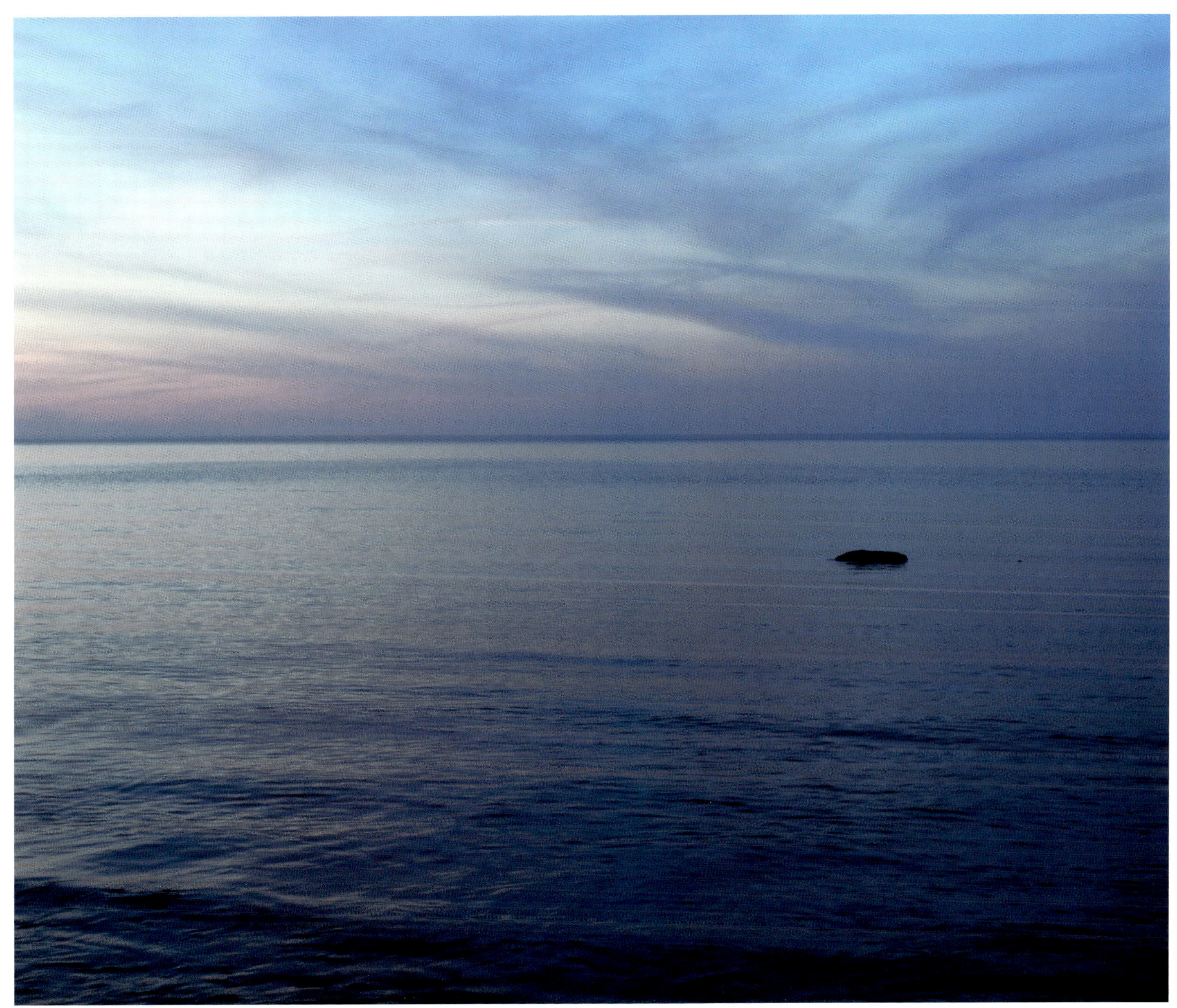

As the earth tilts steadily and more directly toward the warming sun, the glow of sunset in early spring takes on a new light.

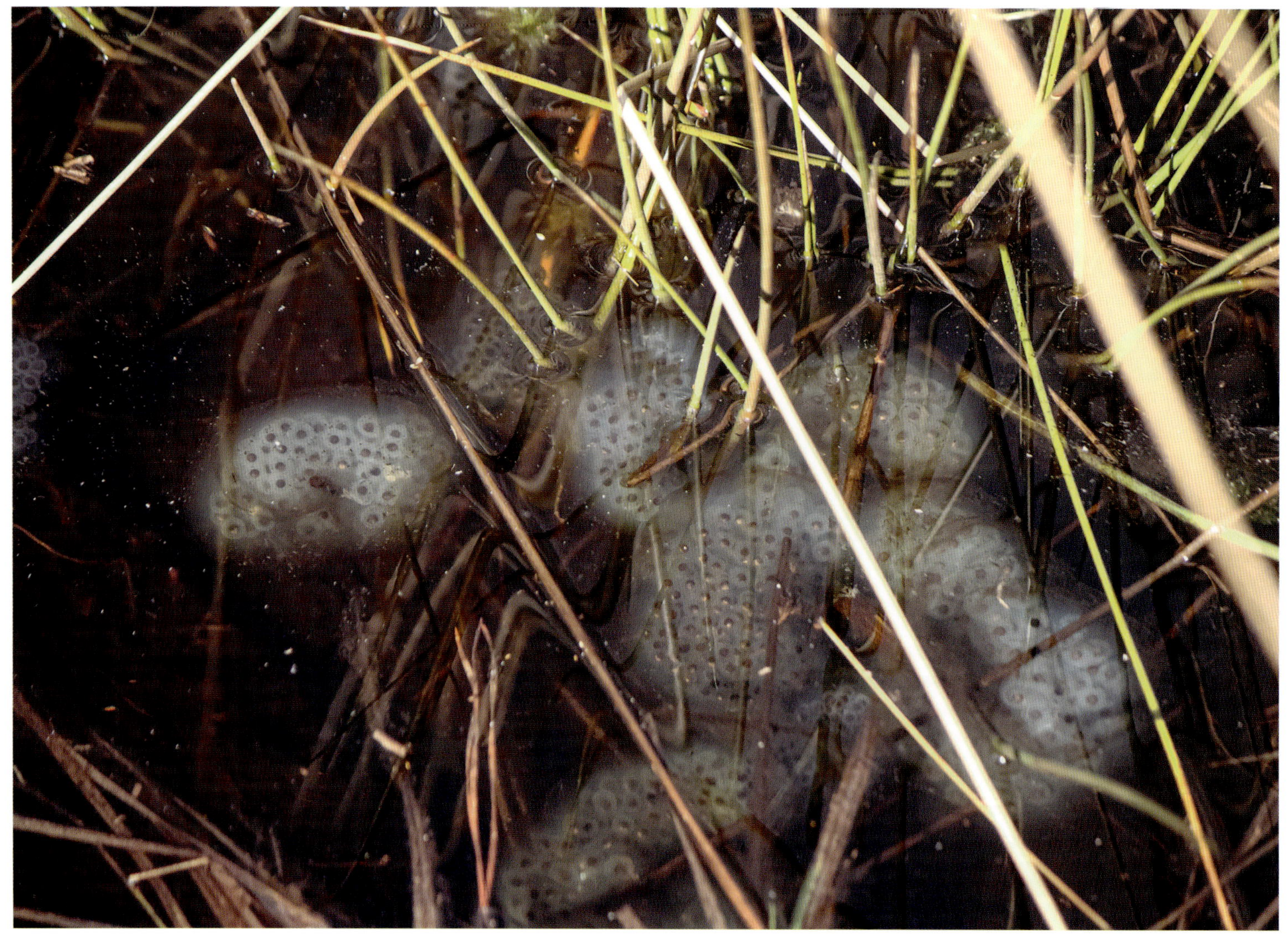

One of the most significant events of nature's year is the March full moon. On the first rainy night after this celestial event, amphibians emerge from their winter hibernation and begin a breeding frenzy; their deafening chorus heralds the onset of spring like nothing else. Spotted salamanders (*pictured top right*) crawl and clamor over the woodland floor, emerging from their underground winter torpor, to a nearby vernal pool, where hundreds may be seen on any rainy night in a black-and-yellow whirling mass. The males and females "dance" to form a pair bond, after which the males deposit tiny packets of sperm called spermatophores on the pool bottom. Then the females, with cloacal lips designed to grasp the sperm packets, tuck them into their bodies, where the eggs are fertilized internally. These gelatinous-looking egg masses may be seen attached to grass or twigs in the water (*above*). Meanwhile, thousands of inch-long frogs, called spring peepers, not much bigger than a cranberry (*as pictured bottom right*), emerge from hibernation and perch along wetland edges and nearby vegetation, peeping in a glorious chorus to announce their presence and confirm their territory.

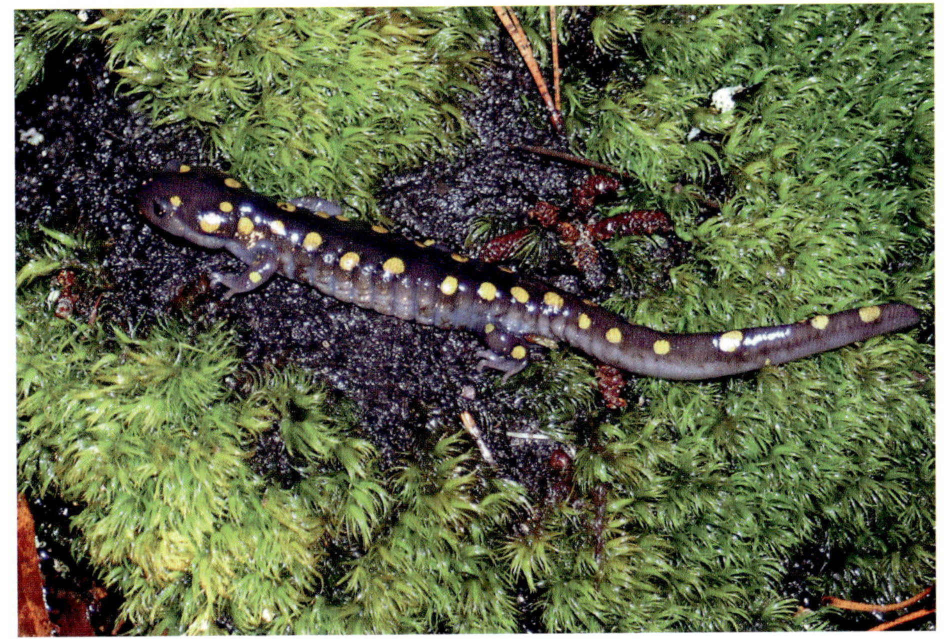

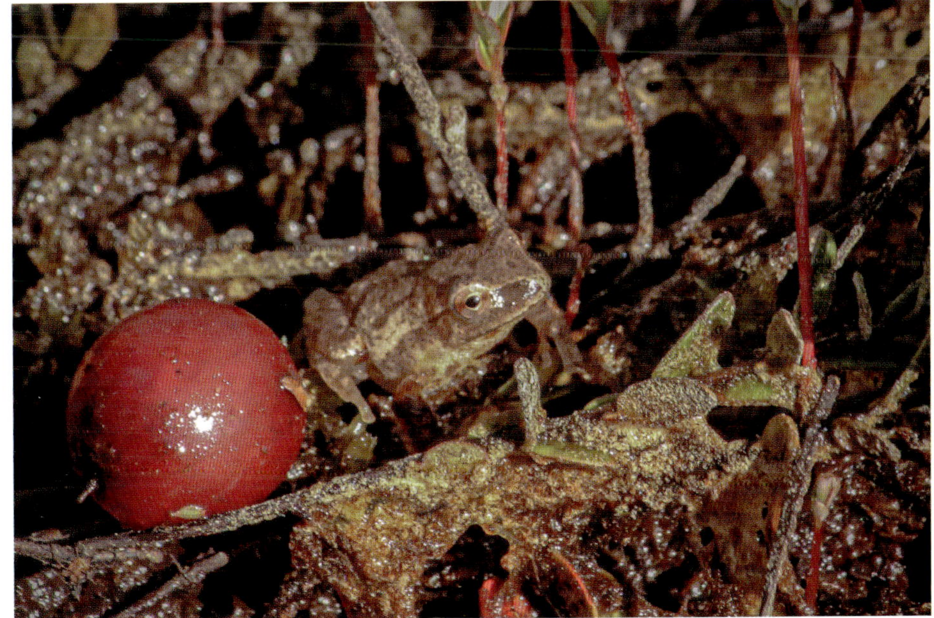

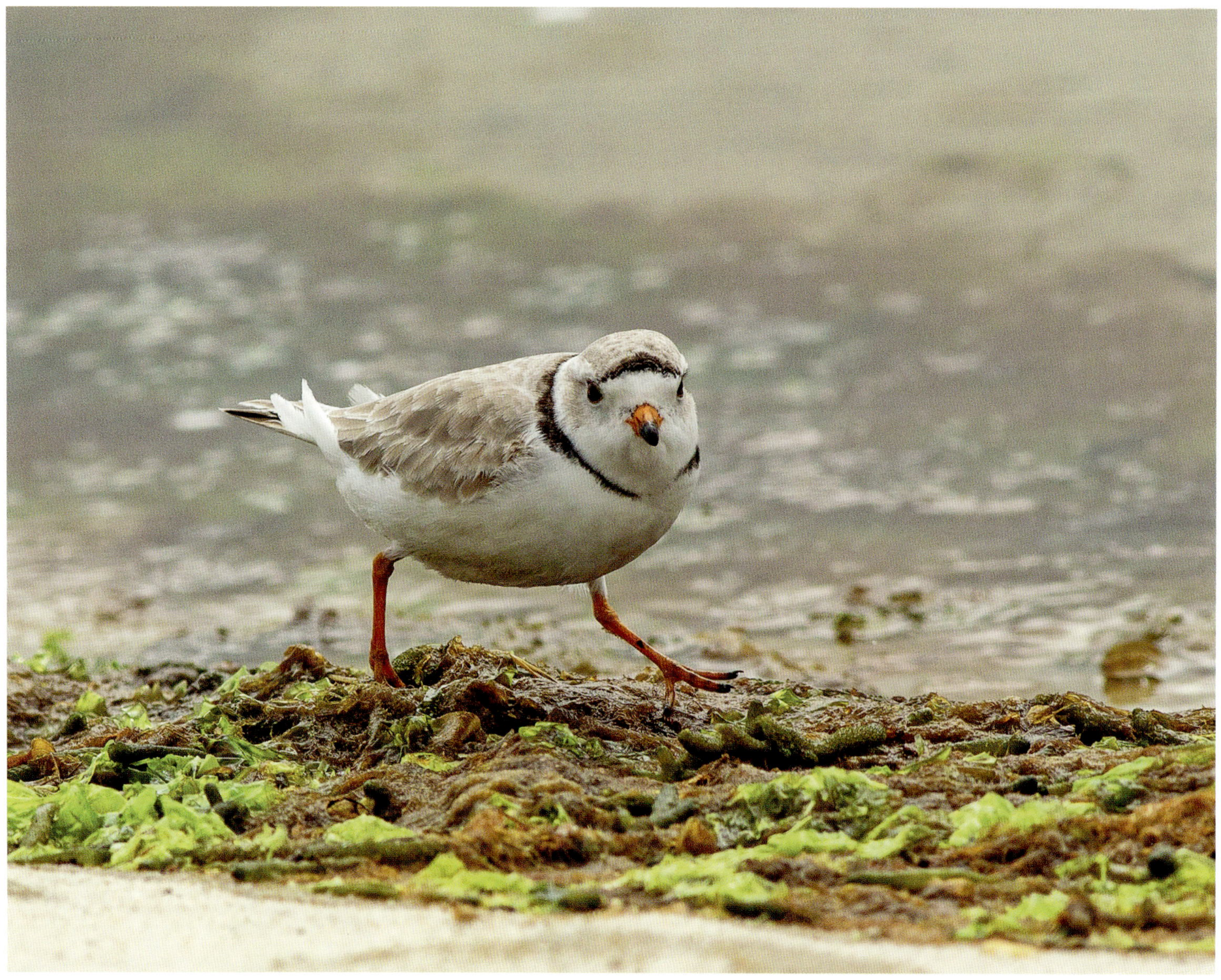

Listed as a federally threatened species in Massachusetts, the petite, cryptic piping plover arrives along the Cape Cod shores in late March and early April to begin its annual breeding cycle. They are a true symbol of the cape's beaches, nesting singly along the sandy shores. Adults, chicks, and nests with eggs are virtually invisible to the untrained eye, so their nesting areas are often posted with stakes and symbolic string fences to protect them from beachgoers. When approached too closely, the adults may feign injury to lead the intruder or predator away from the nest.

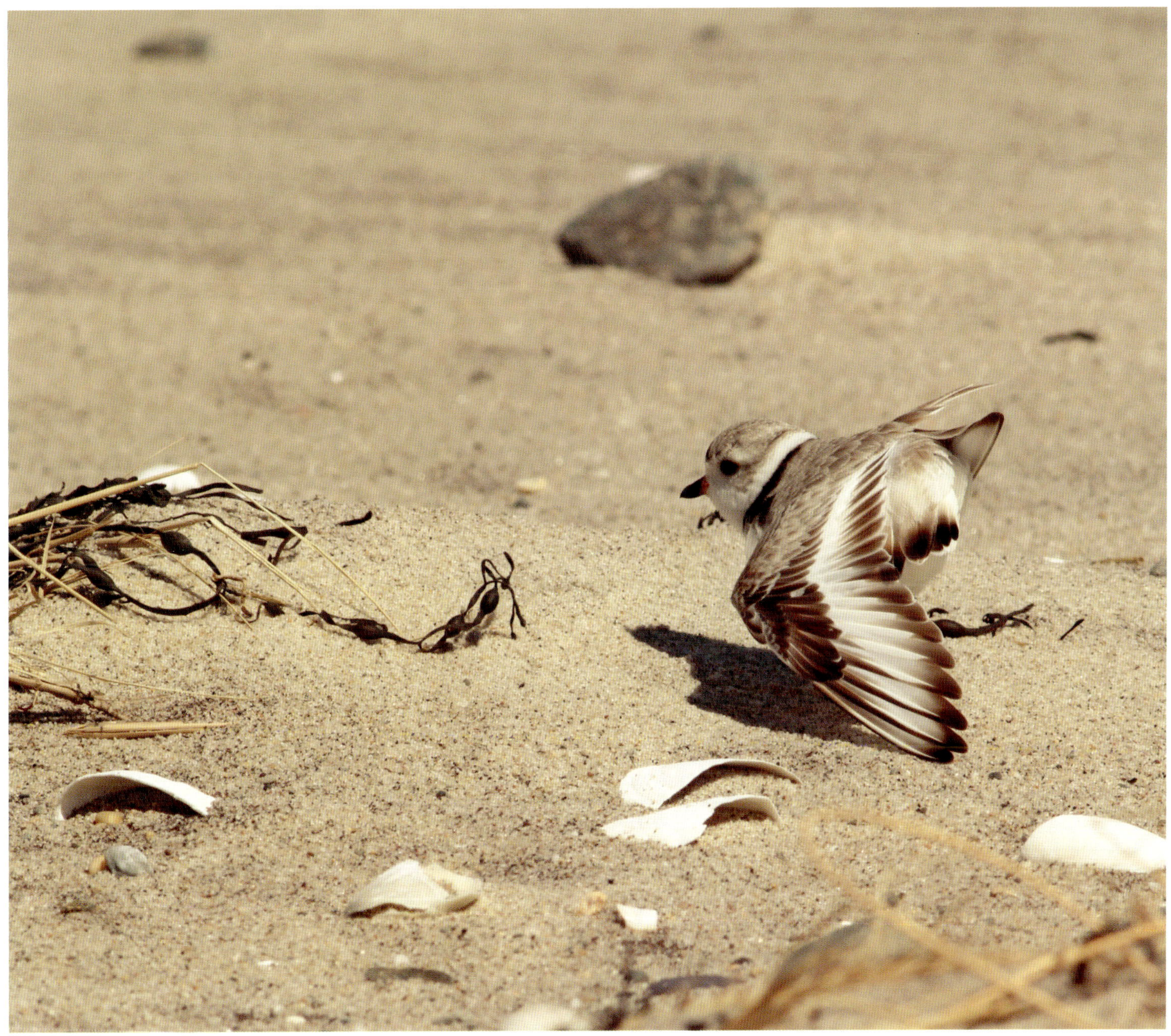

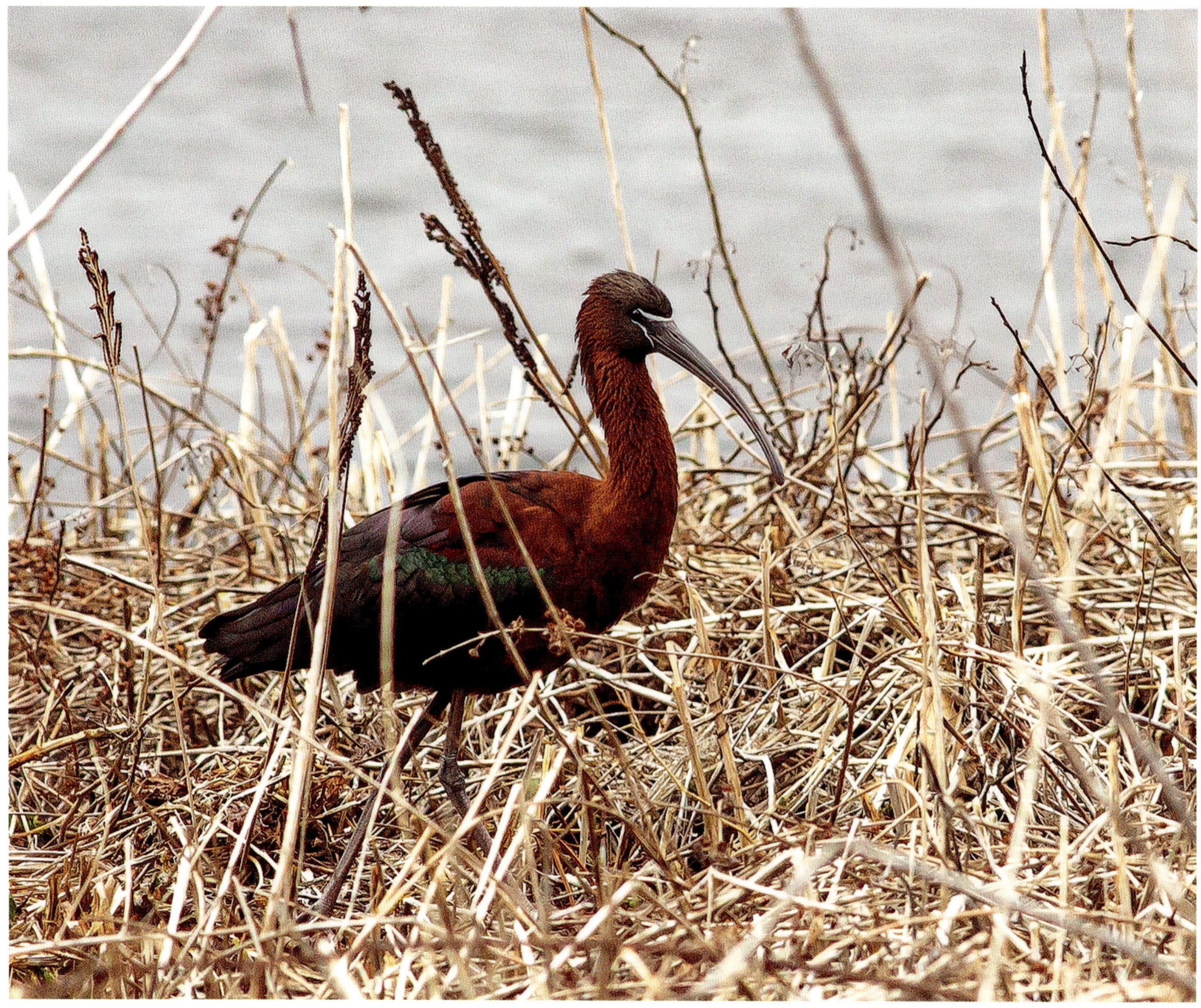

The glossy ibis, a regular April migrant, is sought after by birders. Found in marshes, often in the company of snowy egrets, it is a wading bird with a distinctive sicklelike beak and a contrasting body of rust, glossy green, and black. A remarkable bird!

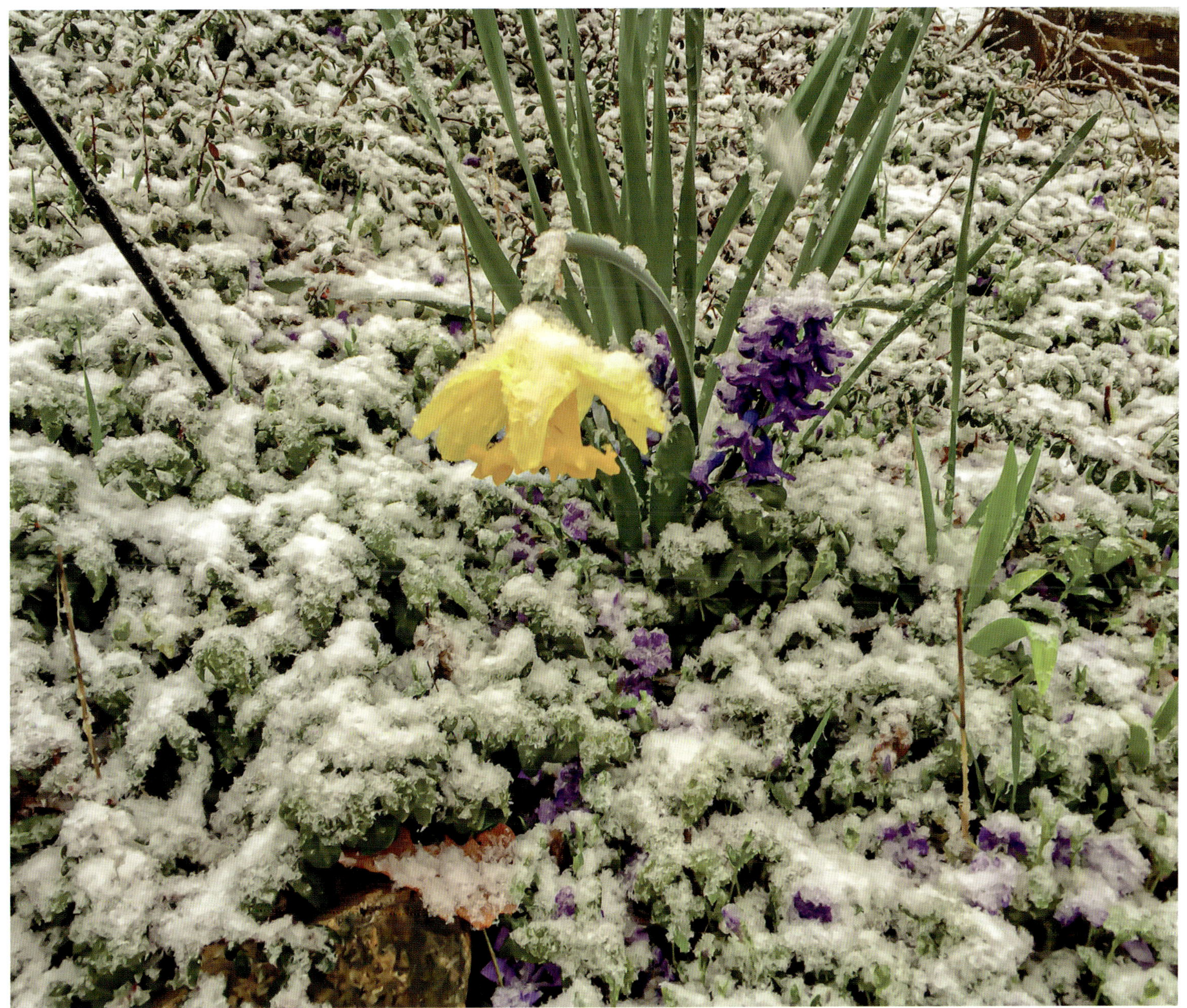

Any meteorological event is possible during April on Cape Cod, from 80-degree tanning days to snow on the daffodils.

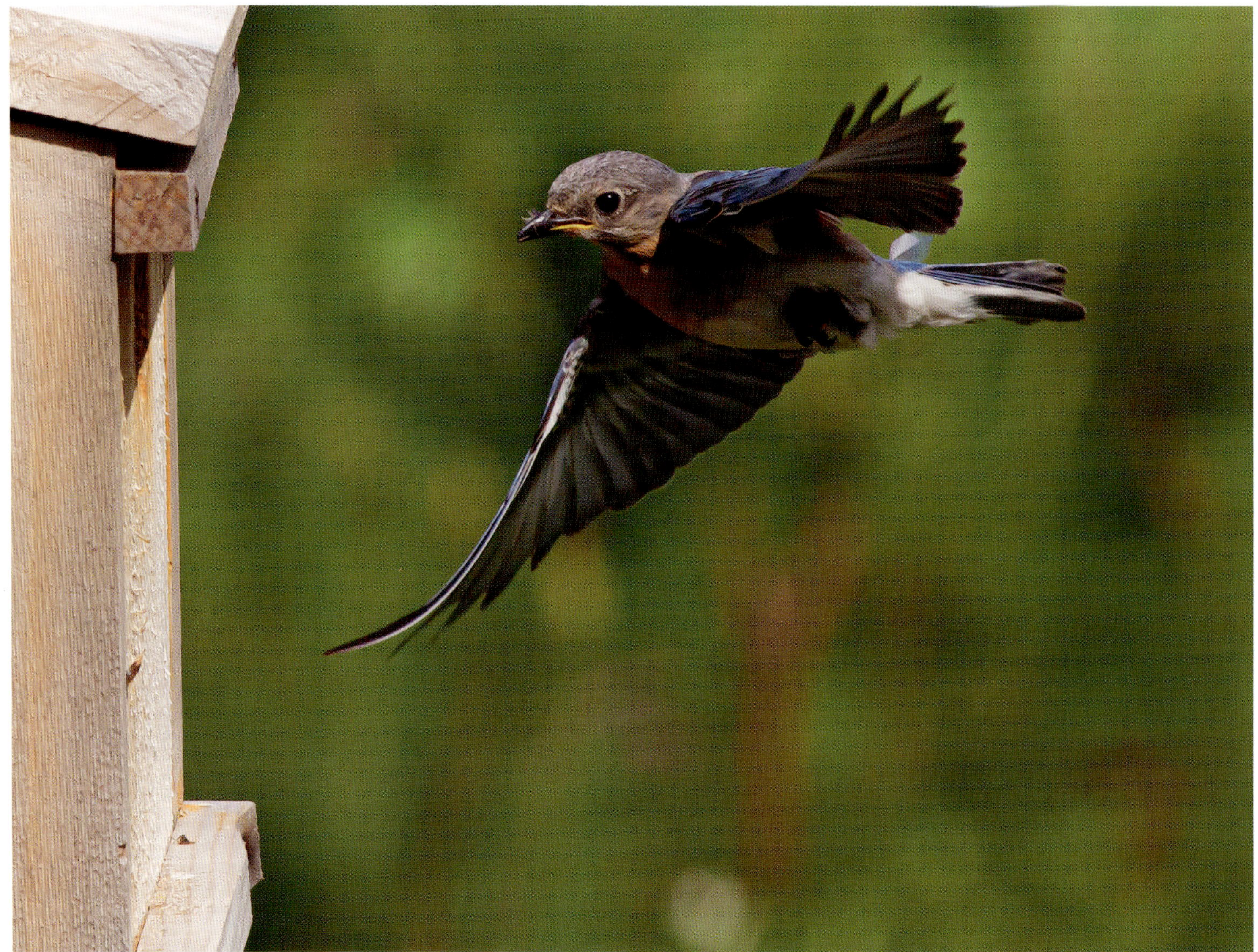

The beautiful eastern bluebird, which may or may not winter over on the cape, has built a nest and laid eggs by early to mid-April. As is the case with most birds, established pairs will return, often independently, to a previous year's nesting site, especially if they successfully raised young. The concept that birds "mate for life," as many people like to say, doesn't mean they spend the years of their lives together. It simply means that they return to a previous year's successful nest site (called site tenacity), meet up with each other, recognize each other through calls and behavior, and get right down to business, sooner and more efficiently than birds that have to establish a new pair bond. Simply put, it makes sense to breed with someone you know. Bluebirds take readily to nest boxes if they are the right size and placed in a favorable location (*above*). By late April, chicks are being fed (*right*).

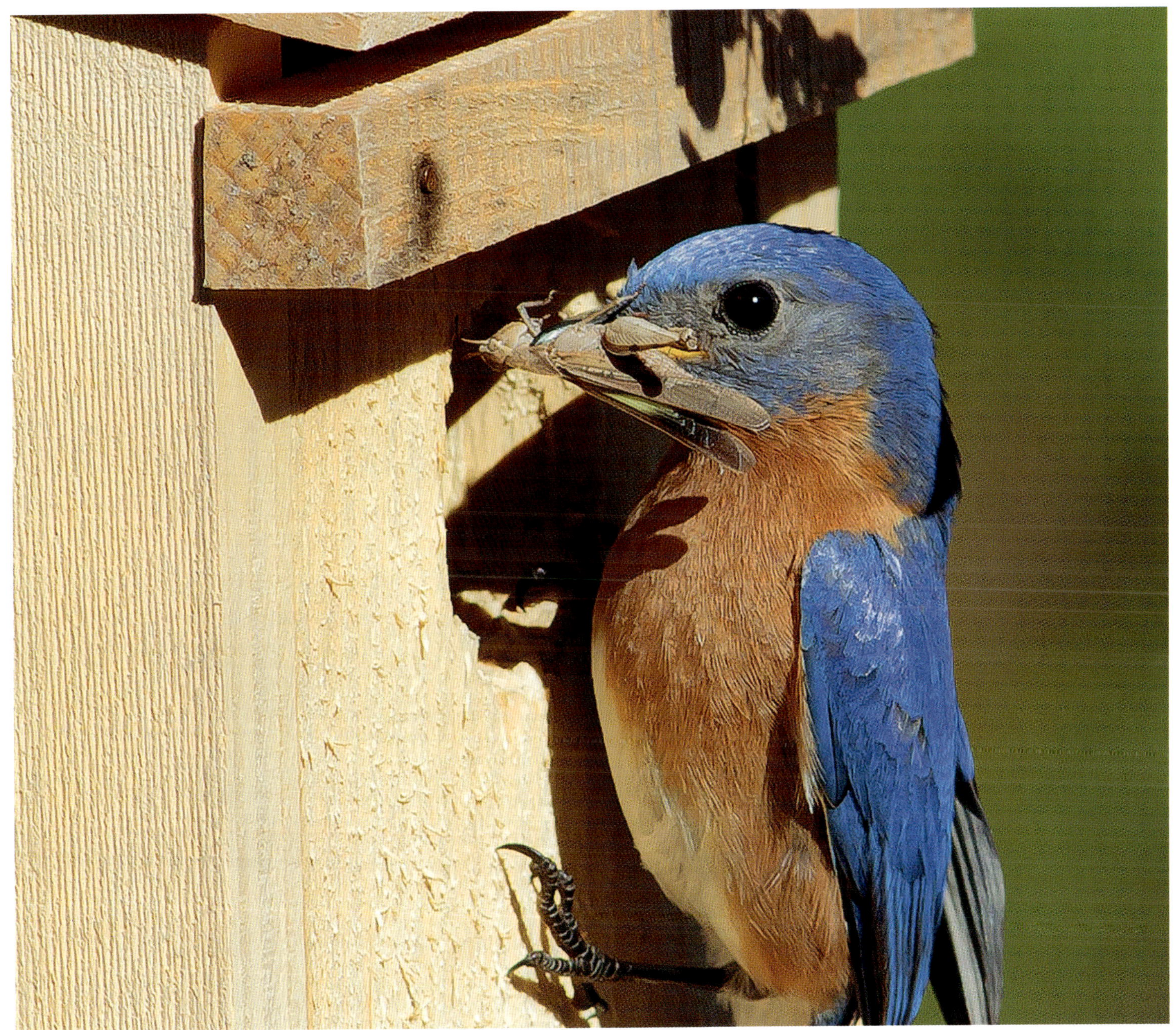

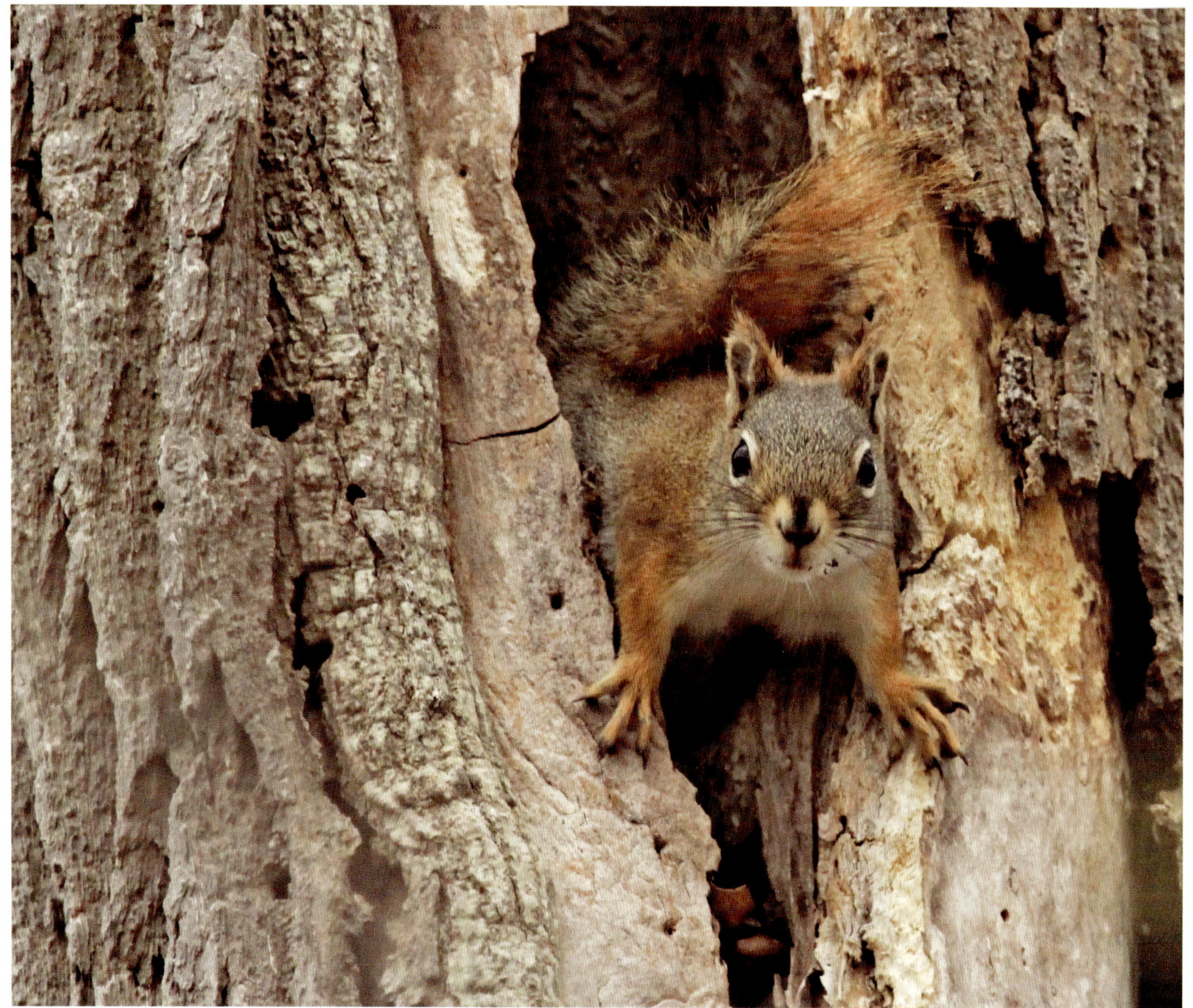

With the warming days of spring, mammals become more visible, like the chattering, busybody red squirrel, posing for the camera.

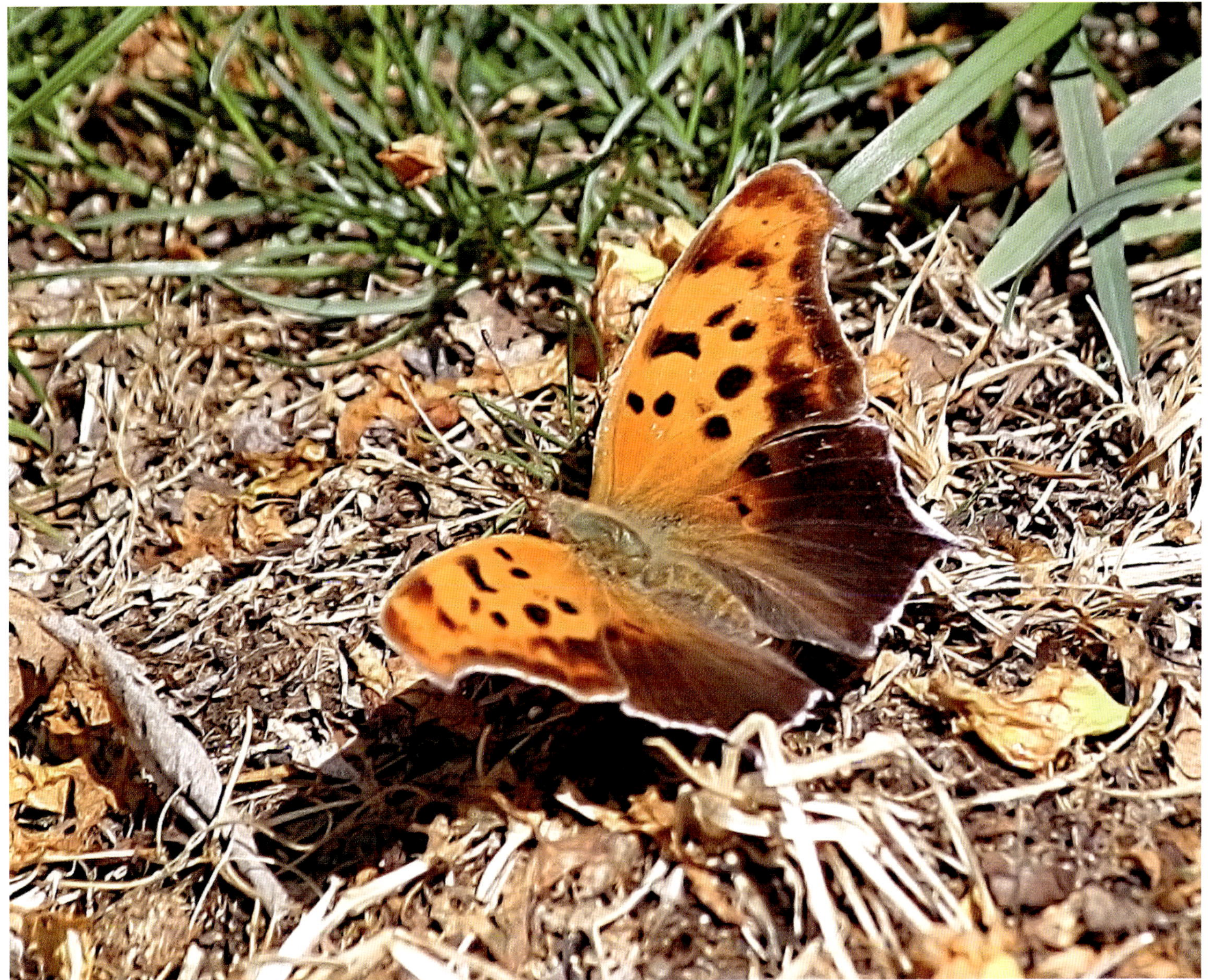

This beautiful, uniquely shaped butterfly, called a question mark, is one of the earliest butterflies to emerge in spring. This is a tough little butterfly (if there is such a thing). The question mark may hibernate beneath tree bark or plant crevices rather than migrate. It gets nutrients from plants as well as from animal droppings, carrion, or minerals from muddy shorelines. Look for question marks on tree trunks on sunny April days.

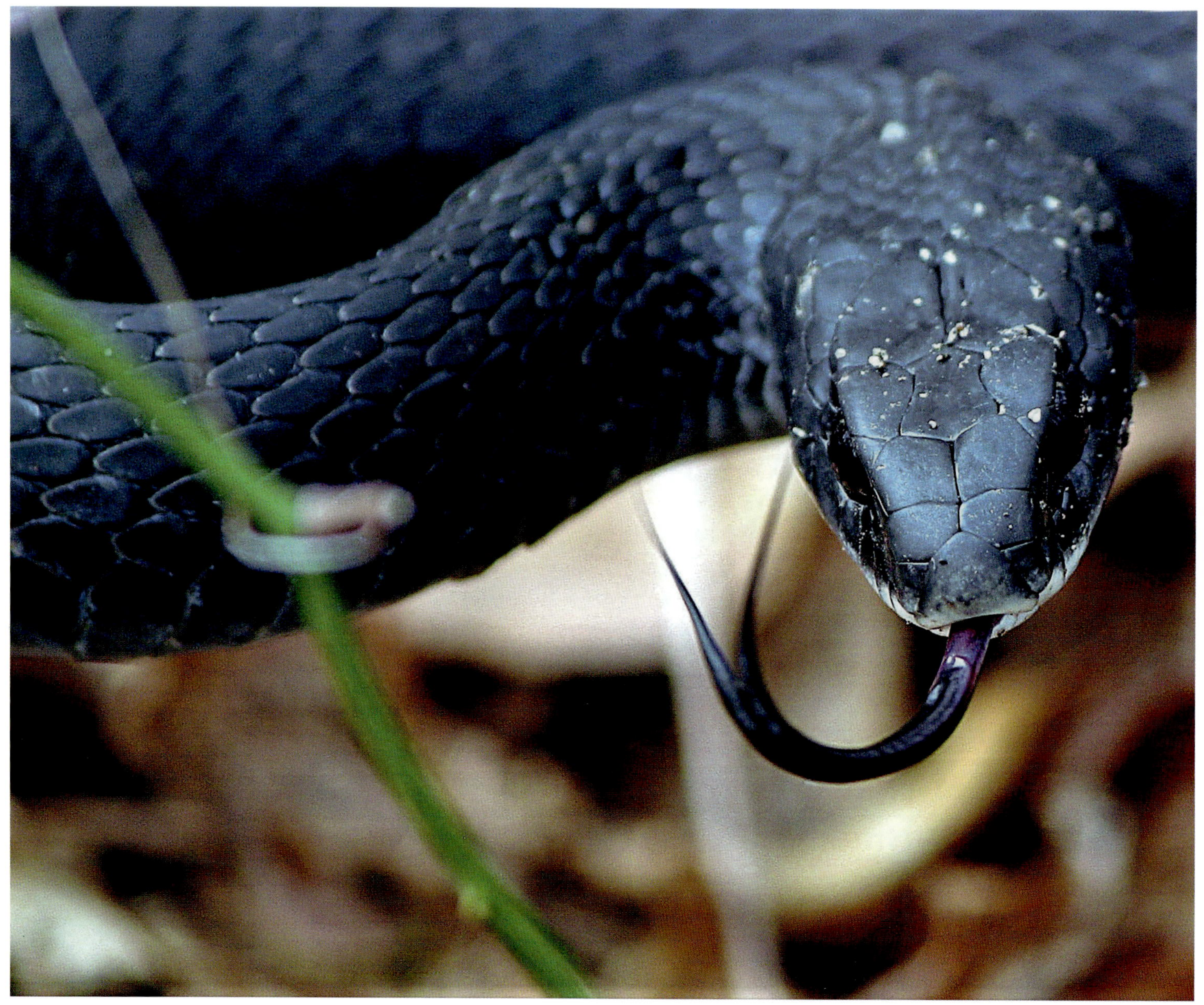

As the ground warms, terrestrial reptiles emerge from their winter hibernation. This black racer is an impressively long but harmless predator, unless you're a small rodent. A great snake to have around.

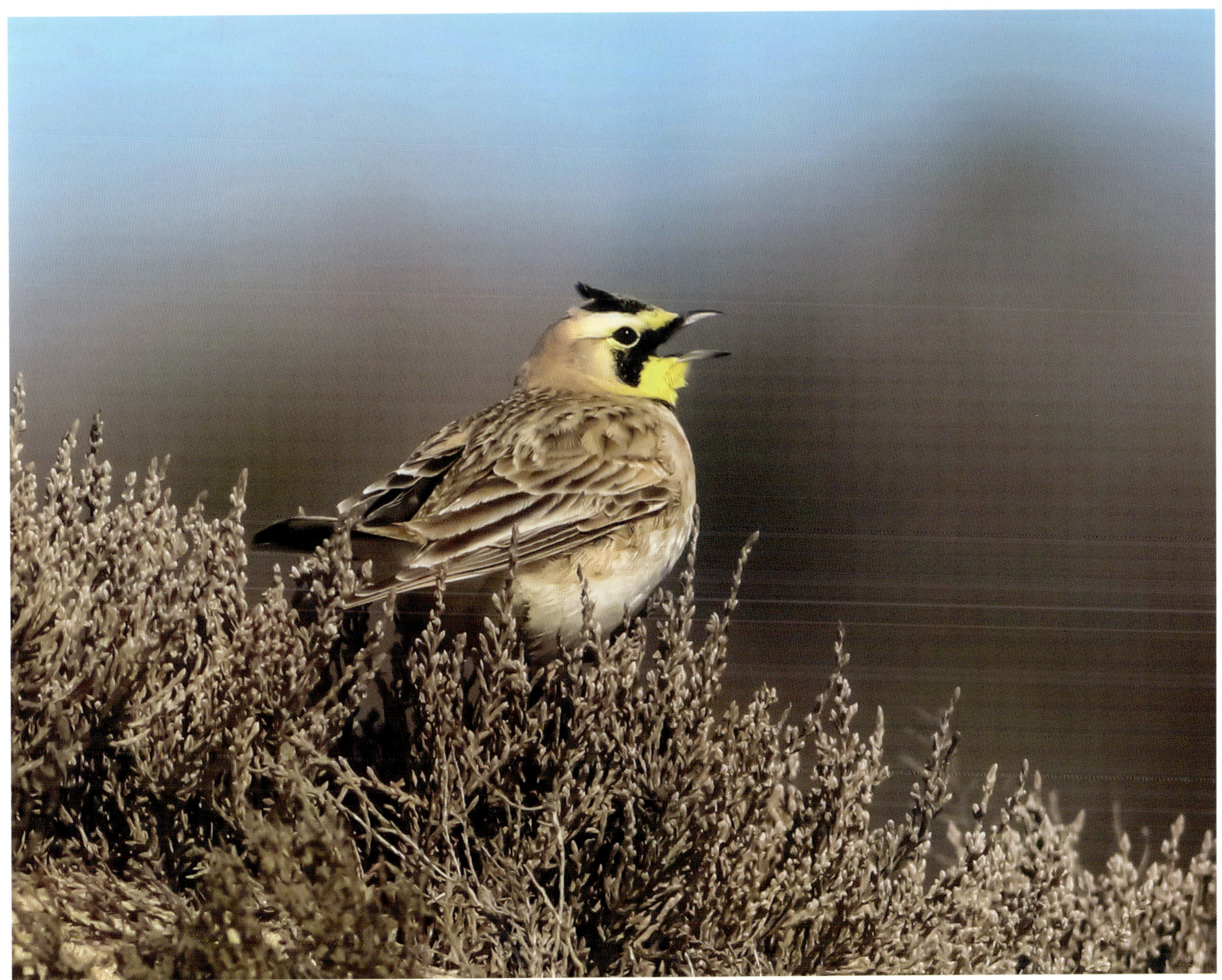

During mid- to late April, the horned larks that may winter along the beaches and in the dunes begin to molt into their spring colors. Though the perennial poverty grass may still exhibit the dull colors of winter dormancy, the singing male horned lark displays the yellow throat and feather tufts that give this beach-nesting bird its name. Note the black streak below the eye, evolved to cut the glare of sun on beach sand. Athletes copy nature's adaptations by streaking black below their eyes to deflect stadium lights and bright sunlight.

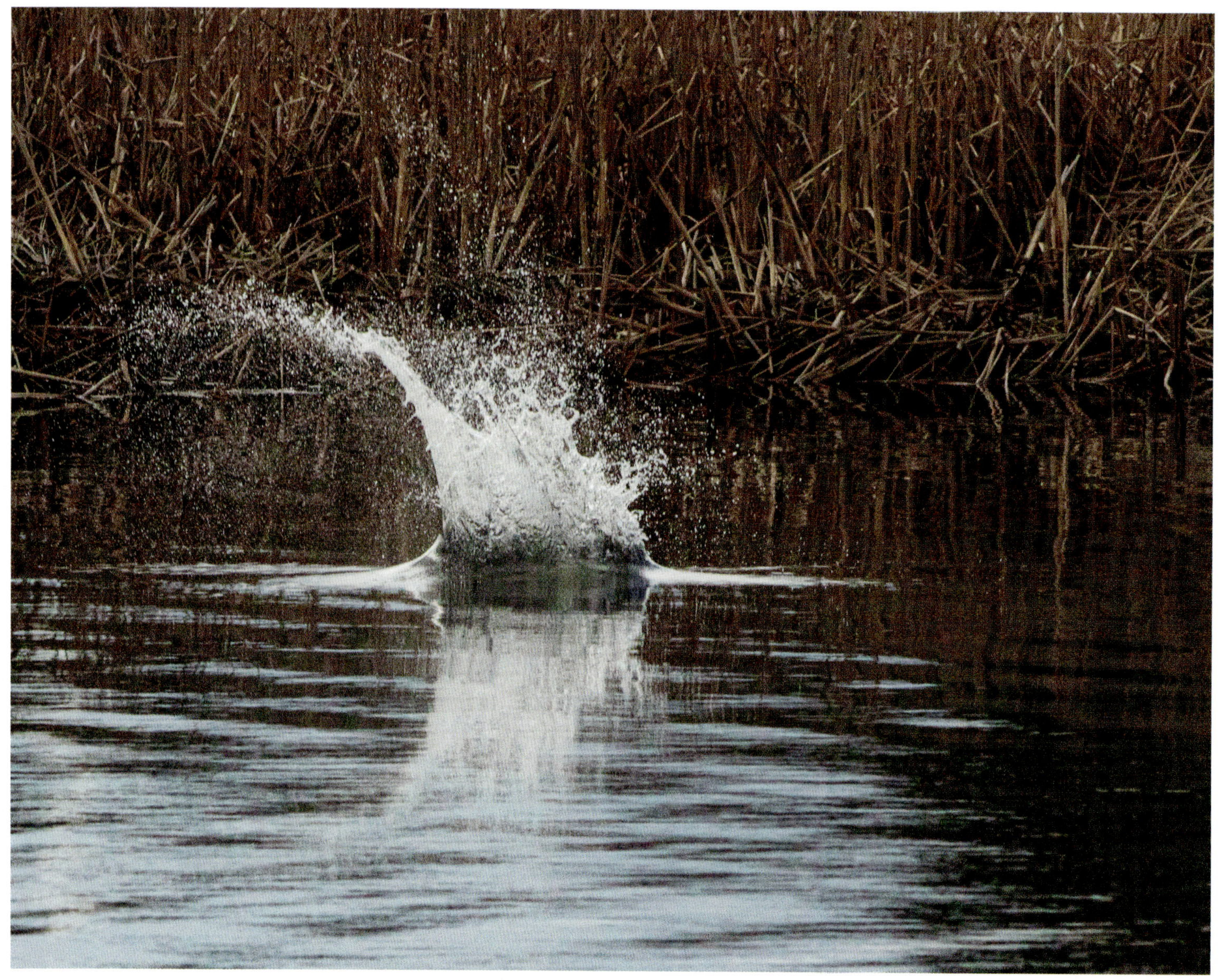

Osprey is a species of fish-eating bird of prey. Sometimes called fish hawks, osprey winter in Central America and South America and return to Cape Cod in April. Osprey feed on live fish in both fresh water and salt water. During April, the herring runs are regular haunts for these dynamic diving birds. They hover above the water, find their fish, then plunge feet first, grabbing the slippery prey with long, needlelike talons, and disappear in a huge splash!

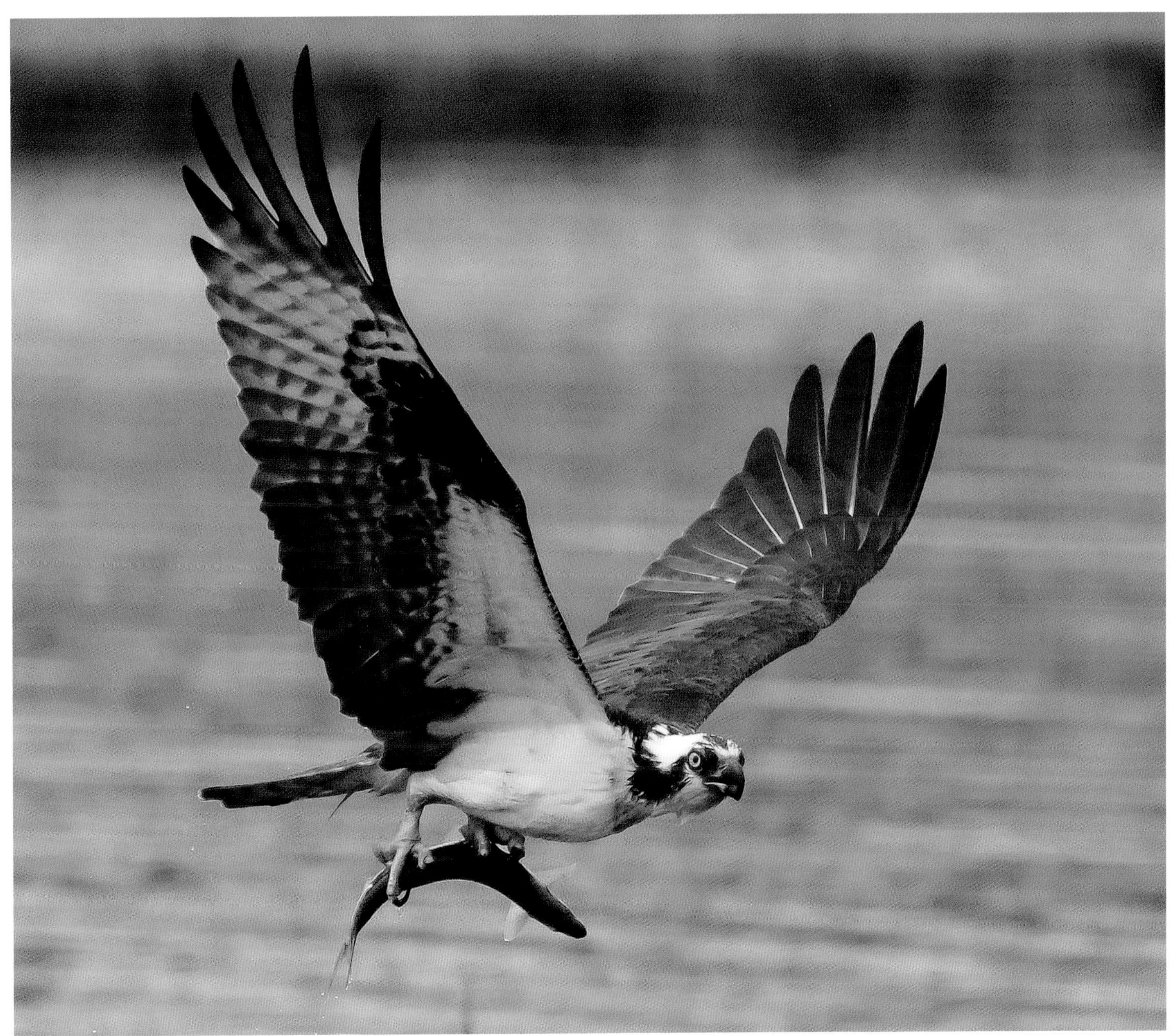

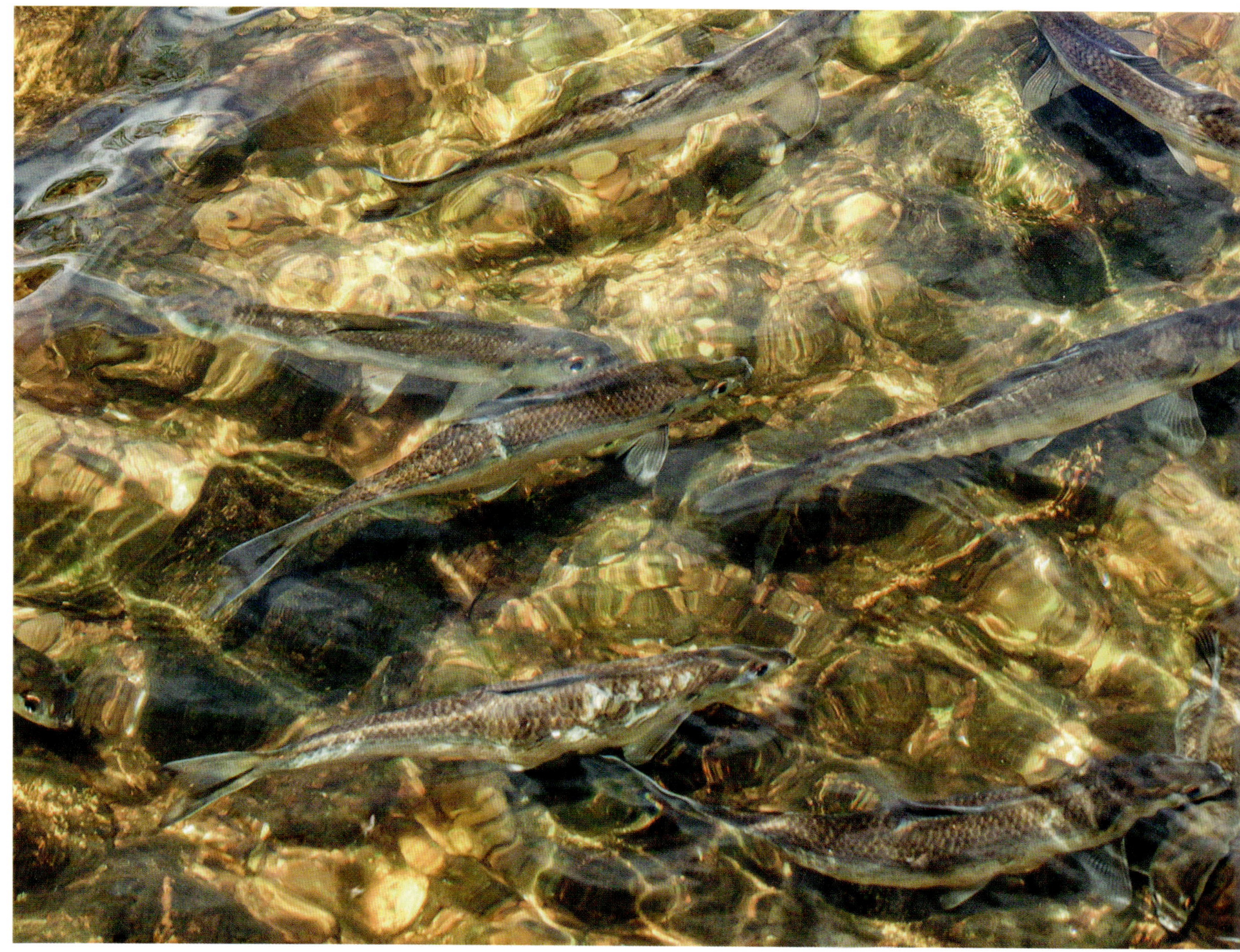

The herring run from mid- to late April. The Grist Mill on Stony Brook Road in Brewster attracts thousands of people to witness one of nature's most powerful displays of survival, Alewives, commonly known as herring, spawn in fresh water. They come from the open reaches of the North Atlantic Ocean, where they live most of their adult life, swimming in huge numbers to the freshwater coastal-plain ponds where they were born. Osprey, several species of herons, raccoons, and, of course, herring gulls (*top right and bottom right*) exploit this seemingly overabundant food supply.

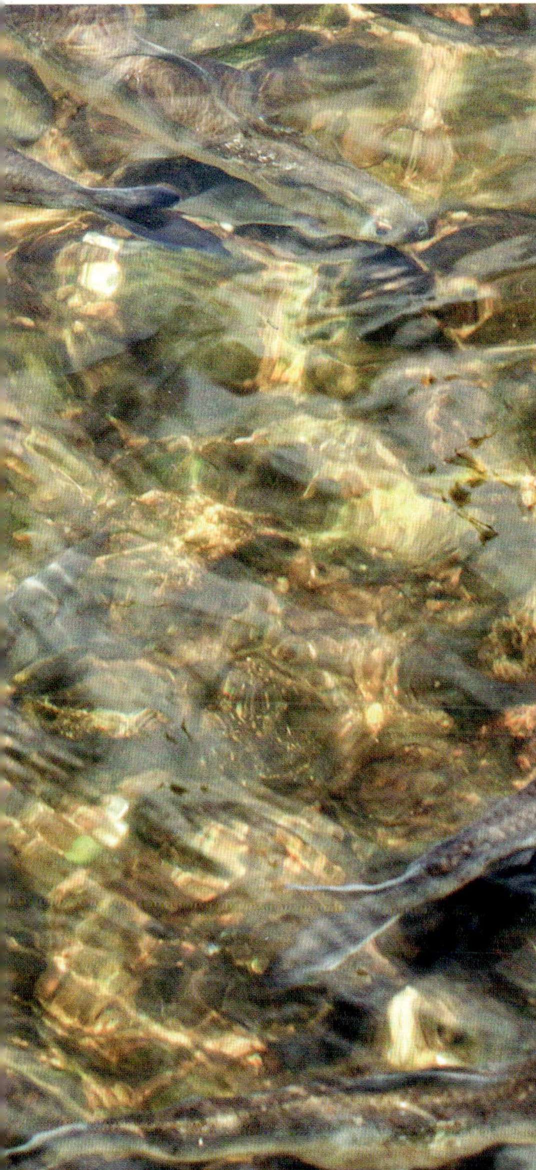

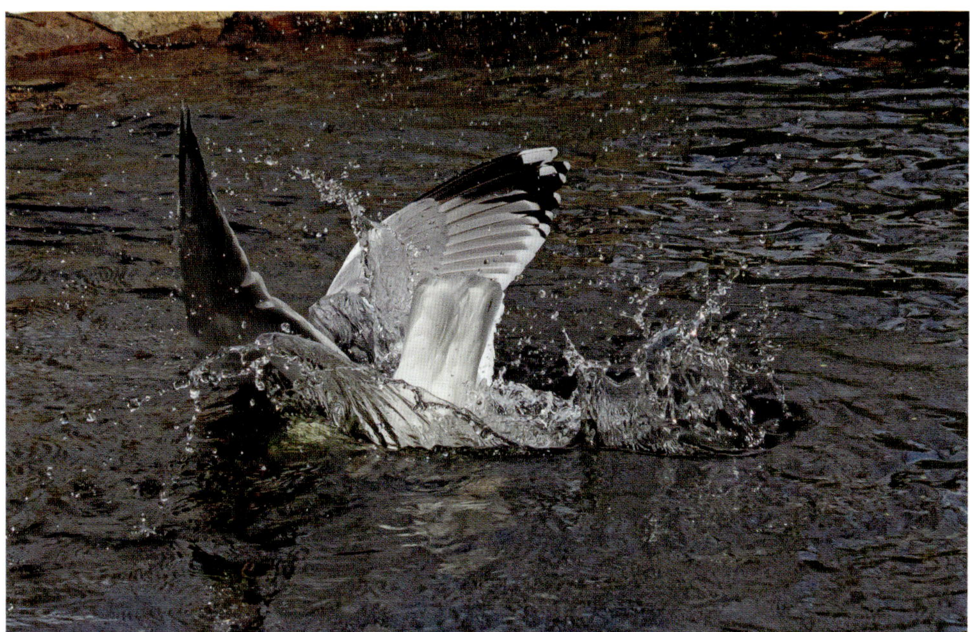

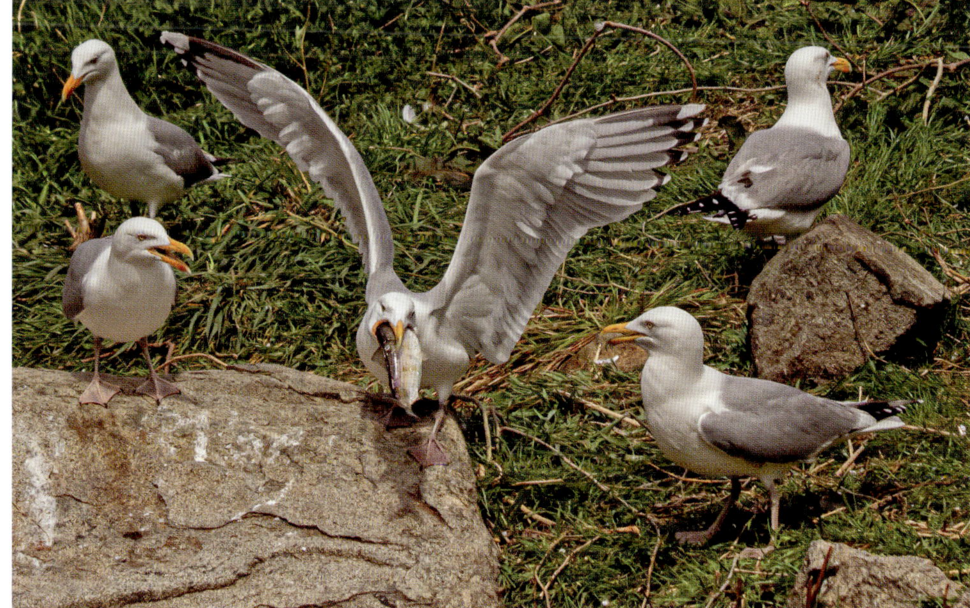

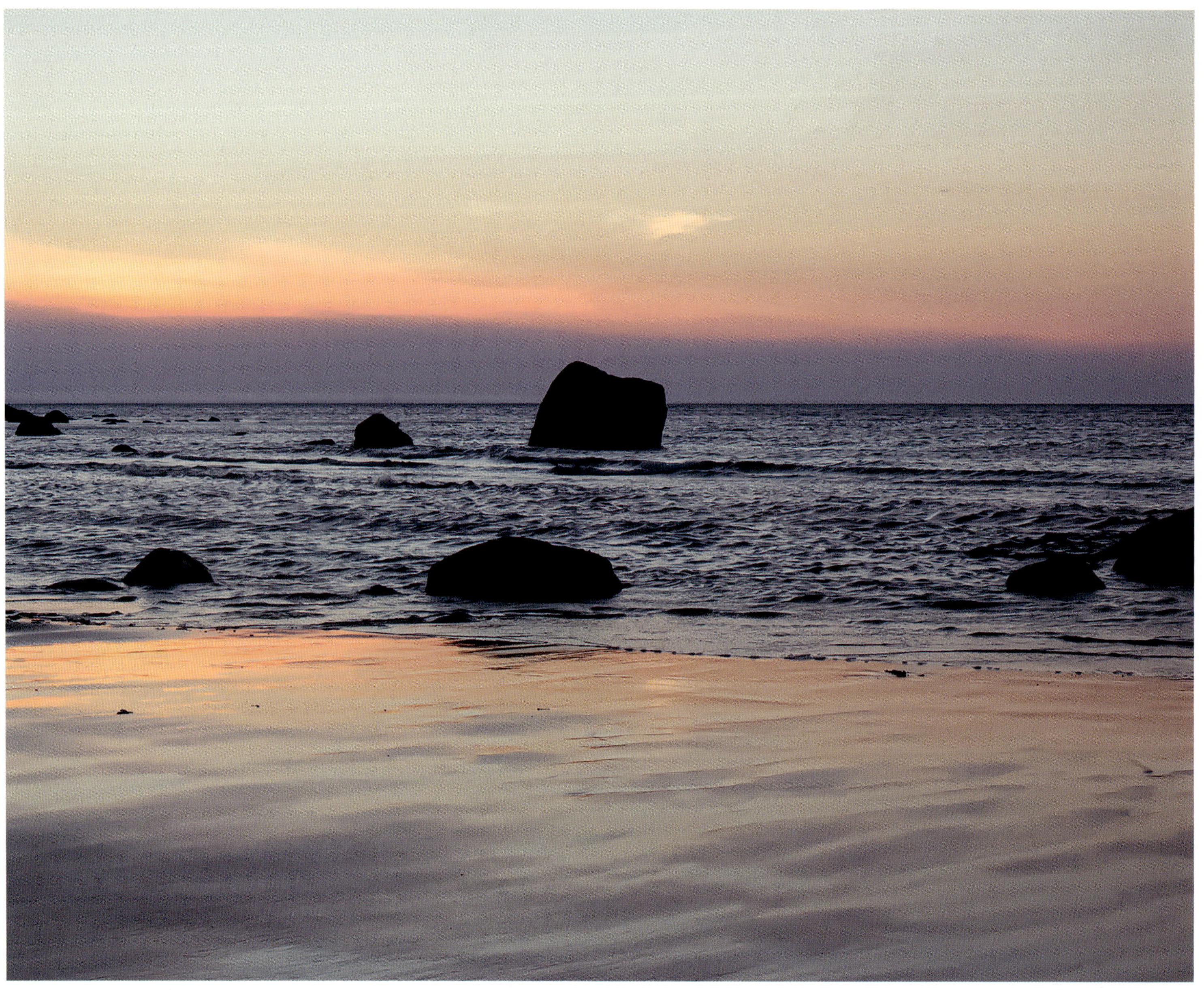

Are these the colors of spring or summer? As the lengthening days of April announce the onset of warmer days and warming water, the glow of sunset shows the imminent and continuing rejuvenation of the natural world. We're seeing the emergence of amphibians, reptiles, flowers, and summerlike temperatures. As we close the story of nature's year, a calmness and tranquil darkness fall over Cape Cod Bay.

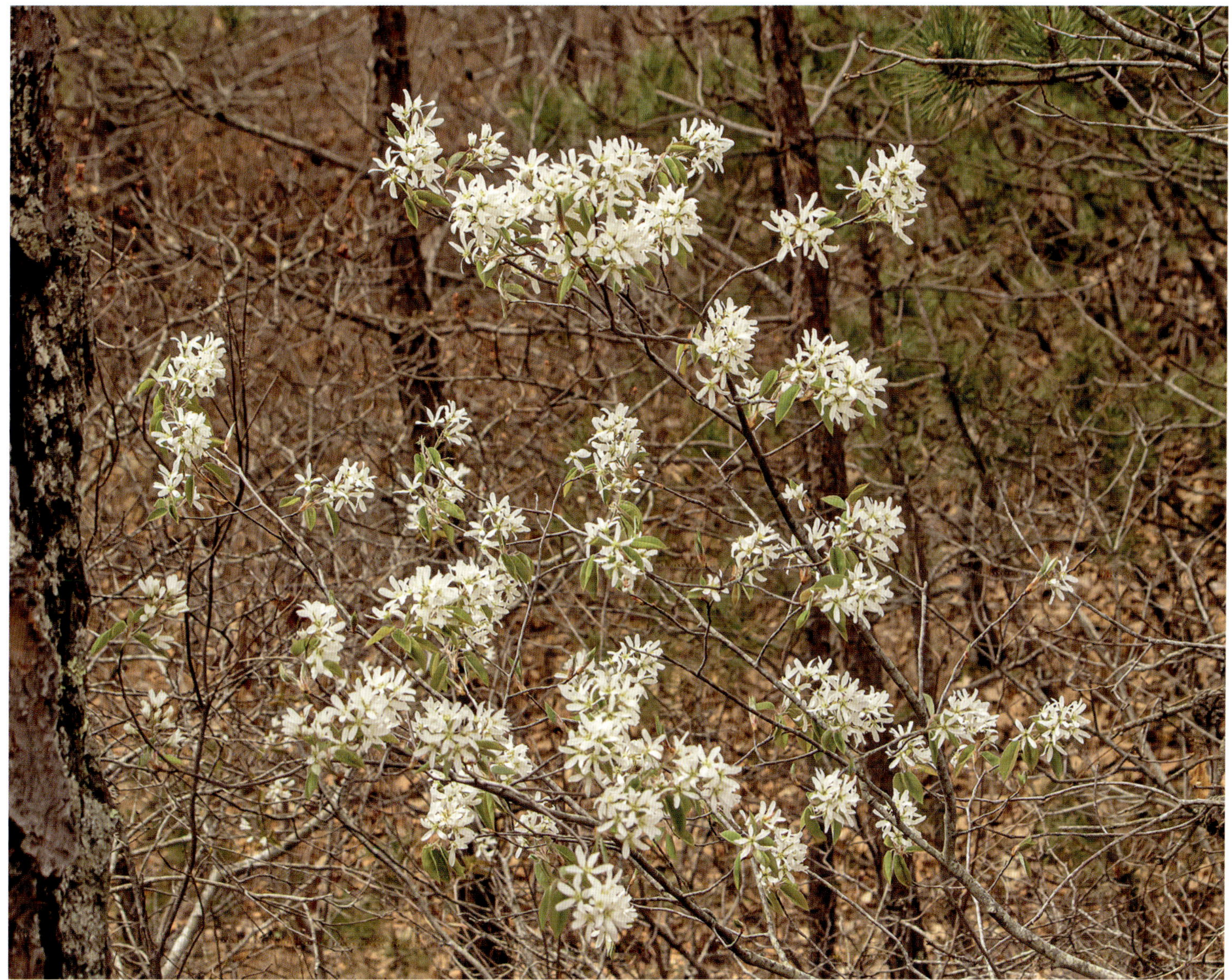

We've done it. We have followed nature's calendar of events through the seasons, through the storms, and from birth to death. As we look toward May and June, we begin yet another exploration of this great interwoven fabric we call the natural world. Look to the resurgence of new blossoms and bright plumage. Along roadsides and woodland edges, shadbush brightens the early May days, while Baltimore orioles sing a cheerful, liquid song from the treetops, announcing nature's colorful canvas of rebirth.

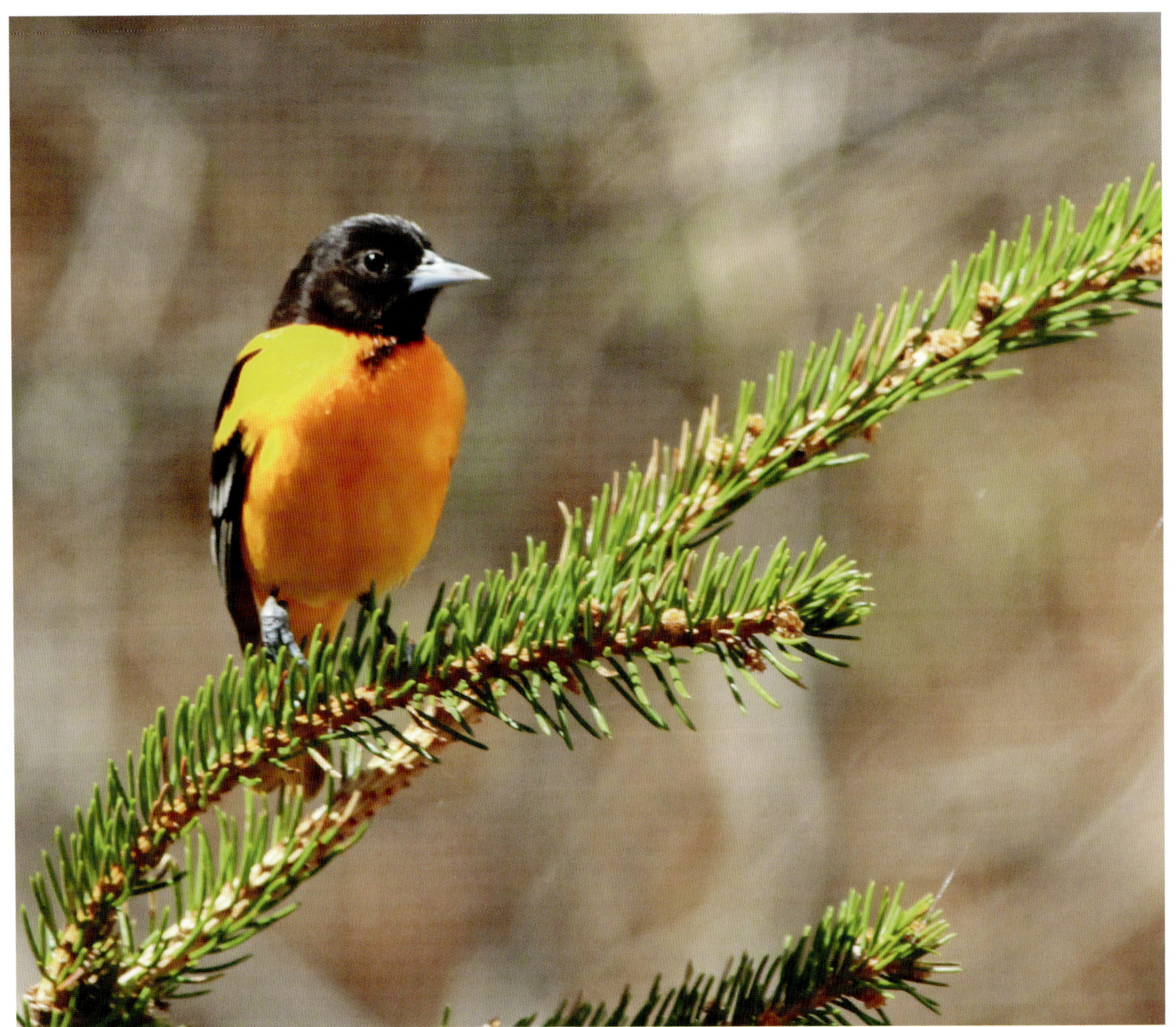

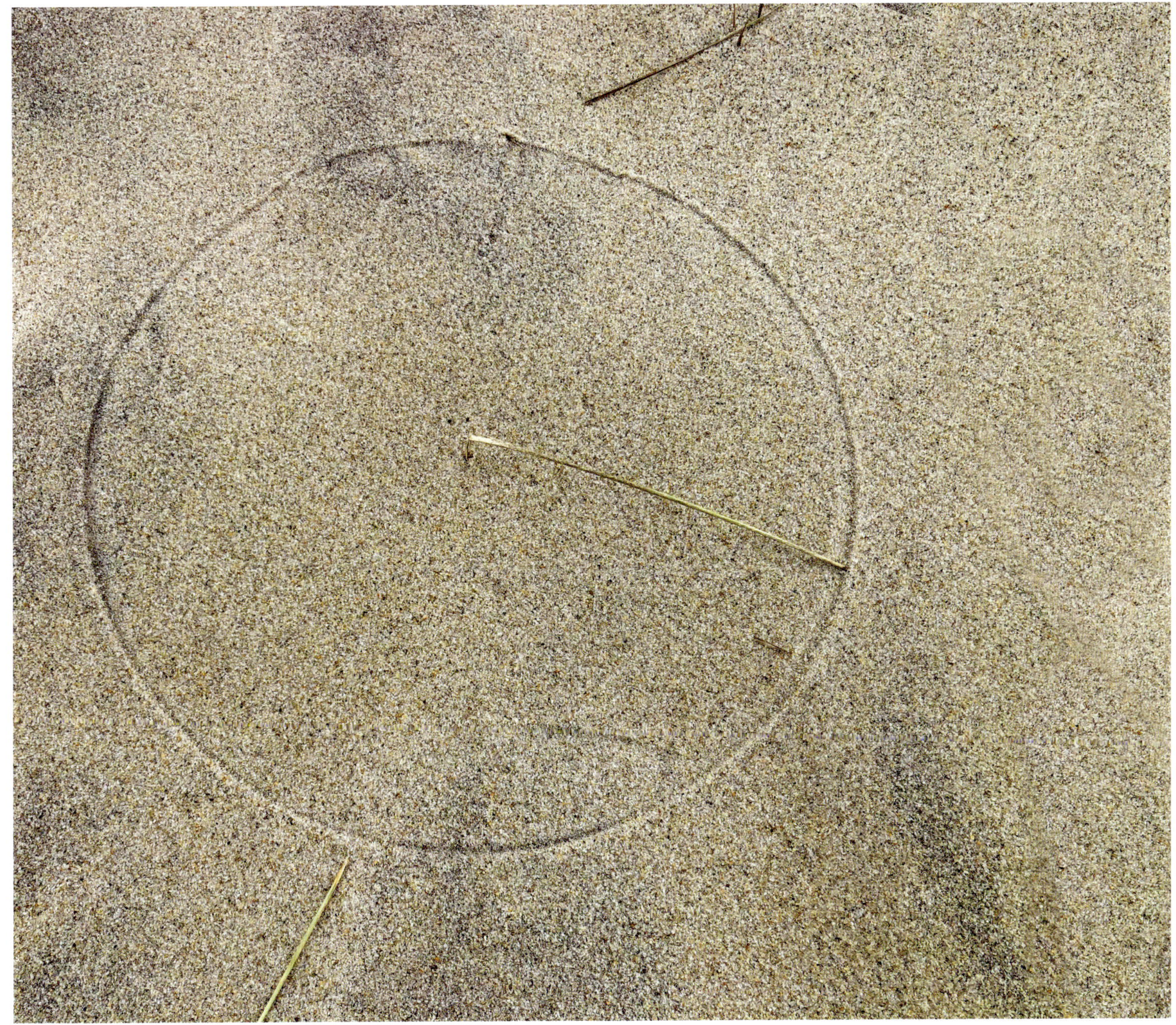

Acknowledgments

Susannah Remillard was a catalyst and inspiration in the concept of this book, and I am forever grateful for her initial encouragement. No matter what my confidence level or depth of knowledge as a field naturalist and researcher may be, there are always questions to be asked and new things to learn. During the years of preparation, writing, and photography for this project, I sought advice and answers from several people with a great range of expertise and backgrounds. Mark Wilson changed my entire outlook and methodology on the art of photography. His perfectionism and extensive skill, along with his often-humbling critique of my work, has raised my consciousness of, and love for, the art. Artists Carol and Mary Elizabeth Trull brought their expert eye to my photo compositions and techniques. I reached far and wide to answer questions related to the behavior, taxonomy, identification, and location of some of my subjects. I wish to thank the following people: Donald Schall, Steven Whitebread, Tyan Basset, Blair Nikula, David Wiley, Bob Cook, Sue Finnigan, Tom Walker, and Ian Nisbet. And, of course, a sincere debt of gratitude extends to my editors, Cheryl and Max. Cheryl has shown patience and understanding through it all. Max nurtured and pulled together the final product, working tirelessly between me and the design team. Thank you, Max. Each of these friends and colleagues helped make this book educational and informative. I am truly grateful for your help and advice.

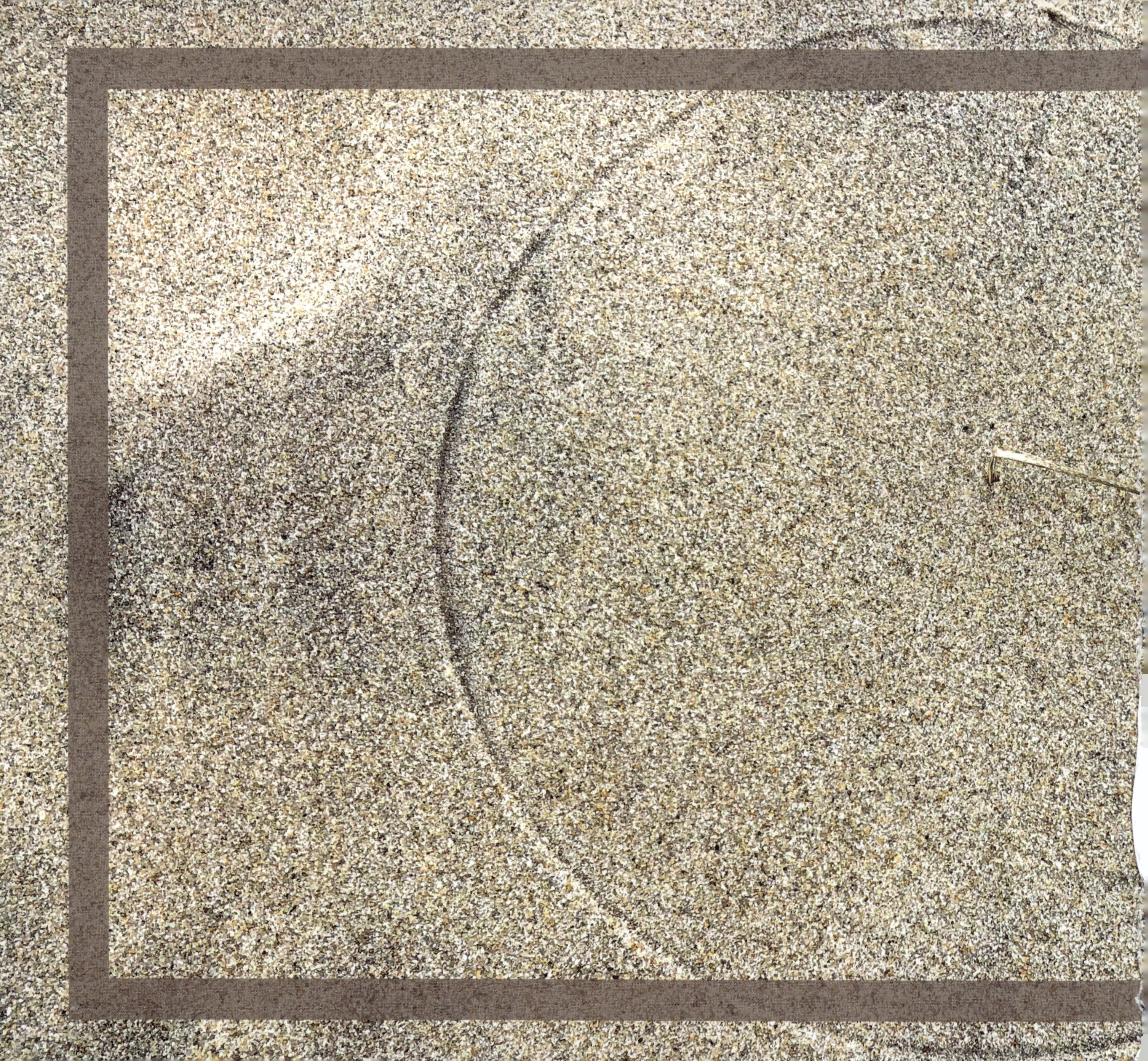